Better Homes and Gardens®

ENCYCLOPEDIA
of
COOKING

Volume 7

Plump, juicy Stuffed Cornish Game Hens are filled with a
savory rice and almond stuffing. A red wine glaze brushed on
during the last hour of baking permeates the golden brown hens.

On the cover: Hilo Franks and pineapple slices brown over
a table-side hibachi. The apricot-preserves glaze gives the
sizzling meat and fruit a tempting, tart-sweet coating.

BETTER HOMES AND GARDENS BOOKS
NEW YORK • DES MOINES

©Meredith Corporation, 1970. All Rights Reserved.
Printed in the United States of America.
First Edition. Second Printing, 1971.
Library of Congress Catalog Card Number: 73-129265
SBN 696-02007-6

ENGLISH COOKERY—Toad in the hole, kippers, bangers 'n mash, shephard's pie, bubble and squeak. These evocative names do not belong to gourmet fare, but they rather are names of simple English dishes: sausages in batter, salted herring, sausage and mashed potatoes, minced meat cooked in potatoes, and fried potatoes and cabbage, respectively.

This, after all, is English cookery—simply prepared foods that are noted for their heartiness and home-style flavor. English food has been drawn from a mingling of recipes and techniques introduced by successive invaders who, generally influenced a different section of the country.

Under Roman domination, the earliest English tribes were exposed to civilized dining. But, with the subsequent fall of the Roman Empire and the conquest of England by barbaric peoples, these culinary advances virtually disappeared.

Even though they were less cultured than the Romans, the Germanic invaders of the fifth century, who were known as Anglo-Saxons, are credited with establishing hearty foods as the basis for the national cuisine. From their homeland, they brought the arts of baking, brewing, making butter and cheese, and raising livestock. They utilized the food of the land by hunting wild boars, partridges, and rabbits, catching fish, and picking wild berries. And by the eleventh century, the Anglo-Saxons' love of lavish meals and incessant feasting had resulted in the evolution of new ways with food.

The conquering Normans abruptly altered the Anglo-Saxon's food culture. The imaginative Normans prepared refined bread products as well as pastries and meat pies. Foods were seasoned with exotic spices such as ginger, cloves, nutmeg, and cinnamon. To replace the Anglo-Saxon's conglomerate meals, the Normans served dinners in a series of courses.

Internal changes rather than external influences marked the fourteenth-through sixteenth-century advances.

Many basic fruit and vegetable varieties were introduced and salads were promoted. In addition, housewives were offered the first cook book written by an English author, *The Boke of Cookery.*

The growing acceptance of sweets, which developed during the Elizabethan Age (1558-1603) was the most notable cuisine change of this period. Queen Elizabeth I became so fond of sweets that she would often excuse herself from the royal dining table to eat sweets she had hidden in her room. A myriad of dishes including cakes, pastries, custards, and jellies were popularized—so much so, in fact, that sweets were soon being served at the beginning of, between, and after meals.

Foreign cooking influences were revived in England during the following centuries. As a mark of respect to William of Orange, Patrick Lamb, who had headed the royal kitchens of England for over 50 years, introduced Dutch cooking methods to England in 1710 with his book, *Royal Cookery.* With increased communication between the American colonies, "all-American" dishes became well known. French cuisine so attracted wealthy Englishmen that they began importing French chefs.

A large portion of the English population, however, did not readily accept French cooking. The English claimed to be better cooks than the French (a claim that is still made) and attempted to prove their superiority by producing more cook books than any other nation. For nearly 100 years, all French cookery was obliterated from English texts.

In the late 1700s this rivalry subsided. And in a unique turnabout, a native Frenchmen, Alexis Soyer, became the most renowned English chef and cook book author of the nineteenth century.

Most of the typically English recipes of today are modernized versions of the inherited dishes. Each generation has adapted the old ideas to incorporate current ingredients and techniques.

Characteristics of English cookery: English dishes are consistently substantial in nature and are planned for use in a well-defined meal pattern.

Christmas dinner is a typical example of how hearty English foods make a substantial meal. Just reading Charles Dickens' *A Christmas Carol* brings a mouthwatering picture to the imagination. Although today a turkey may replace the

Cratchit's roasted goose, the enormity of the meal remains the same. Everyone is expected to take at least second and sometimes third helpings of golden brown roast turkey, sage and onion stuffing, baked or fluffy mashed potatoes, steaming gravy, and applesauce. This is followed by a blazing plum pudding with hard sauce, tiny mince pies, jellies (gelatin), custards, and an assortment of confections.

Common to all of England is a wide array of meats. Although often called "a nation of beef-eaters," mutton, venison, veal, lamb, and ham are also popular for roasts, chops, meat pies, and stews. Suckling pig, boar's head, and large and small game such as Cornish game hens are served at meals celebrating special occasions.

Since England is an island, fish and seafood are among the most abundant and favorite foods. Interestingly, however, pagan Britains did not eat fish, but used it in sacrifices to their gods. Fresh fish are available daily in most areas of England. Shops specializing in newspaper-wrapped fish and chips (batter-fried fish and deep-fat fried potato strips) abound. Oysters, prawns, sole, and salmon are plentiful. Herring are lightly salted and briefly smoked (bloaters) or more liberally salted and heavily smoked (kippers).

Of the traditional English meal pattern —hearty breakfast, moderate lunch, late afternoon tea, and course-by-course dinner —the style of breakfast and teatime are the most unique to this cuisine.

Although the current trend is toward a hurried breakfast of tea and toast, the English are long-remembered for their large breakfasts. The upper-classes breakfasted buffet-style with oatmeal porridge (more recently cornflakes), bacon, eggs, fried bread, hot toast with marmalade, and large quantities of hot tea. Fish, fruit, fried mushrooms, or grilled tomatoes were sometimes included. The lower-classes were not so lavish but still made the first meal of the day a large one: hot porridge, kippers, fried bread, lashings of marmalade (usually orange) and toast, and mugs of hot, scalding tea (with sugar and milk).

England's worldwide culinary fame is closely linked with tea, a term that denotes both the nation's favorite beverage and a meal as well. Introduction of this beverage to England is credited to seventeenth-century Dutchmen who brought tea back with them from East Indian trading posts. However, just when tea took on the added meaning of a meal is not clear. The Duchess of Bedford is said to have introduced the afternoon tea to dispel a five o'clock "sinking feeling."

The meal called tea has two different connotations which depend on whether it is served during the week or on weekends. During week days, tea is similar to the American habit of drinking a cup of coffee in the late afternoon, except that the British have a cup of tea with a bun or small cake. On weekends, tea, with the possible inclusion of dainty sandwiches of watercress, or shrimp, ham, thinly sliced cucumber, and tomatoes; cookies, crumpets; lemon-filled tarts; Scottish scones with jam and cream; an assortment of cakes and small sweet rolls; or platters filled with sausage rolls and slices of pork pie, takes the place of a full evening meal.

One of the most typical weekend teas consists of pork pie, lettuce, celery sticks, bread and butter, possibly jam (preserves), cake, and a pot of tea. This style of dining probably came about because the British often entertained company by having a meal on Sunday afternoon.

Regional English cookery: The groups of people that established homes in England tended to concentrate in certain regions of the country: Normans in the north, Celts in the southwest, and Anglo-Saxons in the southeast. Many of the well-known recipes are still primarily prepared in the region of their origin, but others such as steak and kidney pie and plum pudding have become so naturalized to the English cuisine as a whole that their origin has been somewhat obscured. Yorkshire pudding (a popoverlike bread always served

English Christmas dinner

With turkey serve stuffing, sweet and mashed → potatoes, broccoli, cranberries, and Regal Plum Pudding (see *Plum Pudding* for recipe).

with a joint of beef roast) and Lancashire hot pot (England's version of Irish stew) have retained regional names but are popular throughout the island.

Northern Englishmen rely on heavy foods to sustain them through colder weather much like their Norman ancestors and Scottish neighbors. Hearty main dishes include the thin stew lobscouse (or scouse for short) and hot pots (stews baked in casseroles). Large round scones called singing hinnys and cakelike breads known as fat rascals are griddle-baked in Scottish fashion. Spicy gingerbread is a common and very popular northern dessert.

Middle England, known as the midlands, is the home of world-famous Cheshire and Stilton cheeses as well as some unique desserts. Cheshire cheese's characteristic saltiness is due to the cows feeding on the grasses of Cheshire county's extremely salty soil. Because of this, Cheshire cheese cannot be reproduced in any other part of the world. Stilton, first made around Stilton, England, is a mellow, blue-veined cheese based on very rich milk. A tour of the countryside also uncovers cream-filled brandy snaps, Mothering Sunday and Easter simnel cake (a spicy cake topped with 12 marzipan balls), and Banbury tarts (pastries filled with spiced dried fruit).

Because the early Celtic tribes were little troubled by foreigners, the southwest region of England, which includes Cornwall, Devon, Somerset, and Dorset counties, contains some of the most unique cooking traditions. A myriad of fish and seafood dishes as well as dairy products are used. Specialties such as Cornish pasties (meal-in-one meat pies), Devonshire cream, Cheddar cheese, rich and sweet Sally Lunn cakes, and caraway-flavored Bath buns had their beginnings with these people.

London and the surrounding area of southeastern England includes a conglomerate of the cuisine styles found throughout the island. Some of its own contributions include fruit tarts and teacakes such as Richmond's maids of honor.

As can be seen, English cookery embraces many kinds of delicious foods. Although many are closely allied to traditional feasts and reserved for special occasions, others are used in everyday meals.

Stuffed Cornish Game Hens

Cook 1½ cups long-grain rice according to package directions. Add ⅓ cup dry red wine, 1½ teaspoons sugar, ¾ teaspoon salt, ⅛ teaspoon pepper, ⅛ teaspoon ground nutmeg, and ⅛ teaspoon ground allspice; mix well. Add ⅓ cup toasted, slivered almonds; stuff lightly into cavities of 6 Cornish game hens, 1 to 1½ pounds each. Place hens in shallow roasting pan; cover loosely with foil.

Roast at 400° for 30 minutes. Uncover and bake 1 hour more, basting occasionally with *Wine Glaze:* Combine ¼ cup dry red wine, 3 tablespoons melted butter or margarine, and 1½ teaspoons lemon juice. Makes 6 servings.

Beef and Kidney Pie

In saucepan combine 1 beef kidney, 1 quart lukewarm water, and 1 teaspoon salt. Soak 1 hour; drain. Cover kidney with cold water. Bring to boiling; simmer 20 minutes. Drain; remove kidney membrane and hard parts, if any. Cut meat in ½-inch cubes; set aside.

Coat 1 pound beef round steak, cut in ½-inch cubes, with ¼ cup all-purpose flour. In Dutch oven brown beef steak cubes in 2 tablespoons hot shortening. Add 1 medium onion, sliced, and 2 cups water. Cover; simmer steak and onion till tender, about 30 minutes.

In shaker mixer combine ½ cup cold water, ¼ cup all-purpose flour, 1 teaspoon salt, and dash pepper. Stir flour mixture into hot steak-onion mixture. Cook, stirring constantly, till mixture is thickened and bubbly. Add cooked kidney cubes; heat through. Pour meat mixture into 2-quart casserole. Cover with Pastry Topping. Turn under edge and flute. Cut slits for escape of steam. Brush top of pastry with milk. Bake at 450° till golden, 20 to 25 minutes.

Pastry Topping: Sift together 1 cup all-purpose flour and ½ teaspoon salt; cut in ⅓ cup shortening with pastry blender till pieces are the size of small peas. Sprinkle 1 tablespoon cold water over part of mixture. Gently toss with fork; push to side of bowl. Repeat sprinkling with 2 to 3 tablespoons more water till all is moistened. Form pastry into a ball.

Flatten on lightly floured surface by pressing with edge of hand 3 times across in both directions. Roll the dough in circle ½ to 1 inch larger than the casserole dish.

Crispy English Muffins are baked to a delicate brownness on a top-of-the-range griddle. The cooled muffins are split and toasted, then spread with lots of butter and marmalade.

ENGLISH MUFFIN—A small, round yeast bread baked on a griddle. The baked muffins are usually split and toasted, then spread with butter and jam or marmalade. They can also be used under creamed foods in casseroles or other such dishes.

These muffins were once sold by street vendors in England; hence, they are called English muffins. (See also *Bread*.)

English Muffins

Spread liberally with butter and jam—

    1 **package active dry yeast**
5¾ **to 6 cups sifted all-purpose flour**
    2 **cups milk**
   ¼ **cup shortening**
    2 **tablespoons sugar**
    2 **teaspoons salt**

In large mixer bowl combine yeast and 2¼ *cups* flour. Heat milk, shortening, sugar, and salt just till warm, stirring occasionally to melt shortening. Add to dry mixture in mixing bowl. Beat at low speed with electric mixer for ½ minute, scraping sides of bowl constantly. Beat 3 minutes at high speed. By hand, stir in enough of the remaining flour to make a moderately stiff dough. Turn out on lightly floured surface; knead till smooth (8 to 10 minutes). Place in greased bowl, turning once. Cover; let rise till double (1¼ hours).

Punch down; cover and let rest 10 minutes. Roll dough to slightly less than ½ inch on lightly floured surface. Cut with a 3-inch round cutter. (Reroll edges.) Cover; let rise till very light (1¼ hours). Bake on top of range on medium-hot griddle; turn muffins frequently till done, about 30 minutes. Cool thoroughly. Split muffins with a fork; toast both sides. Serve at once. Makes 24 muffins.

ENGLISH MUSTARD—A powder made from ground mustard seeds. Before using, this powder is mixed with water, vinegar, or flat beer. The resulting mustard sauce is very hot. (See also *Mustard.*)

EN PAPILLOTE *(än pa pē yôt')*—The French word for food enclosed in a paper bag and baked. This method aids in retaining the food's shape and juiciness.

ENRICHED—Flour, cereal, or bakery products to which small amounts of vitamins and/or minerals have been added to improve their nutritive quality. The addition of these vitamins and minerals does not change the food's appearance or flavor.

In the late 1930s, nutritionists became concerned about the deficiency of certain vitamins and minerals in the average American's diet. This concern led to the enrichment, beginning in 1941, of several cereal foods including white bread, all-purpose flour, macaroni products, farina, white rice, and cornmeal. Although this enrichment is not mandatory, over half the states have adopted enrichment laws.

Today, almost all the all-purpose flour sold on the retail market is enriched. In the United States, enriched foods contribute a significant part of the thiamine, riboflavin, niacin, and iron consumed.

ENTRECOTE *(än truh kōt')*—A French word meaning "between the ribs." On a menu, an entrecote beef cut indicates a boneless steak similar to a sirloin steak.

ENTRÉE *(an' trā)*—A French word meaning "entrance." Originally entrée referred to the first course of a meal or the course served between the soup and roast. In the United States, however, it now refers to the main course of a meal.

ENTREMET *(än truh mā')*—A dish served in addition to the main course. In France, an entremet is the sweet course (other than cake or pastry), served after the cheese.

ENZYME *(en' zīm)*—A protein substance produced by living cells in plants and animals that causes chemical changes without being changed itself.

The enzymes in foods are responsible for both desirable and undesirable changes. Enzyme action is important in the ripening of fruits and vegetables. However, once the food has reached maturity, continuing enzyme action results in spoilage characterized by browning, soft spots, and off-flavors. The darkening of cut, fresh fruits such as apples and bananas is caused by enzymes. One of the enzymes in uncooked pineapple breaks down gelatin protein so the gelatin won't set. Therefore, fresh or frozen pineapple must be cooked before it is used in gelatin dishes.

The knowledge that enzymes are inactivated by acids, foods, or heat is applied in several cooking techniques. Apple, banana, pear, and peach pieces will not darken as fast if dipped in lemon juice. The heating of canned foods inactivates enzymes to prevent spoilage from enzyme action. Although freezing foods will slow down enzyme action, it does not inactivate the enzymes. Vegetables, for example, are blanched (heated for a short period of time) before being frozen.

EQUIPMENT—Apparatus used in performing an activity such as food preparation.

Ever since man learned to cook his food over the campfire, he has been using cooking equipment. The remnants of utensils found by archeologists have been extremely important in piecing together the story of man. The first cooking utensil was probably a green stick used to hold food over the fire. Shells were also used by early man as a spoonlike tool. As man became more advanced, he covered woven baskets with clay mud and when they had dried, he used them as water vessels.

After the discovery of metal, man began using metal cooking utensils and tools. Later a reflector-type oven was made for baking bread. In ancient Egypt, an enclosed oven was made. Glass, which was made by fusing sand and soda ash, was another cooking utensil of ancient Egypt.

Through the centuries, man has perfected these ancient materials and equipment designs and has discovered so many new things that today we have an abundant choice of cooking equipment in a variety of materials, colors, sizes, and styles.

Basic kitchen needs: In cooking, the production of the finished dish depends not only on the proper handling of food materials but also on the use of proper equipment and utensils. The equipment needed for food preparation can be broken down into five groups—storage, preparation, cooking, cleaning, and serving. In each of these groups, there are numerous articles available. The box at right, however, is limited to the equipment needed to initially supply a kitchen. As money and need arise, other convenient but less essential equipment can be added.

How to select: Food preparation is one of the homemaker's basic duties, so it is important to select kitchen equipment carefully. Since this group includes a broad range of items, it is difficult to give specific selection guides. The following points, however, should be considered when purchasing any kitchen equipment.

1. Materials and structure. Is this piece of equipment sturdy and durable? Is the material easy to clean and suitable for this piece of equipment? (Metal handles might get hot and plastic measuring cups may bend and not give accurate measurements.) Will the material stain or rust? Will the finish peel off? Are all the handles securely fastened? Are all the electrical terminals safely recessed?

2. Design. Are there any hard-to-clean cracks or crevices? Does the design coordinate with the other kitchen equipment? Are there any sharp edges?

3. Storage. Is there space to store this where it will be readily available?

4. Use. What can this be used for? Does another model offer features that will increase the possibilities of use?

5. Price. Will another model or another store give more for the money?

6. Seals of approval, standards, and testing. Gas appliances should have American Gas Assocation seal. Look for the Underwriters' Laboratory seal on electrical appliances. Measuring utensils should have "U.S. Standard Measures" on the package to show they have been standardized.

7. Manufacturer and dealer. Will they stand behind the product? Do they provide servicing? Are they well known?

Basic kitchen equipment

Storage

refrigerator/freezer	cupboards
assorted refrigerator-	bread box
freezer dishes	canisters
foil; clear plastic wrap	waxed paper

Preparation

can opener	utility slicer
grater or shredder	carving knife
vegetable peeler	potato masher
kitchen shears	vegetable brush
pair of tongs	strainers
2 paring knives	colander
serrated knife	electric mixer
nested set of dry	wooden spoons
measuring cups	flour sifter
measuring spoons	rotary beater
set of mixing bowls	bottle opener
liquid measuring cup	rubber spatula
rolling pin with cover	pastry cloth

Cooking

covered skillets (10-	range with oven
and 7-to 8-inch)	tube pan
covered saucepans (1,	square pans
2, and 4 to 6 quarts)	coffee maker
wire cooling rack	pancake turner
long-handled fork	toaster
long-handled spoon	jelly roll pan
oblong pan (13x9x2)	round cake pans
loaf dish (8½x4½x2½)	muffin pan
roasting pan, rack	custard cups
casserole with cover	cookie sheets
pot holders; hot pads	pie plates

Cleaning

sink	dishpan
dishcloth and towels	wastebasket
draining rack, mat	garbage pail

Serving

serving bowls	platter
dinner and salad plates	sauce dishes
cups and saucers	glasses
table linen	silverware

ESCALLOPE, ESCALLOPED—To bake foods, topped with crumbs, in a cream sauce in a casserole or individual baking dish. At one time the term was used to refer to foods that were served in scallop shells, hence the term escalloped. (See also *Scalloped*.)

ESCARGOT (*e skar gō'*)—The French word for an edible, land snail. Escargot is often used on restaurant menus for snails or dishes made of snails. (See also *Snail*.)

ESCAROLE (*es' kuh rōl'*)—Broad-leafed variety of endive most often used for salads. Native to the East Indies and known to have been grown in ancient Greece and Egypt, escarole was introduced to the United States by early colonists.

The flattened escarole bunches, with broad, slightly curled leaves, have a firm texture. The green leaves shade into yellows close to the center of the head. Because escarole has a slightly bitter flavor, it is usually combined with other greens and fresh vegetables for salads.

Escarole is often considered a winter salad green but is available all year around. When selecting a head of escarole in the market, look for tender, crisp, fresh, green leaves enclosing a heart of blanched creamy white or yellow white leaves. The leaves should snap easily between the fingers. Toughness and excessive bitterness of this endive variety are indicated by wilted and brownish outer leaves.

A head of escarole should be thoroughly washed before using to remove any sand. If any sand remains, soak the head for a short time. Then cut off and discard the bitter roots. The clean salad green is then torn into pieces instead of being cut with a knife. Escarole should be chilled in the refrigerator, as any salad green, well before serving time.

As a salad ingredient, escarole can be tossed with oil and vinegar, or mixed with other salad greens and served with any favorite salad dressing. You can also use it as a boiled and lightly salted table vegetable with cheese and cream sauces poured over it. Or, use it as part of a delectable soup. Preparation methods and recipes for endive and chicory can also be used for escarole. (See also *Endive*.)

Slightly bitter escarole has green outer leaves shading to yellow closer to center. Well-branched heart appears bleached.

ESCHALOT (*esh' uh lot', esh' uh lot'*)—The French word for shallot, a member of the onion family. The gray or brownish bulbs are divided into cloves similar to garlic. This mild, delicate-flavored herb is used in meat dishes, fish, poultry, and sauces, or when combined with onions, is often used in salads and soups.

ESPAGNOLE SAUCE (*es' puhn yōl', -pan-*)—A basic brown sauce from which other sauces can be made. Espagnole sauce is made with a rich stock of brown roux or bouillon and simmered several hours. It becomes quite thick after it has boiled down. French cooks take espagnole sauce a step further and make it into a demi-glace. The sauce may contain tomatoes or tomato paste, fruit juices, or vegetable stocks. It may be flavored with sherry wine, if desired. (See also *Sauce*.)

ESPRESSO COFFEE (*e spres' o*)—A dark, strong coffee made in a special coffee machine by forcing hot water or steam pressure through finely ground roasted coffee. To make espresso coffee in the home, purchase an imported machine from a specialty shop, or use a three part coffee maker similar to a drip-type coffeemaker. Instant espresso coffee is also available in some shops or supermarkets for those people not wanting to invest in the special equipment required to brew espresso coffee.

Originally Italian, the after-dinner espresso coffee is usually served in small demitasse cups; for an added delight, garnish it with a lemon twist or serve it with tiny dollops of whipped cream on top of the coffee. (See also *Coffee.*)

ESSENCE—Concentrated, oily liquid or extract possessing the smell, taste, nutritive value, or color of some plant or food. The commercial preparation is obtained by distillation or infusion.

Jellylike meat essences, such as beef essence, are made from concentrated meat juices and are used to enhance the flavor of dishes such as soups, sauces, stews, and gravies. The rich, essential oils in alcoholic solutions are usually volatile.

Essences resemble extracts in that they are flavor additions in concentrated form.

EST EST EST—A golden, semisweet wine made from the Moscatello grapes of Montefiascone in the Lazio region (north of Rome), Italy. There are two different types of the Italian wine that vary in sweetness, with the sweetest one most often preferred.

The name "Est! Est! Est!" (It is! It is! It is!) was given to this renowned beverage in honor of a wine-loving German bishop, who used to take long journeys and would send a trusty servant ahead to check the lodging and to taste the wines.

Whenever the servant came across an acceptable lodge offering good wines he was to write "Est!" on the wall. Upon tasting the superb wine of Montefiascone, the servant wrote "Est! Est! Est!" on the wall. The bishop agreed with his enthusiasm after arriving and proceeded to drink himself to death. (See also *Wine and Spirits.*)

ESTOUFFADE (*es' tōō fad'*)—1. A rich meat stew cooked very slowly in a covered casserole dish with seasonings and a small amount of liquid. 2. A light brown stock made of meats, vegetables, and seasonings used to dilute sauces for meats and casseroles and used in jellies and stews.

ESTRAGON (*es' truh gon'*)—The French name for the herb terragon. The mysterious sweet, bitter taste resembling anise makes estragon an excellent companion to vinegars and sauces, and fish or chicken dishes. Mix the fragrant estragon leaves with butter and serve with cold dishes.

ÉTOUFFÉ (*e tu' fe*)—A French cooking method in which foods are simmered, sometimes covered, in very little liquid. The liquid may be water, stock, or wine. The foods, either meats, poultry, or vegetables, are smothered in their own juices.

Shrimp Étouffé

  1 medium onion, finely chopped
  2 green onions, finely chopped
  3 or 4 cloves garlic, minced
  ¼ cup chopped celery
  ½ cup butter or margarine
  2 tablespoons all-purpose flour
  1 10½-ounce can tomato purée
  2 bay leaves
  1 tablespoon Worcestershire sauce
  4 drops bottled hot pepper sauce
  1 teaspoon salt
  ½ teaspoon sugar
  ½ teaspoon dried thyme leaves, crushed
  ⅛ teaspoon pepper
  3 cups cleaned raw shrimp (about 1½ pounds)

Cook onion, green onions, garlic, and celery in butter till tender. Add flour; cook and stir till lightly browned. Add all remaining ingredients except shrimp. Stir in 2½ cups water.

Simmer, uncovered, stirring occasionally, till almost of desired consistency, about 25 minutes. Add shrimp; cook 15 minutes more. If desired, garnish with wedges of hard-cooked egg.

EVAPORATED MILK—Milk from which about 60 percent of the water has been removed during processing for canning. The two types are evaporated milk, made from whole fresh milk, and evaporated skimmed milk, made from skimmed milk. The concentrated canned milk is lower priced than the same amount of fresh milk in terms of milk solids. No sugar is added to the evaporated milk which must conform to federal standards. The sterilized milk is easy to store and efficiently transported without refrigeration.

How evaporated milk is produced: Evaporated milk is made by heating whole milk in a vacuum evaporator. About 60 percent of the water is removed in the process and the milk is homogenized, then cooled and put in 6- or 14½-ounce cans or 6¾-pound institutional cans.

The sealed cans are then sterilized for ten to fifteen minutes at 245° to 250° F. This sterilization prevents any bacterial spoilage and makes storage without refrigeration possible. A stabilizer is often added to the evaporated milk.

Nutritional value: According to federal regulation, evaporated milk must contain not less than 7.9 percent milk fat and not less than 25.9 percent total milk solids. All brands of evaporated milk have vitamin D added to fortify nutrition.

How to store: Store unopened cans of evaporated milk on the kitchen shelf. Store opened cans of evaporated milk in the refrigerator and use within a few days as you would any fresh milk product.

How to use: Add equal amounts of water to evaporated milk to use as whole, fresh milk. For some recipes, it is interesting to reconstitute the milk with vegetable liquids, fruit juices, or broths.

For a smooth texture, use evaporated milk in creamed and scalloped dishes, custards, sauces, and candies. It is also excellent when used for binding, coating, and emulsifying purposes. (See also *Milk.*)

How to whip evaporated milk

Freeze milk in freezer trays till soft ice crystals form around the edges. Whip the evaporated milk until stiff peaks form and the mixture triples in volume. Sweeten whipped evaporated milk with sugar to taste.

Tomato Aspic Soufflé

Pour one 6-ounce can evaporated milk into freezer tray. Freeze milk till soft ice crystals form around edges. In medium saucepan blend 2 cups tomato juice with 2 bay leaves; 4 black peppercorns; ½ teaspoon onion salt; ¼ teaspoon celery salt; and ¼ teaspoon dried oregano leaves, crushed. Simmer mixture, covered, for 5 minutes; strain with sieve.

Soften 2 envelopes (2 tablespoons) unflavored gelatin in an additional ½ cup cold tomato juice; stir into hot mixture till gelatin is dissolved. Cool thoroughly. With rotary beater, gradually beat an additional ½ cup tomato juice into two 3-ounce packages softened cream cheese; stir into gelatin mixture.

Chill mixture till partially set. Whip icy cold evaporated milk till stiff peaks form; fold whipped milk into gelatin mixture. Pour mixture into 6½-cup mold; chill till firm. Unmold at serving time. Makes 10 to 12 servings.

Chicken Loaf

    4 **cups coarsely ground, cooked chicken (1 4- to 5-pound stewing chicken)**
1½ **cups soft bread crumbs (about 2½ slices bread)**
    1 **6-ounce can evaporated milk**
    2 **slightly beaten eggs**
⅓ **cup chicken broth**
⅔ **cup finely chopped celery**
¼ **cup chopped canned pimiento**
¾ **teaspoon salt**
    Dash pepper
    Dash dried rosemary leaves, crushed
    Dash dried marjoram leaves, crushed
    Dash ground nutmeg
    Mushroom Sauce

Lightly combine all ingredients except Mushroom Sauce. Line bottom of greased 8½x4½x2½-inch loaf dish with foil; grease foil. Turn mixture into dish. Bake at 350° till center is firm about 45 minutes. Invert on platter; remove foil. Serve with Mushroom Sauce.

Mushroom Sauce: Combine one 10½-ounce can condensed cream of mushroom soup with ⅓ cup milk; heat thoroughly. Makes 6 servings.

Pumpkin-Orange Crunch Pie

1 cup brown sugar
1 tablespoon cornstarch
1½ teaspoons pumpkin pie spice
1 16-ounce can pumpkin (2 cups)
1 14½-ounce can evaporated
    milk (1⅔ cups)
2 slightly beaten eggs
1 *unbaked* 9-inch pastry shell
    (See *Pastry*)
1 tablespoon brown sugar
1 tablespoon butter or margarine
1 tablespoon all-purpose flour
½ cup chopped walnuts
2 teaspoons grated orange peel

Combine 1 cup brown sugar, cornstarch, pie spice, ¼ teaspoon salt, and pumpkin. Stir in milk and eggs. Pour into pastry shell. (Crimp edges high—filling is generous.) Bake at 400° for 40 minutes. Meanwhile, combine remaining ingredients. Spoon mixture over pie; return to oven and bake till knife comes out clean, about 5 to 10 minutes more. Cool.

Apple-Walnut Cobbler

½ cup sugar
½ teaspoon ground cinnamon
¾ cup coarsely chopped walnuts
4 cups thinly sliced, peeled
    tart apples

• • •

1 cup sifted all-purpose flour
1 cup sugar
1 teaspoon baking powder
¼ teaspoon salt
1 well-beaten egg
½ cup evaporated milk
⅓ cup butter or margarine, melted

Mix ½ cup sugar, the cinnamon, and ½ *cup walnuts*. Place apples in bottom of a greased 8¼x1¾-inch round ovenware cake dish. Sprinkle with the cinnamon mixture. Sift together dry ingredients. Combine egg, milk, and butter; add dry ingredients all at once and mix till smooth. Pour over apples; sprinkle with remaining walnuts. Bake at 325° till done, about 55 minutes. Spoon warm cobbler onto dessert plates. If desired, top with cinnamon whipped cream or ice cream. Makes 8 servings.

Honey-Banana Mold

Pour one 6-ounce can evaporated milk into freezer tray. Freeze milk till soft ice crystals form around edges of freezer tray.

Dissolve one 3-ounce package orange-flavored gelatin in 1 cup boiling water; cool mixture. Peel 2 ripe medium bananas; mash in large mixer bowl with electric mixer. Beat in ¼ cup honey and 3 tablespoons lemon juice, then cooled gelatin. Chill till mixture is partially set.

Whip mixture at low speed with electric mixer while gradually adding icy cold milk. Increase to high speed; continue whipping till mixture is double in volume and thick. Pour into 4½-cup mold. Chill till firm. Serves 4 to 6.

Asparagus with Two-Cheese Sauce

Wash and cook fresh asparagus spears, covered, in small amount boiling, salted water for 10 to 15 minutes; drain thoroughly.

Beat one 8-ounce package softened cream cheese till smooth; gradually beat in ½ cup evaporated milk. Cook and stir over medium heat till hot. Stir in dash salt and 1 tablespoon grated Parmesan cheese. Pour over hot cooked asparagus spears; sprinkle with an additional 1 tablespoon Parmesan cheese. Makes ¾ cup.

EXTRACT—Concentrated flavorings secured by boiling or distillation. The condensed flavors are extracted from meats, vegetables, liquids, or seasonings. The degree of evaporation is controlled to produce a liquid extract, such as vanilla, or a solid extract, such as a bouillon cube.

The liquid extracts of vanilla, mint, lemon, peppermint, almond, and others are dissolved in an alcohol solution and are volatile. Of the two liquid types, pure and imitation extracts, imitation has fuller flavor. Both liquid and solid extracts are used as flavoring additions.

EXTRA DRY—Term used to indicate the opposite of sweet when speaking of wines and spirits. The grape sugar is fermented into alcohol resulting in a light flavor good for most food accompaniments. Champagne is an example of an extra dry wine. (See also *Wine and Spirits*.)

F

FAGOT (*fag' et*) – 1. A *bouquet garni* made by tying seasonings and vegetables with a string. 2. A pork liver pattie that is most often baked in the oven.

Season soups and stews as well as braised meats or vegetables with a fagot used as a bouquet garni. The bundle, tied securely with a string, most often includes celery, bay leaf, parsley, thyme, and other herbs specified by the recipe or personal taste. Before serving, the fagot is easily removed from the stew or meat.

Fagot pork patties made of pork liver, crumbs, seasonings, and pork fat are sold in some meat departments ready to bake.

FANTAN ROLL – Dainty rolls made by stacking long strips of dough and cutting through strips for each roll. The rolls are placed with cut side down in muffin pan and allowed to bake.

For variation, fantan rolls are brushed with melted butter and sprinkled with sesame or poppy seed before baking. The tops of the rolls fan out slightly as they bake and become lightly browned.

Use convenient ready-to-bake butterflake rolls for quick and easy preparation of the classic fantan rolls. Make them for special occasions by separating the sections slightly and brushing with an herb-flavored butter which would be compatible with the particular meal. (See also *Roll*.)

Fantans

Divide Basic Roll Dough (see *Roll*) in 3 equal pieces and round each in a ball. Cover; let rest 10 minutes. Roll each ball in a 14x9-inch rectangle, about ¼ inch thick. Brush with melted butter or margarine.

Cut each rectangle lengthwise in 6 strips, 1½ inches wide (see picture). Pile all 6 strips on top of one another; cut in 1½-inch lengths, making 9 pieces (see picture). Place cut side down in greased muffin pans. Cover rolls and let rise in warm place till double in size, about 1 to 1½ hours. Bake at 375° till done, about 15 minutes. Makes 27 rolls.

Parsley Fantans

> 2 tablespoons butter
> 1 teaspoon lemon juice
> 2 tablespoons snipped parsley
> 2 tablespoons snipped chives
> 6 brown-and-serve butterflake
>   rolls

Melt butter; add lemon juice. Combine parsley and chives. Partially separate sections of brown-and-serve rolls. Brush sections with some butter; sprinkle with part of parsley-chive mixture. Place in muffin cups. Brush with remaining butter; sprinkle with parsley and chives. Brown at 400° for 10 minutes.

Cut Fantans from 14x9-inch rectangle of Basic Roll Dough. Slit each rectangle lengthwise in six strips 1½-inches wide.

Stack six strips on top of another and cut in nine 1½-inch lengths. Place Fantans cut side down in greased muffin pan.

FARCE — A French word meaning stuffing or forcemeat, generally ground meat, used as a filling. Farce is made from finely ground meats, poultry, or fish combined with a wide variety of seasonings and vegetables. Combinations include pork and herb, rice and kidney, and ham and mushroom.

Fix-up Parsley Fantans in a hurry with ready-to-bake butterflake rolls. Serve with a salad for a light lunch.

FARCI — 1. French word meaning stuffed or filled. 2. Any one of a number of stuffed French food dishes. Various food dishes which originated in the southern part of France are referred to as farci. The most commonly served farci dish is stuffed cabbage leaves cooked in stock.

FARFEL — Pastalike mixture of flour, eggs, and water cooked in boiling water to use as an accompaniment or in dumplings. The egg mixture is formed into noodles which become quite crumbly. A speciality of Jewish cookery, farfel is often used as a substitute for potatoes and can be served with goulash to complete a meal.

FARINA — The granular, center portion of hard wheat kernel from which bran and germ have been removed. The finely ground cereal is sometimes combined with protein splitting enzymes and a salt to cause the particles to swell faster and cook more quickly. This is why it is important to check the label when cooking farina.

Farina is most often enriched with iron and the various B vitamins. This makes farina valuable as a breakfast cereal and baby food. Because of its bland flavor, farina combines well with other foods to make puddings, muffins, baked desserts, and dumplings. (See also *Wheat.*)

FARMER CHEESE—A pressed-curd cheese related to cottage cheese. Also known as farm cheese and pressed cheese, farmer cheese was originally made in France. Processing methods differ according to locality, so all farmer cheese is not the same. The tangy-flavored farmer cheese made in the United States cuts smooth without crumbling. (See also *Cottage Cheese*.)

FASTNACHTKUCHEN (*fash' näkt ko͞ok uhn, fäs-, -kûh-*)—The Pennsylvania-Dutch name for rectangular or round doughnuts. Traditionally served the night before fasting began for Lent, the word means fastnight cake. (See *Doughnut, Pennsylvania-Dutch Cookery* for additional information.)

FAT—A class of foods from animal and vegetable sources; in solid form called fat and in liquid form called oil. Fats are a source of essential fatty acids, carry fat-soluble vitamins, and contribute energy in concentrated form. Every cook knows the value of fats for adding flavor and aroma to many foods, as a shortening in baked foods, and as a preservative.

Nutritional value: Besides supplying essential fatty acids and making fat-soluble vitamins available to the body, fats provide more energy per gram than any other food source. In fact, nutritionists figure nine calories per gram for fats to four calories per gram for proteins or carbohydrates. Fats are stored in the body and converted to energy as needed; thus protein is not needed for energy and can be used for body-building purposes instead. Also, although easily digested, fats are absorbed slowly and delay the return of the sensation of hunger.

Fats are eaten as spreads on bread or as an ingredient in other foods. One tablespoon of butter or margarine contains 100 calories. Of course, calories are contributed to any food to which fat is added.

Currently, there is much discussion and research on the relationship of dietary fats and cholesterol. The terms saturated, unsaturated, and polyunsaturated refer to how the hydrogen atoms in a fat molecule are linked together. Saturated fats contain single-bond linkages; unsaturated fats have one double-bond linkage; and polyunsaturated fats contain more than one double-bond linkage.

Types and kinds: Fats that are solid at room temperature include butter, margarine, hydrogenated shortening, and lard. Fats that are liquid at room temperature are usually referred to as oils.

By law, butter must contain 80 percent natural milk fat. Margarine, similar to butter in flavor, color and cooking uses, can be made with animal or vegetable fat combined with milk or cream.

Today, shortenings used in the home and commercially include vegetable shortenings, vegetable and animal fat combinations, and lards that are processed from pork fat. The shortening grandmother used most often was lard rendered from animal fats and was quite different from the soft, white lards that supermarkets now stock.

Salad oils and cooking oils are made principally from cottonseed, corn, and soybean oils, although olive, peanut, and safflower oils are also used. Vegetable oils are refined to produce a bland, odorless product without added moisture.

Although many of these fats are used interchangeably, butter and margarine are used primarily as spreads, lard, and vegetable shortening are used most often for baking and frying, and the oils are basic ingredients in homemade and commercial salad dressings and mayonnaise.

How products from fats and oils are processed: With the exception of butter which is churned from cream, the processing of fats and oils, regardless of ultimate use, begins with three steps that remove undesirable elements: refining removes impurities; bleaching removes color-producing substances; deodorization eliminates undesirable aromas and flavors. When manufacturers wish to turn a liquid oil into a semisolid shortening with improved stability and excellent creaming properties, they expose the oil to hydrogen in a process called hydrogenation.

Cooking value: Fats and oils probably have a wider range of table and cooking uses than any other kind of food. The most obvious example of their versatility is the use of butter and margarine as flavor enhancers for spreading on bread, and for seasoning cooked vegetables.

Another popular use of fats and oils is for frying. When properly prepared, fried foods are wholesome and easily digested. Select the type of fat according to the temperature to be used for frying. Butter and margarine, for instance, smoke at a fairly low temperature, called the smoke point, and thus are suitable only for sautéeing and quick, light frying.

For high-temperature and deep-fat frying, vegetable oils (except olive), all-purpose shortenings (hydrogenated or not), and some high-quality lards are best because they have high smoke points.

The word shortening describes the action of the fat in baking and explains how fats create tenderness in pastries and other baked goods: the fat, surrounding the flour particles, breaks up or "shortens" the gluten strands that form the framework of the cake or bread; hence a more tender product. When creamed for baked products, the shortening traps air in the batter for leavening. In pastry the shortening melts during baking leaving air spaces which produce the desired flakiness. As the shortening melts, it also dissolves and blends the seasonings. Shortenings include butter, margarine, lard, hydrogenated shortening, and a very large variety of vegetable oils.

The emulsifying properties of oils determine the textures of salad dressings. Commercial salad dressings and mayonnaise must contain a certain percentage of fat and oil as specified by law.

As a preservative, fats and oils prevent exposure of foods to air which can cause drying and decomposition. That is why canned fish is often packed in oil. Since oils do not blend readily with other liquids, a thin layer will keep the air from reaching the liquid's surface. Try it on an unfinished bottle of wine. Just put a drop of oil on the surface of the wine to preserve its flavor and good quality.

How to select: Table spreads are marketed by the pound or quarter pound, in tubs, and in whipped form. Oils are available in bottles or cans, in liquid or ounce measures. Lards and vegetable shortenings are packed in one- to three-pound containers. Purchase the right size and kind of fat by considering your family's needs, tastes, and size. Another important point to consider is the size of your refrigerator; fats require careful storage.

How to store: Exposure to air, heat, light, or moisture causes a chemical change in most fats and oils; a decomposition and unpalatable taste and aroma called "rancidity." Some fats and oils are specially processed to contain antioxidants that retard rancidity. Because oxygen in the air causes rancidity, and heat speeds the damage, proper storage of fats and oils at home is important. Butter and margarine absorb odors quickly and should be kept tightly covered in the refrigerator. Salad oils should be stored in a cool place. Some lards need to be refrigerated, others may be kept on the kitchen shelf if the room is relatively cool. Keep all lards covered and check the labels for storage directions. All-purpose shortenings have been stabilized during processing and need only be kept in a closed container at room temperature to maintain and prolong their nutritional value. (See *Nutrition,* individual fats and oils for additional information.)

How to measure fats and oils

Correct measuring methods using standard measuring equipment are important to the quality of the recipe being prepared.

Solid fats

Press firmly in a measuring spoon or individual measuring cup, making sure all air bubbles are pressed out.

Cut with a knife at tablespoon equivalents marked on moisture-proof wrappers of quarter pound butter or margarine.

Oils and melted fats

Measure, as you do any liquid, in a measuring spoon or liquid measuring cup.

FATTIGMANN—A Norwegian deep-fat fried Christmas cookie. The name means poor man, and the cookie may be served either plain or with a jam or jelly. (See also *Scandinavian Cookery*.)

Fattigmann

        6 egg yolks
     ¼ cup sugar
        1 tablespoon butter or margarine, melted
     ⅓ cup whipping cream
        2 cups sifted all-purpose flour
        1 teaspoon ground cardamom
     ½ teaspoon salt

Beat egg yolks till thick and lemon-colored; gradually beat in sugar. Gently stir in butter or margarine. Whip cream till soft peaks form. Fold into egg mixture. Sift together flour, cardamom, and salt; gradually fold just enough flour into yolk mixture to make a soft dough. Chill dough thoroughly.

Divide dough in half. On lightly floured surface, roll each half to an ⅛-inch thickness. Cut dough in 2-inch wide strips, then slash diagonally at 3-inch lengths to make diamonds. Cut slit in center of each diamond and pull one end through. Fry a few at time in deep hot fat (375°) for 1 to 1½ minutes, till very light golden brown. Drain on paper toweling. While warm, sift a little confectioners' sugar over cookies, if desired. Makes about 5 dozen.

Shape Scandinavian Fattigmanns by pulling one end of the diamond-shaped piece through slash cut in center. Deep-fat fry.

FAVA (*fä' vuh*)—The Italian name for big, broad beans similar to lima beans. The heavy beans, growing up to eighteen inches long, are often removed from the pod (purchased in pod) before cooking. The beans may also be peeled before cooking. If the beans are young and fresh, the complete bean and pod is eaten.

Known also as the broad bean in Italy, fava beans are boiled till tender in salted water. Sometimes they are then mashed with butter or other oil till of mashed potato consistency. The beans can also be puréed and dressed with cream or cheese and served with pork, chicken, or a variety of other meats. (See also *Bean*.)

FELL—A thin, paperlike membrane covering the outside fat of lamb cuts, such as leg of lamb or lamb chops. The homemaker often removes the fell from most lamb cuts before cooking, except for the larger cuts such as leg of lamb. If the leg of lamb is to be marinated or brushed with a sauce during cooking, the fell should be removed so the flavoring substance can penetrate the meat more thoroughly.

Some homemakers prefer to leave the fell on the leg of lamb cut during cooking. The larger cut of meat will hold its shape better if the fell is left intact. Because the juices are held in by the membrane, the lamb cut will cook faster and be juicier. The fell does not affect the taste of the meat. (See also *Lamb*.)

FENNEL (*fen' uhl*)—An aromatic plant of the parsley family with a celerylike texture and an anise flavor. Native to southern Europe and the Mediterranean, fennel has enjoyed a number of contrasting uses. The plant was long used as a condiment by the ancient Chinese, Indians, and Egyptians. The Italians and Romans cooked fennel roots and stalk as a vegetable. For medicinal purposes, fennel was used to remedy snake bites, strengthen eyesight, and combat diseases.

The herb was a symbol of success to the Greeks, and was used in the Middle Ages to enhance witchcraft ideas and ceremonies. Early colonists staved off hunger by chewing on sugar coated fennel seed during church services.

The hardy perennial grows from a seed in a moderate climate. After the fennel seeds have turned a greenish gray color and are somewhat hard, they are harvested and dried. Argentina, Bulgaria, and India are among the chief exporters of fennel to the United States.

A small, dwarf variety, known as sweet fennel or Florence fennel, has a broad bulbous base and thick leaf stalks. The sweet fennel bulb and stalks are cooked like a vegetable and have a flavor similar to that of celery.

Fennel, surprisingly rich in vitamin A, is available throughout the year whole (seeds) or ground. The sweet-scented herb is appropriately used for breads, confections, fish, pastry, stews, and pickles. The licorice-flavored fennel is popular in Scandinavian and Italian dishes.

The long-needled leaves are often included in fish sauces and pickles. The leaves can also be minced and the bulbous roots sliced to be used in a fresh salad. The seeds yield an oil adaptable for use in cough drops, pickles, perfumed cosmetics, and licorice candies. (See also *Herb*.)

American Pizza

    ¾ pound ground beef
    ⅓ cup chopped celery
    ⅓ cup chopped onion
    3 tablespoons chopped green pepper
    1 small clove garlic, minced
    ½ teaspoon dried oregano leaves,
        crushed
    ¼ teaspoon fennel seed
            • • •
    1 15½-ounce package cheese pizza
        mix
    2 ounces sharp process American
        cheese, shredded (½ cup)

In skillet cook meat with vegetables till meat is browned and vegetables are tender. Drain off excess fat. Stir in seasonings. Prepare pizza dough following package directions. Roll or pat out to fit 12-inch pizza pan. Crimp edges. Spread pizza sauce (from package mix) over dough. Top with meat, American cheese, then grated cheese (from package mix). Bake at 425° for 25 to 30 minutes. Makes 1 12-inch pizza.

FENUGREEK (*fen′ yŏŏ grēk′*) — An aromatic herb of the bean family cultivated for its seed. Native to Asia and southeastern Europe, fenugreek was used by the Egyptians as quinine is used for medicinal purposes today in medicines.

The fenugreek plant is important as a spice, food in the form of a vegetable, cattle forage, and is used sometimes as a medicinal ingredient. The annual plant is grown commercially from a seed. Chief export countries include Argentina, Egypt, France, India, and Lebanon. The small seeds, yellow brown in color, have an irregular shape. The aroma of the seed, available either whole or in ground form, is strong but pleasant.

The flavor of fenugreek, similar to burnt sugar, is well known in the kitchen as it is used commercially in imitation maple syrups, maple flavorings, and maple-flavored candies. The spice, which supplements protein nutritive value as well as adding flavor, is also used in chutneys, curry powders, mango pickles, and condiments. (See also *Herb*.)

FETTUCINI (*fet′ uh chē′ nē*) — An Italian specialty made of flat egg noodles, cheese, butter, and sometimes cream. The noodles are made of the same flour paste as spaghetti. (See also *Italian Cookery*.)

FIDDLEHEAD GREENS — The tightly curved sprouts of a fern plant that are eaten as a vegetable. The name comes from the violinlike appearance of the curving frond (leaf) of the plant. Growing along the edges of streams, the fern is a well-known vegetable in Maine, in northern New England, and in Canada.

When the sprouts have grown to a length of two inches, in early spring, they are picked. Cooked in boiling, salted water, the fiddlehead greens offer a unique flavor and crunchy texture when served as a hot vegetable. The flavor of fiddlehead greens can best be described as a cross between asparagus and mushrooms.

The greens may also be cut and tossed with an assortment of salad greens and then be dressed with vinegar and lemon juice. Canned fiddlehead greens are available in specialty grocery stores.

FIELD SALAD—A salad green, both wild and cultivated, recognized by its spoon-shaped leaves. Field salad contributes a slightly bitter flavor. Field salad varieties are also called corn salad, lamb's lettuce, fat hen, and hog salad. (See also *Vegetable*.)

FIG—The small, sweet edible fruit of the fig tree grown in warm climates. The fig originated in Asia, Africa, and southern Europe and was introduced to America by early Spanish missionaries.

How figs are produced: California is the chief commercial producing state. Some fig trees are self-pollinating and others must be cross-pollinated by a fig wasp. The blossoms are actually inside the fruit, which explains why the tree has no visible blossoms and why there are such a great number of seeds inside the fruit

Fresh figs are marketed immediately upon becoming ripe. Dried figs are allowed to fully ripen on the tree until heavy with sugar. Partially dried when they drop to the ground, the figs are then dried in the sun, graded, and cleaned.

Nutritional value: The soft fruit is an excellent source of natural fruit sugars which contribute quick energy. Dried figs are rich in iron, calcium, and phosphorus.

Types and kinds: From six to eight hundred varieties of figs, varying in size and color, are grown throughout the world.

The original planting of figs by missionaries in California has led to the development of the many varieties now grown in this country. The Calimyrna is grown in California along with the Adriatic, Black Mission, and Kadota. The varieties, differing in color and size, are sold fresh, dried, or preserved.

The figs common in the southeastern states and Texas and grown chiefly for canning and preserving include the Brown Turkey, Celeste, and Magnolia also called New Brunswick. Each variety is recognized by a different skin and pulp color.

How to select: A fresh fig should feel soft to touch and have a bright, clear color representative of the variety. A charac-

Figs vary in color from green to yellow, brown, purple, or black, depending on variety. The sweet fruit is seed-filled.

teristic aroma, produced by fermentation, is obvious if the fig is not fresh. Fresh figs are available June through October. Figs may also be bought dried or preserved.

How to store: Refrigerate and use fresh figs soon after purchased. Store dried figs in a covered container in a cool place. Refrigerate canned figs after opening.

How to prepare: Peel fresh figs and serve with sugar and cream. Dried figs used for stewing require a short soaking and quick-cooking period. Prepare plump dried figs, for cakes and candies, by soaking them in hot water up to 30 minutes.

How to use: Fresh, dried, and canned figs are used in desserts and confections such as cakes, candies, and puddings. Toss plump figs in salads and fruit compotes. Use figs in dumplings, fritters, breads, and marmalades. (See also *Fruit*.)

fig 885

Applesauce-Fig Loaf

6 tablespoons butter or margarine
⅔ cup sugar
1 egg
1 teaspoon vanilla
2 cups sifted all-purpose flour
1 teaspoon baking powder
1 teaspoon baking soda
½ teaspoon ground cinnamon
¼ teaspoon ground nutmeg
1 cup applesauce
1 cup finely snipped dried figs
½ cup chopped pecans

Cream butter or margarine and sugar till fluffy. Add egg and vanilla; blend well. Sift together flour, baking powder, baking soda, cinnamon, and nutmeg; add to creamed mixture alternately with applesauce. Stir in figs and nuts. Pour into greased 9x5x3-inch loaf pan and bake at 350° till done, about 1 hour. Cool in pan about 20 minutes; remove and cool on rack.

Fig-Nut Squares

½ cup butter or margarine
1¾ cups brown sugar
4 well-beaten eggs
1 teaspoon grated lemon peel
1 teaspoon grated orange peel
2 cups snipped dried figs *or* dates
1 cup chopped walnuts
1½ cups sifted all-purpose flour
1 teaspoon baking powder
½ teaspoon salt
. . .
Creamy Hard Sauce

Melt butter; stir in brown sugar. Add eggs; mix well. Stir in lemon and orange peel, *half* the figs, and *half* the nuts. Sift together dry ingredients. Blend into batter. Pour into greased 13x9x2-inch baking pan. Sprinkle batter with remaining figs and nuts. Bake at 325° for approximately 50 to 55 minutes.

Creamy Hard Sauce: Thoroughly cream together ¼ cup butter or margarine and 2 cups sifted confectioners' sugar. Add 3 tablespoons milk and 1 teaspoon vanilla; mix well. Whip ½ cup whipping cream; fold into creamed mixture. Pass with fig squares. Serves 12.

Fig Bars

1 cup shortening
½ cup granulated sugar
½ cup brown sugar
1 egg
¼ cup milk
1 teaspoon vanilla
3 cups sifted all-purpose flour
½ teaspoon salt
½ teaspoon baking soda
. . .
Fig Filling

Cream shortening and sugars. Add egg, milk, and vanilla; beat well. Sift together dry ingredients. Stir into creamed mixture. Chill at least 1 hour.

On well-floured surface roll ¼ of dough at a time into 8x12-inch rectangle. Cut crosswise in six 2-inch strips. Spread about 2 tablespoons Fig Filling down center of three strips. Moisten edges and top with remaining strips. Press lengthwise edges together with floured fork. Cut in 2-inch lengths. Bake on *ungreased* cookie sheet at 375° about 10 minutes. Makes 4 dozen.

Fig Filling: Combine 2 cups finely chopped dried figs, ½ cup granulated sugar, 1 cup orange juice, and dash salt. Cook, stirring occasionally, till mixture is thick, about 5 minutes. Cool.

Fig Fruit Salad

½ cup dried figs
1 8¾-ounce can crushed pineapple
. . .
1 3-ounce package cream cheese, softened
1 tablespoon mayonnaise or salad dressing
1 tablespoon honey
. . .
2 medium unpared apples, diced
2 medium bananas

Steam figs in a sieve over hot water about 20 minutes; cool. Clip stems; cut figs in thin strips. Drain pineapple, reserving 2 tablespoons syrup. Beat syrup, cheese, mayonnaise, and honey together till smooth. Toss figs, apples, and drained pineapple with dressing. Chill. Before serving, peel and slice bananas; toss with fruit mixture. Serves 6.

FILBERT—A small, thick-shelled nut grown on a bushy shrub or oriental hazel tree. The shell is smooth, medium brown in color, and has a light-colored tip. The nut meat is covered with a thin brown skin which may or may not be removed.

Named for St. Philbert of France, the French people set aside August 22 to recognize him and to gather filberts. The filbert is now used commercially and has been since the early 1900s. Although filberts are also known as hazelnuts, hazelnut refers to a wild nut.

Filberts are imported from Italy, Turkey, and Spain, but are also grown commercially in the northwestern United States. The cultivated varieties are larger and more flavorful than wild hazelnuts.

Available all year round, shelled or unshelled, filberts are sold by the pound. When buying nuts in the shell, be sure the shell is smooth and clean and so well-filled it does not rattle. Store filberts in a cool place away from light.

Filberts can be used in most recipes calling for nuts. They contribute a mild, sweet flavor. The nuts can be ground, sliced, or chopped satisfactorily. Blanch the nuts by toasting in a warm oven for 20 minutes or till the skins rub off.

Filberts are excellent flavorings for desserts, coffee cakes, and ice creams. Add chopped filberts to candies and use whole nuts for garnishing desserts. Give texture to salads and main dishes with sliced filberts. (See also *Nut.*)

Filbert Meringues

Fancy shells to bake ahead of the party—

Beat 2 egg whites to soft peaks. Gradually add ½ cup sugar, beating till very stiff peaks form and sugar is dissolved. Fold in ½ cup finely chopped filberts.

Cover baking sheet with plain paper. Draw 6 circles 3½ inches in diameter; spread each with ⅓ cup meringue. Using back of spoon, shape into shells. Bake at 275° for 1 hour. (For crisper meringues, turn off heat; let dry in oven with door closed about 1 hour.)

Fill with coffee ice cream or top with chocolate sauce, if desired. Makes 6 shells.

Filbert Macaroons

> 1 3½-ounce package whole
>   unblanched filberts (about 1 cup)
> 2 egg whites
> 1 teaspoon lemon juice
> 1 cup sifted confectioners' sugar
> ¼ teaspoon ground cinnamon
>   Whole filberts (optional)

Grind filberts, using coarse blade of food grinder. Beat egg whites with lemon juice till stiff peaks form. Carefully fold in confectioners' sugar, ground nuts, and cinnamon. Drop macaroons onto greased cookie sheet, using 2 teaspoons mixture for each. Top each with nut. Bake at 350° for 15 to 20 minutes. Makes 24.

Filbert Sponge Cake

Coffee powder provides a flavor bonus—

> 1 cup unblanched filberts
> 1 tablespoon instant coffee powder
> 6 egg yolks
> 1 teaspoon vanilla
> 1½ cups sifted cake flour
> 2 teaspoons baking powder
> ¾ cup sugar
> 6 egg whites
> ½ teaspoon salt
> ¾ cup sugar

Grind filberts, using fine blade. Dissolve coffee powder in ½ cup water. Beat egg yolks till thick and lemon-colored. Add coffee and vanilla; beat well. Sift cake flour, baking powder, and ¾ cup sugar together two times. Add to yolk mixture; mix smooth. Stir in nuts.

Wash beaters. Beat egg whites with salt till soft peaks form. Gradually add ¾ cup sugar, beating till stiff peaks form. Fold batter into egg whites, ⅓ at a time. Turn into *ungreased* 10-inch tube pan and bake at 325° for 60 to 65 minutes. Invert to cool.

Elegant nut cake

Sprinkle with confectioners' sugar and perch → whole filberts atop Filbert Sponge Cake. Slice thin and serve with coffee.

Filbert Ice Cream Cake

> 1 pint vanilla ice cream
> 1 cup snipped dates
> 1 cup boiling water
> 1 cup butter or margarine
> 1 cup sugar
> 2 eggs
> ½ teaspoon orange extract
> 1¾ cups sifted all-purpose flour
> ¼ cup unsweetened cocoa powder
> 1 teaspoon baking soda
> ½ teaspoon salt
> 3 ounces chopped filberts,
> toasted (¾ cup)
> 2 squares semisweet chocolate,
> grated or shaved (2 ounces)

Stir ice cream to soften; spread evenly in foil-lined 8x1½-inch layer cake pan. Freeze firm. Combine dates and boiling water; cool. Cream butter or margarine and sugar till light and fluffy; beat in eggs and orange extract. Sift together flour, cocoa powder, soda, and salt; add to creamed mixture alternately with date mixture, beating after each addition. Turn into two greased and lightly floured 8x1½-inch layer cake pans. Sprinkle toasted filberts over batter. Bake at 350° till cake tests done, about 30 to 35 minutes. Cool layers thoroughly, nut side up, on racks; sprinkle with grated chocolate, and chill. Place one cake layer on serving plate; add ice cream layer and top with second cake layer. Serve immediately.

FILÉ *(fuh lā', fē lā')*—Powdered sassafras leaves used as a thickening and flavoring agent particularly in gumbo and other creole dishes which gives the texture of okra. Choctaw Indian squaws taught New Orleans creole cooks that the powdered leaf should be added to the dish after it has been removed from the heat or it will become stringy. (See also *Creole Cookery.*)

FILET MIGNON *(fi lā' min yon', min' yon)*— A small, boneless steak taken from the beef tenderloin. The boneless, tender, and usually expensive beef cut is generally broiled with bacon wrapped around the outside edges. For optimum flavor the filet mignon should be cooked to the rare stage of doneness. (See also *Beef.*)

Filet Mignon Princess

Accompanied by butter-fried potatoes—

In skillet cook 1 tablespoon finely chopped onion in 1 tablespoon butter till tender, but not brown. Mince 2 cups fresh mushrooms; add to onions; cook till liquid is almost gone. Add 2 tablespoons lemon juice and ½ cup red Burgundy wine; reduce to half. Remove from heat. Slightly beat 1 egg yolk; add small amount hot mixture to egg yolk; return to hot mixture; cook and stir till thickened. Fill 4 artichoke cups* with mushroom mixture; keep hot. In another skillet, melt 1 tablespoon shortening; season four 8-ounce center-cut filet mignons with salt and pepper; panbroil 20 minutes, or to desired doneness. Remove from heat; place on stuffed artichoke cups. Pour excess fat from skillet; add ½ cup red Burgundy wine to pan; reduce to half; pour over meat. Place 3 cooked asparagus tips on each steak; top each with 1 tablespoon Béarnaise. Serve with hot panfried potato strips. Serves 4.

Béarnaise Sauce: In small saucepan, combine 3 tablespoons tarragon vinegar, 1 teaspoon minced shallots, 4 crushed peppercorns, and a bouquet of a few tarragon and chervil leaves; simmer till liquid is reduced to half. Strain; add 1 tablespoon cold water to herb liquid. Beat 4 egg yolks in top of double boiler (not over heat); slowly add herb liquid. Have ½ cup butter at room temperature. Add a *few tablespoons* of the butter to egg yolks; place over *hot, not boiling,* water. Cook and stir till butter melts and sauce starts to thicken. Continue adding butter and stirring till all has been used and sauce is smooth as thick cream. Remove from heat at once. Salt to taste and add 1 teaspoon minced fresh tarragon leaves. (Or, add ¼ teaspoon dried whole tarragon leaves and strain sauce.) Makes about 1 cup sauce.

*Available in cans. (These are artichoke bottoms, or *fonds,* 2 inches in diameter.)

FILLED COOKIE—Name given to cookies of rolled, chilled dough cut and filled with jam or sweet mixture. The cookies are filled before baking by sealing the filling between two dough rounds or pulling two ends of a square together over the filling. The baked cookie should have a delicate brown color. (See also *Cookie.*)

Enjoy traditional filet mignon dinner by serving elegant Filet Mignon Princess. Béarnaise Sauce flows atop tower of artichokes, mushroom purée, asparagus tips, and filet mignon.

Date-Filled Sugar Cookies

  1 cup shortening
  ½ cup granulated sugar
  ½ cup brown sugar
  1 egg
  3 tablespoons milk
  1 teaspoon vanilla
  3 cups sifted all-purpose flour
  ½ teaspoon baking soda
    Date Filling

Cream shortening and sugars till fluffy. Add egg, milk, and vanilla; beat well. Sift together dry ingredients and ½ teaspoon salt; add to creamed mixture; mix well. Chill dough 1 hour. On floured surface roll *half* dough at a time to less than ⅛ inch. Cut with 2½-inch round cutter. With tiny cutter or thimble, cut small hole in center of half the cookies. Place scant tablespoon Date Filling on each plain cookie. Top with cutout cookie; press edges with inverted teaspoon tip to seal. Bake 1 inch apart, on *ungreased* cookie sheet at 350° for 10 to 12 minutes. Makes 2½ dozen.

Date Filling: Combine 2 cups snipped dates, ⅓ cup sugar, and ½ cup water. Bring to boiling; cover and simmer about 5 minutes, stirring occasionally. Add 2 tablespoons lemon juice and ¼ teaspoon salt. Cool filling before placing atop cookie dough circles.

Use your fingers to pinch two opposite corners of rolled cookie dough squares together to encase jam or filling in filled cookie.

FILLED MILK — Fresh milk from which natural milk fat has been removed and replaced with another fat, usually coconut oil. The milk used is either nonfat dry milk reconstituted with water, or fluid skim milk. The latter product sometimes contains extra milk solids. Filled milks are subject to numerous state regulations; nutritionally, they may or may not be similar to whole milk. In any event, the use of coconut oil does not reduce the cholesterol value of filled milk. (See also *Milk*.)

FILLET (*fil' it*) — 1. Boned flesh or meat removed from fish, poultry, or game. 2. The process of removing meat from bones of fish, poultry, or game. The word is often confused with filet which refers to the French delicacy, filet mignon.

A large fish can be filleted successfully by cutting down the middle of the back (starting at tail end) carefully slicing flesh away from the center bone section just to the head. This flat slice often makes an individual serving.

The fillet of beef refers to the tenderloin cut or a portion of the sirloin. The fleshy part of the thigh becomes the fillet of veal and mutton. Poultry and winged game fillets come from the underside or the breast of the animal.

FILLING — A sweet or nonsweet food mixture used in sandwiches, pastry shells, and desserts. Filling often refers to a stuffing for meat or poultry, too. The filling not only adds flavor to the food but also provides contrast in texture and color.

Some fillings are smooth, such as frosting or whipped cream between cake layers. Other fillings contain meat, egg, or cheese and are used to make sandwiches.

Types and kinds: Fillings can fall into one of two categories—sweet or nonsweet. The ingredients used to make the filling determine the category.

1. Nonsweet fillings are used for sandwiches and for nonsweet pastry shells, such as those that are used for some hors d'oeuvres and meat-vegetable pies. The fillings include foods such as meats, fish, cheese, and eggs along with olives, pickles, relishes, and vegetables.

When making nonsweet sandwich fillings, be sure the mixture is soft enough to spread without tearing the bread. Also spread softened butter or margarine, as well as salad dressing or mayonnaise, over the bread before adding the filling.

The filling is prepared with crisp vegetables and mayonnaise or salad dressing just before serving: cream butter before mixing with fish, meats, or vegetables for butter fillings. When making rolled sandwiches, choose a moist filling that helps hold the sandwich together. A tiny appetizer sandwich should be savory and appealing. Select a colorful garnish that is appropriate to the filling.

Tuna Rounds

        1 6½- or 7-ounce can tuna, drained
        ½ cup mayonnaise or salad dressing
        1 5-ounce can water chestnuts,
            drained and chopped
        1 tablespoon minced onion
        1 teaspoon lemon juice
        1 teaspoon soy sauce
        ½ teaspoon curry powder
            Party rye bread

Combine ingredients and mix thoroughly. Spread tuna mixture on slices of small rounds of rye bread. Trim each open-face sandwich with a pimiento-stuffed green olive slice, if desired. Makes about 36 open-face tea sandwiches.

Most sandwich fillings may be stored in the refrigerator in a covered container. Avoid storing cream cheese fillings as they turn yellow and dry out with storage. Sandwiches to be frozen should be spread with butter instead of salad dressing before filling so they do not become soaked.

2. The second type of filling, sweet filling, embellishes cakes, pies, and other desserts to make them deliciously rich. Ingredients used for sweet fillings include fruits, nuts, dates, raisins, mincemeat, and coconut, along with whipped cream, honey, and buttery syrups.

Cake fillings are often the frosting used between the layers, or they may be a specially prepared filling such as a fruit or a cream filling. To fill a layer cake, make sure all the layers are approximately the same thickness. Slice off any humps after baking to make the layers uniform in thickness. Brush crumbs from the cake and lay the first layer bottom side up. (This makes the cake stand straighter.) With spatula, spread about one cup of the filling to the edges. (Spread to within one inch of edge if the filling is very soft.)

The cake filling should be at least 3/16 inch thick for flavorful eating. Spread filling quickly and position second layer with top side up. If the cake has more than two layers, position all layers except the top one with bottom sides up. Place the top layer with the top side up. Allow filling to firm a few minutes before frosting the outside of the cake.

Elegant torte desserts layered with proportioned amounts of cake, filling, and fruit are an excellent party or family treat. Some traditional torte recipes require many hours of preparation, while others use quick and easy shortcuts.

Della Robbia Torte

Prepare 1 package lemon chiffon cake mix according to package directions. Grease the *bottoms only* of three 9x1½-inch round pans. Divide batter among pans and bake at 350°, 30 to 35 minutes. Invert to cool. If desired, brush tops of cake layers with rum, using ½ cup white rum; let layers stand 20 minutes.

Prepare one 3- or 3¼-ounce package *regular* vanilla pudding mix according to package directions *but use only 1½ cups milk.* Add 1 teaspoon vanilla. Cover mixture; chill in the refrigerator, stirring once or twice. Beat smooth; fold in 1 cup whipping cream, whipped.

Spread pudding between layers. To make glaze, melt ½ cup apple jelly; stir in 1 tablespoon lemon juice; cool. Arrange one 8½-ounce can pineapple slices, drained and halved; 5 drained, canned pear halves; 5 drained, canned apricot halves; and 11 maraschino cherries over the top of the cake. Position the pineapple slices around outer edge with pears in center and cherries dropped atop. Spoon cooled glaze over fruit. Chill 5 to 6 hours.

Easy-to-prepare Della Robbia Torte uses packaged lemon cake mix, vanilla pudding mix, and canned fruits to create a rich dessert that looks as though it took hours to make.

Jelly cake rolls lend themselves to delicious filling recipes. Jam or jelly fillings may be used when the dessert is served at room temperature. Chill the jelly roll before cutting when serving it with a filling of either whipped cream or pudding.

Walnut Cream Roll

Beat 4 egg yolks till thick and lemon-colored. Combine 4 egg whites, 1 teaspoon vanilla, and ½ teaspoon salt. Beat till soft peaks form; gradually add ½ cup sugar, beating till stiff peaks form. Fold egg yolks into whites; carefully fold in ¼ cup sifted all-purpose flour and ½ cup finely chopped walnuts. Spread batter evenly in greased and floured 15½x10½x1-inch jelly roll pan. Bake at 375° till done, about 12 minutes. Test for doneness with pick.

Immediately loosen the sides and turn out on towel sprinkled with confectioners' sugar. Starting at narrow end, roll cake and towel together; cool on rack. Unroll; spread with 1 cup whipping cream, sweetened and whipped. Roll cake; chill before serving.

Cookie fillings are most often sandwiched between two rolled dough cookie rounds. The edges are carefully pinched together to seal the filling so that it does not escape during baking. Delicious date and raisin fillings with nuts are popular for tasty filled cookies and cakes.

Date–Nut Filling

Combine 1½ cups pitted dates, cut up; 1 cup water; ⅓ cup sugar; and ½ teaspoon salt in saucepan; bring to boiling. Cook and stir over low heat till thick, about 4 minutes. Remove from heat; cool. Fold in ½ cup chopped walnuts. Makes about 1½ cups. *Note:* If cake is being topped with Seven-Minute Frosting (See *Frosting*), reserve ¼ cup of the frosting and fold in filling mixture.

Mouth-watering pie fillings of fruit, custard, chiffon, pumpkin, and others in a delicate, flaky pastry are sure signs of an excellent cook. There are as many types of fillings as there are favorite kinds of pies. Rich, creamy fillings are soft and smooth, yet firm enough to hold their shape.

Cream Filling

Use plain or flavored variations—

⅓ cup granulated sugar
3 tablespoons all-purpose flour
¼ teaspoon salt
1¼ cups milk
1 beaten egg
1 tablespoon butter or margarine
1 teaspoon vanilla

In saucepan combine sugar, all-purpose flour, and salt. Gradually add milk; mix well. Cook and stir over medium heat till mixture thickens and bubbles; cook and stir 2 minutes longer. Very gradually stir in the hot flour mixture into the beaten egg; return to saucepan. Cook and stir till mixture just boils. Stir in butter and vanilla; cover surface of filling with waxed paper or clear plastic wrap. Cool. (Don't stir during cooling.) Makes 1½ cups.

Butterscotch Filling: Prepare Cream Filling, *substituting* ⅓ cup brown sugar for ⅓ cup granulated sugar. *Increase* butter from 1 tablespoon to 2 tablespoons.

Chocolate Filling: Prepare Cream Filling, increasing granulated sugar from ⅓ cup to ½ cup. Cut up one 1-ounce square unsweetened chocolate. Add with milk.

Sometimes fillings for individual deep-dish pies are prepared separately from the crust. The crust can be baked on a cookie sheet or baking dish and put over the pie filling just before serving.

Flavorful fruit pies can be prepared with canned or fresh fruits from the market. The filling is often thickened with cornstarch, flour, or egg. Eggs also contribute added flavor and richness to the pie.

Many fillings are put in a baked pastry shell and chilled, such as chiffon pies based on gelatin, egg whites, and cooked custard. Frozen ice cream pies are chilled in the freezer. Creamy, jellied fillings use no egg whites and are put into a baked pastry and chilled.

Lemon Filling

Pour creamy fruit filling in baked, flaky pastry—

¾ cup sugar
2 tablespoons cornstarch
Dash salt
¾ cup cold water
2 slightly beaten egg yolks
1 teaspoon grated lemon peel
3 tablespoons lemon juice

. . .

1 tablespoon butter or margarine

In saucepan combine sugar, cornstarch, and salt; gradually add cold water. Stir in beaten egg yolks, grated lemon peel, and lemon juice. Cook and stir over medium heat till thickened and bubbly. Boil 1 minute; remove from heat. Stir in butter or margarine. Cool to room temperature without stirring. Makes 1⅓ cups.

Lime Filling: Prepare Lemon Filling *substituting* 1 teaspoon grated lime peel and 3 tablespoons lime juice for lemon peel and lemon juice. Add drop green food coloring and butter.

Orange Filling: Prepare Lemon Filling, *substituting* ¾ cup orange juice for the ¾ cup water and the 3 tablespoons lemon juice. Omit 1 teaspoon grated lemon peel.

Delicious breads and coffeecakes warm from the oven with rich, spicy fruit and nut fillings are a welcome sight to anyone. Fill rich dough with nutmeats, candied fruits, fruit peels, and spices.

Jeweled Banana Bread

⅔ cup sugar
⅓ cup shortening
2 eggs
1¾ cups sifted all-purpose flour
2¾ teaspoons baking powder
1 cup mashed banana (2 large)

. . .

¾ cup mixed candied fruits and peels
½ cup chopped walnuts
¼ cup raisins

In a bowl cream sugar and shortening till light. Add eggs, one at a time, beating well. Sift together flour, baking powder, and ½ teaspoon salt; add to creamed mixture alternately with banana. Fold in the remaining ingredients. Pour into a greased 8½x4½x2⅝-inch loaf pan. Bake at 350° till done, about 60 to 70 minutes. Cool bread in pan 20 minutes.

Spread walnut-flavored cake roll with sweet whipped cream and roll to make Walnut Cream Roll dessert for the coffee crowd. Top with whipped cream and crunchy walnut halves.

Pineapple Crisscross Coffee Cake

> 2 packages active dry yeast
> 4½ to 4¾ cups sifted all-purpose
>   flour
> 1¼ cups milk
> ½ cup sugar
> ¼ cup shortening
> 2 eggs
> 1 teaspoon grated lemon peel
> 3 tablespoons butter or margarine
>   melted
>   Pineapple-Coconut Filling

In a large mixer bowl combine yeast and 2½ *cups* of the flour. Heat together the milk, sugar, shortening, and 2 teaspoons salt just till warm, stirring occasionally to melt shortening. Add to dry mixture in mixing bowl; add eggs and lemon peel. Beat at a low speed with electric mixer for ½ minute, scraping sides of bowl constantly. Beat for 3 minutes at high speed. By hand, stir in enough of remaining flour to make a soft dough. Turn out on a lightly floured surface. Knead till smooth and satiny, about 8 minutes. Place in a greased bowl, turning once to grease surface. Cover and let rise till double, about 1¾ hours.

Punch down and divide dough into 3 portions; cover and let rest 10 minutes. Roll each portion into 12x8-inch rectangle and place on greased baking sheet. Brush dough with melted butter and spread Pineapple-Coconut Filling lengthwise down center third of dough. With scissors, make cuts 2 inches in from the side at 1-inch intervals along edges of dough. Alternately fold strips over filling in herringbone fashion. Cover and let rise till double, 45 minutes. Brush top with slightly beaten egg white and sprinkle with ½ cup toasted almonds, if desired. Bake at 350° for 25 to 30 minutes.

Pineapple-Coconut Filling: Combine one 20-ounce can crushed pineapple, well drained; one 3½-ounce can shredded coconut, toasted; ½ cup brown sugar; and ¼ teaspoon cinnamon.

Bake bread in the morning

← Bake Apricot Bubble Balls, Double-Decker Coffee Strips, Cranberry Wagon-Wheel Rolls, Pineapple Crisscross or Cherry Lattice Coffee Cake for a special brunch.

Double-Decker Coffee Strips

Rich dough contains a rich prune filling—

Soften 1 package active dry yeast in ¼ cup warm water. Cool ⅓ cup scalded milk to lukewarm; stir into yeast mixture; set aside.

Combine 2 cups sifted all-purpose flour, ¼ cup sugar, 1 teaspoon grated lemon peel, and ½ teaspoon salt. Cut in ¼ cup shortening till it resembles coarse cornmeal. Add the yeast-milk mixture and 1 beaten egg; mix. Place in a greased bowl, turning to grease surface. Cover and let rise till double (1¼ to 1½ hours).

Punch down and turn out on floured surface. Roll to 12x10-inch rectangle; place on greased baking sheet. Combine 1 cup chopped, cooked prunes, 3 tablespoons sugar, 1 teaspoon lemon juice, and ⅛ teaspoon ground cinnamon. Spread prune mixture lengthwise over half the dough; fold remaining dough over filling and seal. Cover; let rise till double, about 45 minutes. Bake at 350° for 15 minutes. Cool; frost with confectioners' icing, if desired.

Apricot Bubble Balls

Filling is dropped between rich dough balls—

In a large mixer bowl combine 2 packages active dry yeast and 1½ cups sifted all-purpose flour. Heat together ¾ cup milk, ⅓ cup sugar, ⅓ cup shortening, and 1 teaspoon salt just till warm, stirring to melt shortening. Add to the dry mixture in a mixing bowl; add 2 eggs. Beat at low speed with electric mixer for ½ minute, scraping sides of bowl. Beat 3 minutes at high speed. By hand, stir in 1½ to 2 cups sifted all-purpose flour to make soft dough. Place in greased bowl, turning to grease surface. Cover; let rise till double (2 hours).

Punch down; divide dough into 3 portions. Cover; let rest 10 minutes. Divide portions into 9 pieces; shape into balls. Roll balls in ¼ cup melted butter or margarine; then in mixture of ½ cup sugar and 1 teaspoon ground cinnamon. Arrange in layers in greased 10-inch tube pan, staggering balls; drop ⅔ cup apricot preserves from teaspoon between balls and sprinkle with nuts. Cover; let rise till double, about 45 minutes. Bake at 350° till done, about 35 to 40 minutes. Cool 10 minutes in pan. Invert and remove from pan.

Cranberry Wagon Wheel Rolls

    2 packages active dry yeast
    4¾ to 5¼ cups sifted-all-purpose
         flour
    1⅓ cups milk
    ½ cup sugar
    ½ cup shortening
    1¼ teaspoons salt
    2 eggs
        Cranberry-Apple Filling

In a large mixer bowl, combine yeast and 2½ cups of the flour. Heat together the milk, sugar, shortening, and salt just till warm, stirring occasionally to melt shortening. Add to dry mixture in mixing bowl; add eggs. Beat at low speed with electric mixer for ½ minute, scraping sides of bowl constantly. Beat 3 minutes at high speed. By hand, stir in enough of the remaining flour to make a soft dough. Turn out on lightly floured surface; knead till smooth and satiny, about 8 to 10 minutes. Place dough in greased bowl, turning once to grease surface. Cover and let dough rise till double, about 1½ hours.

Punch down; divide and form into 2 balls. Let rest 10 minutes. Divide each ball into about 8 pieces and form each of these into a bun. Place the buns about 2 inches apart on a greased baking sheet; flatten slightly. Cover and let rise till double. Make an indentation in each bun, leaving ½-inch edge around roll. Fill in with Cranberry-Apple Filling. Bake at 400° till done, about 15 minutes. Remove from baking sheet immediately and sprinkle rolls with sifted confectioners' sugar, if desired.

Cranberry-Apple Filling: In blender container at low speed chop 1½ cups cranberries and 2 small apples. Add ¾ cup sugar and 1½ teaspoons ground cinnamon; blend.

Cherry Lattice Coffee Cake

    1 package active dry yeast
    ¼ cup warm water
    ⅔ cup butter
    ⅓ cup sugar
    1 teaspoon salt
    4 beaten eggs
    4 cups sifted all-purpose flour
    ¾ cup milk
        Cherry Filling
    ¼ cup sifted all-purpose flour

Soften the yeast in warm water. Cream together butter, ⅓ cup sugar, and salt. Reserve 1 tablespoon of beaten eggs for use later and add remaining eggs to creamed mixture; beat well. Stir in the flour alternately with the softened yeast and the milk. Mix, but do not beat.

Set aside 1 cup of dough and spread remainder in 2 well-greased 9x9x2-inch baking pans. Cover with Cherry Filling.

For lattice, blend ¼ cup sifted all-purpose flour into reserved dough. Divide into 12 parts; roll each between floured hands to make 9-inch strips. Arrange 6 strips in lattice pattern over cherry filling in each pan. Brush the strips with reserved beaten egg. Cover; let rise till double, about 45 minutes. Bake at 375° for approximately 20 to 25 minutes.

Cherry Filling: Combine ½ cup each softened butter, chopped almonds, sugar, and cherry preserves. Mix well.

The ultimate goal is to have a filling with a color, flavor, and texture that is compatible with that of the bread or pastry it supplements. Delicious combinations can be achieved by imaginatively pairing up favorite foods and flavors. (See *Cake, Dessert, Pie* for additional information.)

FILLO *(fē' lō)*—Flaky tissue-paper thin sheets of Greek pastry used in making appetizers and desserts, such as *baklava*. Pastry rolls are made of fillo with honey and nut fillings. Layers of fillo pastry and vegetables, meat, or cheese make interesting luncheon dishes. One-pound packaged rolls of fillo sheets can be found in the frozen foods department of supermarkets in Greek neighborhoods.

FINE CHAMPAGNE—A high-quality French brandy made from certain grapes in the Cognac region of France. It is a blend of Grande and Petite Champagne cognacs. The quality of fine champagne outside France may differ a bit from the splendid brandy that is made in France.

FINES HERBES *(fēn' erbz)*—A French phrase describing a combination of finely chopped herbs used for seasoning. Often, *fines herbes* refers to chopped parsley only. There may be more than two herbs in *fines herbs,* and they may either be chopped or minced. In earlier times, mushrooms and truffles were also added to the *fines herbes* seasoning.

Herbs now used in *fines herbes* include parsley, tarragon, basil, thyme, and chives. If a combination of the seasoning is made at home, it should be stored in a tightly covered container.

This distinct seasoning is used for soups, stews, omelets, salads, steaks, egg dishes, and sauces. (See also *Herb.*)

Pimiento-Onion Relish

⅔ cup water
⅓ cup cider vinegar
½ teaspoon fines herbes
2 tablespoons sugar

. . .

1 4-ounce can or jar whole
    pimientos, quartered
1 medium onion, thinly sliced

Combine water, cider, vinegar, fines herbes, and sugar. Add pimientos and onion; marinate overnight. Drain; serve with meat.

FINISHING SAUCE—A French method of thickening and adding flavor to a sauce by swirling butter into the cooked sauce right before serving. To mix the butter into the sauce, lift the saucepan and move it in a circular motion. Do not stir the butter into the sauce as this will prevent thickening. This method insures a smooth, creamy sauce, an even blend of ingredients, and gives a French taste to the sauce.

FINNAN HADDIE *(fin' uhn had' ē)*—The name for haddock that has been smoked and has a light, golden color. It is believed to have been named after the Scottish fishing port, Findhorn, where finnan haddie were first made. In England, one often finds finnan haddie on the breakfast menu.

Much of what is eaten in the United States comes from the New England area and is prepared from large haddock fillets. As with other fish, finnan haddie is a source of protein and the B vitamins, thiamine, riboflavin, and niacin. A 2½x2½x

¼-inch piece equals 103 calories. A common way of preparing this smoked fish is by baking it in a cream sauce or milk. The creamed fish is tasty served over hot, toasted bread. Use finnan haddie in fish casseroles and main dishes. Or, dab melted butter over pieces of fish and broil the pieces till done. (See also *Haddock.*)

FINO *(fē' nō)*—A dry, Spanish sherry that is blended with other types of sherry and shipped under various brand names. Rated as the best by sherry lovers, fino of sturdy body and clean bouquet is produced in the Jerez region of Spain. This very pale sherry is best served after it has been chilled. The rich, dry flavor is compatible with soups. Fino is sometimes served as an appetizer when entertaining. (See also *Sherry.*)

FINOCHIO *(fi nō' kē ō)*—A succulent bulbous-based Italian vegetable, related to the fennel family. Italian truck gardeners introduced finochio to the American vegetable growers and markets.

The large bulbous base, fleshy and sweet, is the most imporant, useful part of the plant. The ornamental stalk foliage is not used as much as the plant base. The knobs are bleached pure white for two weeks after the bulbous base knobs have reached the sized of hens' eggs. Bleaching is done by banking soil against the roots to ward off the sun. This causes the roots to become pure white. The thick plant, which grows low, yields about two crops a year. One crop appears on the market in the early summer and the second crop usually by early winter.

Sometimes the finochio stalks, if they are young and tender, are eaten with salt as celery is eaten. The stalks have a pleasant taste with a slight anise flavor. Other times the bulb of the plant is cut into strips like celery hearts and carrots and eaten like celery. Finochio may be sliced and served raw or slightly blanched in a salad dressed with vinegars and oils.

The finochio base is also used for appetizers and main dishes. The solid base may be cut and served as hors d' oeuvres. As a hot vegetable, the base is often steamed or braised and served au gratin style or with cream sauce.

FISH

Add variety to the menu with protein-rich fresh- or saltwater fish.

Fish range in size from less than one inch to many feet in length, and are either full-bellied or flat, and range in color from a shimmering translucent to a glorious panorama of yellows, greens, reds, and blues. Some fish are docile, fin flickering creatures, while others are armed with sword-shaped noses, or have gaping mouths filled with file-sharp teeth.

The dictionary defines a fish as "any of a large group of cold-blooded animals living in water and having backbones, permanent gills for breathing, fins, and, usually scales." While this is an accurate definition of a fish, it does not even hint of the manner in which fish have been regarded and used throughout history.

Historically, fish have played a vital role as a religious symbol, as a commercial industry, and, of course, as a food.

Despite their sometimes ferocious appearance, fish were not regarded as food by early Britain's and islanders in the Aegean Sea, but as sacrificial objects for the gods. In fact, many of these pagan people did not eat fish and were quite horrified when they observed dead fish washed up onto the shore for fear that this was a sign of their god's displeasure.

Symbolically the fish has served many purposes. At one time it was used as a substitute for money and as a medium of barter. But its greatest use as a symbol was as a sign of recognition for Christians, in the early days of that religion, when their faith was outlawed by the Romans. When two Christians met, one would sketch out a S in the sand and the other would complete the 8 to indicate that he, too, was a member of the faith.

Religion also has played a vital role in establishing the fishing industry. For example, the Roman Catholic church helped bolster the flagging fishing industries in predominantly Catholic countries by banning meat on Fridays and on Saint days and allowing only fish to be eaten.

The abundance of fish, a natural food which does not require a time of gestation, was probably one of the reasons why the early pilgrims settled near the ocean when they fled from Europe to practice their own religious beliefs in the American colonies. Because of the availability of fish the pilgrims did not have to wait for the season when the crops they had sown ripened and were harvested.

As the pioneers moved inland through the St. Lawrence Valley and up the Mississippi River, they copied the fishing techniques of the Indians and made fish a staple of their diet. And, as they moved across the continent, they established small fish industries—especially on the edge of the Great Lakes.

These fish industries later became vital to the nation's economy. On the East Coast, the New England colonies concentrated on saltwater fishing, while in the hinterland, freshwater fishing prevailed to the extent that in the Great Lakes, by 1865, millions of pounds of fish were being caught and processed each year.

Because of the large volume of fishing done each year, the Bureau of Fisheries was established in 1871 to control grading and to certify the quality of the fish.

Nutritional value: Fish products are rich in protein, contain minerals and vitamins, have a varying amount of fat content, and generally are low in calories.

Fish is an excellent source of protein which is used by the body to build and to repair body tissues. This makes fish particularly good for children, the aged, and those recovering from illness when a large amount of protein is necessary. In fact, a four-ounce serving provides about half the amount of protein needed each day.

In addition to being a source of protein, fish is low in connective tissue—good to keep in mind for those on low-bulk diets.

Fish is also a source of the minerals that are needed for proper functioning of the body. Just a few of the minerals include phosphorus, iron, and potassium. The saltwater varieties of fish contain iodine, which is helpful in the prevention of goiter. Two of the minerals, sodium and chlorine, are not found in great amounts in either freshwater or saltwater fish. This makes fish good for low-sodium diets.

Fishery products also contain vitamins. Some of the fat fish, in particular, are especially good sources of vitamin D. The fish liver oils are good sources of the fat soluble vitamins, especially vitamins A and D. All fish, however, contain at least some of the B vitamins.

The fat content varies with the kind of fish (see chart, page 900). Fish oils contain many polyunsaturated fatty acids, which in some instances, can contribute to the reduction of the blood cholesterol level. The term, fat fish, is not necessarily an indication of the size or shape of the fish, but a guide to the fat content: fat fish contain more than five percent fat; lean fish less than five percent.

What fisherman wouldn't be pleased to have his catch turned into a gourmet entrée? Top the Trout Amandine with a butter sauce and serve the Broiled Lake Trout with Pickle Sauce.

Fat and calorie content of fish

Knowing whether the fish is fat or lean and the calorie count aids in diet planning and in selecting the correct cooking method. (The calorie count is for an uncooked 3½-ounce portion or the serving listed.)

Freshwater Fish	Fat	Lean	Calories
Carp		*	115
Catfish		*	103
Crappie		*	79
Lake Herring		*	96
Lake Trout	*		241
Pickerel		*	84
Rainbow Trout		*	195
Walleye Pike		*	93
Whitefish	*		155
(1 piece 3x3x⅞″)			
Yellow Perch		*	91
(1 medium)			

Saltwater Fish			
Butterfish	*		169
Cod		*	78
(1 piece 3x3x¾″)			
Croaker		*	96
Eel (1 serving)	*		233
Flounder		*	68
(1 piece 3x3x⅜″)			
Grouper		*	87
Haddock (1 fillet)		*	79
Hake		*	74
Halibut		*	100
(1 piece 3x2x1″)			
Mackerel (Atlantic)	*		191
Mullet		*	146
Pollock		*	95
Pompano	*		166
(1 piece 3x3x¾″)			
Red Snapper		*	93
Rockfish		*	97
Salmon (Chinook)	*		222
Sea Bass		*	96
Sole		*	68
(1 piece 3x3x⅜″)			
Swordfish		*	118
(1 piece 3x3x¾″)			
Tuna (fresh)	*		145
Whiting		*	74

For the calorie conscious, you're in for some good news: some fish contain fewer calories than many cuts of beef. Of course, the fat fish will contain a few more calories than lean fish, but both are still good for dieters. If fish is not fried and pouring rich sauces on the fish is avoided, fish is a high-quality protein food especially useful to those counting calories.

Types of fish

With the great number of fish available—over 240 species of finfish and shellfish—the finfish can best be divided into saltwater and freshwater varieties. (Although shellfish are sometimes classified under the category of fish, they differ from finfish because they have a shell and no fins.) (See *Shellfish* for further discussion.)

Finfish can also be divided into two other groups: dermersal, or those that live near the bottom of the water—for example cod, flounder, and sole; and pelagic fish, or those that swim in mid water—for example salmon and mackerel.

There is a difference in flavor between freshwater and saltwater fish and between lake fish and stream fish. This is probably due to various reasons including the feeding habits, which definitely affect flavor.

Sportsmen and commercial fishermen find the Great Lakes and Mississippi Valley especially good sources of freshwater fish. Some of the freshwater varieties include the buffalofish, carp, catfish, chub, lake herring, trout, and whitefish.

Saltwater fish are found in the seas, gulfs, and oceans around the world. In America off the New England coast, however, one can find cod, cusk, eel, flounder of various types, haddock, hake, halibut, Atlantic herring, mackerel, ocean perch, pollock, Atlantic salmon, scup, sea bass, shad, skate, some varieties of smelt, swordfish, tuna, and whiting.

The saltwater fish that are caught in the middle Atlantic coastal area are bluefish, butterfish, cod, croaker, black drum, eel, some kinds of flounder, red and white hake, Atlantic herring, king whiting, mackerel, scup, sea bass, sea trout, shad, skate, spot, striped bass, swellfish, swordfish, tilefish, tuna, and whiting.

In the south Atlantic area from North Carolina down to the east coast of Florida, you can find bluefish, butterfish, croaker, drum, eel, king mackerel, mullet, scup, sea bass, sea trout, shad, sheepshead, Spanish mackerel, and striped bass.

The Gulf of Mexico is another source of saltwater fish, for example, the bluefish, red and black drum, king mackerel, king whiting, mullet, pompano, sheepshead, red snapper, and Spanish mackerel.

On the Pacific coast look for barracuda, cod, halibut, Pacific herring, lingcod, mackerel, rockfish, sablefish, salmon, seabass, shad, Pacific sole, smelt, swordfish, and tuna including the albacore.

Selection of fish

If you are not fortunate enough to have a fisherman in the family, you need not despair of eating fish. You can purchase most types of fish, fresh, frozen, or canned. With the development and improvements over the years of the freezing process, people living almost everywhere are able to enjoy fish all year round.

Fresh fish buying tips: Fresh fish can be purchased in several forms. When buying steaks, fillets, or chunks, choose those cuts that are firm and have a fresh look without a dried-out appearance around the edges. If wrapped, they should be packaged in a moisture-vaporproof material.

When buying a whole or dressed fish or cooking a freshly caught fish, one desirable characteristic to look for is bright, clear, bulging eyes. As the fish becomes stale, the eyes get cloudy and tend to sink. Also, the scales lose their luster and the skin slackens. The flesh, however, should be elastic, yet firm. Avoid fish that has a bad odor as it is probably spoiled.

Market Forms Of Fish

Whole or round: The fish just as it is caught. It has to be scaled and eviscerated (internal organs removed) before cooking. The head, tail, and fins may also be removed.

Drawn: Fish that has been cleaned.

Dressed or **pan-dressed:** Fish that has been cleaned and scaled and usually has had its head, tail, and fins removed. The larger, dressed fish may be cut into steaks or fillets. The term pan-dressed refers to the smaller-sized fish.

Steaks: A cross-section slice from a large, dressed fish. It is usually cut $\frac{5}{8}$ to 1 inch thick. The only bone in the steak is a cross-section of the backbone.

Fillets: Pieces of fish that are cut lengthwise from the sides of the fish away from the backbone. This form of fish is almost bone free. When the flesh is cut from only one side of the fish, it is a single fillet. When it is cut from both sides of the same fish and is held together by uncut meat and skin from the underside of the fish, it is called a butterfly fillet.

Chunks: Cross-section pieces cut from a large, dressed fish. Usually the only bone is a cross section of the backbone.

Portions: Pieces that are larger than sticks, cut from blocks of frozen fish. They can be purchased either as uncooked or partially cooked frozen pieces having a bread coating.

Sticks: Frozen, uniformly-sized pieces of fish cut from a block. They, too, are coated with a batter, then breaded and partially cooked. They must be heated before serving.

Canned: Several varieties and types of fish are processed in this manner and include tuna, salmon, sardines, mackerel, anchovies, fish cakes, soups, stews, chowders, and other products. Advantages of these products are that they can be stored on the shelf and are ready to use.

Cured: Fish that is prepared by either the dry salt method, such as caviar, herring, and mackerel; or brine salted (pickled), such as anchovies, herring, salmon, whiting, or mackerel. After curing some fish are smoked.

Frozen fish buying tips: Fish can be purchased frozen in the following market forms—whole, dressed, steaks, fillets, chunks, portions, and sticks. Look for packages of fish that are solidly frozen with no signs of freezer burn or discoloration. They should have no odor and should be packaged in a moisture-vapor-proof wrap to ensure freshness.

Canned fish buying tips: Anchovies, caviar, cod, haddock, herring, mackerel, and sardines can all be purchased in canned form. However, the two most popular canned fish are tuna and salmon.

Most tuna is packed in vegetable oil or water. However, there is a dietetic pack of tuna that is canned using distilled water and no salt. Tuna is also packed in various-sized pieces—solid pack, chunk-style, grated, and flaked. One can choose either albacore (white) or light tuna.

There are also several canned varieties of salmon from which to choose. The color of the salmon is a good indication of the oil content and the price. The deeper red the color, the higher the oil content, and because of the scarcity and popularity of this fish, the higher the price. Sockeye salmon has the highest oil content and is a deep red color. Pink varieties are lighter in color and have less oil content.

How much fish to buy

The following amounts are for one average main dish serving. When combined with a sauce or served as an appetizer, less will be needed. If diners have hearty appetites, more may be needed.

Whole fish . . . . 12 ounces

Dressed fish . . . . 8 ounces

Fillets, steaks . . . . 5 ounces
    or portions

Fish sticks . . . . 4 ounces

Canned fish . . . . 3 ounces

Storage of fish

Fish is very perishable. In order to maintain the best quality, prepare the fish soon after it is caught or purchased. Fresh fish should be kept iced or refrigerated. If properly wrapped when it is purchased, the fish need not be rewrapped before refrigerating. But to store freshly caught fish, wash under cold water and dry with paper toweling. Wrap tightly in moisture-proof material or place in an airtight container. Be sure to use fresh fish within a day or two after they are caught.

For longer storage, fish should be frozen. Dress and wash the fish, then dip in a salt solution before wrapping and sealing in moisture-vaporproof material. Keep the fish frozen until ready to cook. Do not freeze uncooked, lean fish for longer than six months and fat fish for longer than three months to ensure quality eating.

To store cooked fish, cover tightly and refrigerate not longer than three or four days. Or, if desired, freeze the cooked fish, which has been tightly wrapped, for no longer than three months.

Normally, canned fish should not be stored longer than one year for best quality. Keep it in a cool, dry place.

Preparing fish

The catch of the family's fisherman must be cleaned the same day that it is caught. Have the proper equipment on hand so that cleaning will be easier.

How to clean small fresh fish: After the fish is washed, scrape off the scales with a knife or scraper, working toward the head. Making a ¼-to ½-inch deep cut parallel to the fins, slice along each side of the dorsal fin (large fin on fish's back that is on top of backbone) and anal fin (fin towards the rear, underneath fish). Hold the fish on its back and make a cut right behind the vent on the underneath side. Slip the knife forward under the skin and cut down to the pectoral fins (fins on the sides) on both sides of fish. With the fish laying on its side, make a deep cut on both sides of the fish's body, just behind the pectoral fins.

Break the backbone by pulling the head upward. Tear the head, entrails, pectoral, and pelvic fins (fins towards the front underneath the fish) loose. Remove dorsal and anal fins giving a quick pull forward towards the head so that the root bones will still be attached. Cut off the tail and wash the fish well before cooking.

How to thaw frozen fish: To thaw fish before cooking, place the fish in its original wrappings in the refrigerator. Allow about 24 hours for a 16-ounce package. Or, if time is short, place the fish, sealed in a plastic bag, under cold, running water. This will take about 1 to 2 hours for a 16-ounce package. Once the fish has thawed, use as soon as possible.

Just a few precautions—do not thaw fish sticks or portions before cooking and do not soak unwrapped fish in water.

Cooking fish

Fish is a relatively easy food to prepare, it is versatile, and it cooks rather quickly. It has very tender meat; consequently, correct cooking techniques are very important so that the fish will be served at its best. The flavor of fish is developed and the protein in fish becomes easier to digest as it is cooked. When properly prepared, fish is moist and tender with a very delicate flavor. Because of its versatility, fish is used in many recipes, from appetizers, salads, soups and chowders, to sandwiches and main dishes.

Whether the fish is fat or lean often determines the cooking method. For example, broiling and baking are good methods for cooking fat fish. The fat will keep the fish from drying out during cooking. A lean fish usually is poached, fried, or steamed, but it can be baked or broiled if basted frequently with melted butter or shortening to keep it moist. These are just general guides and almost any fish can be cooked by any method if allowances are made for the fat content of the fish.

The fish is done when the flesh can be easily flaked with a fork and has an opaque appearance. Avoid overhandling the fish during cooking as it is very delicate and tends to flake apart very easily.

Baking: Thaw fish if frozen, and place in a greased, shallow baking pan in a single layer. For fillets, place skin side down and tuck under the thin ends so the fish is an even thickness. A whole fish can be stuffed with a savory mixture before baking. Bake at a moderate oven temperature till fish flakes easily when tested with a fork.

Baked Fish Fillets

  1 **pound fresh or frozen fish fillets**
  1 **tablespoon lemon juice**
 ⅛ **teaspoon paprika**
   Salt and pepper
  1 **tablespoon butter or margarine**
  1 **tablespoon all-purpose flour**
 ½ **cup milk**
 ¼ **cup buttered bread crumbs**
  1 **tablespoon snipped parsley**

Thaw frozen fillets; cut into serving-size pieces. Place in greased shallow baking dish. Sprinkle with lemon juice, paprika, salt, and pepper. In saucepan, melt butter or margarine; blend in flour, dash salt, and dash pepper. Add milk; cook and stir till thickened and bubbly. Pour sauce over fillets. Sprinkle with crumbs. Bake at 350° for 35 minutes. Trim with snipped parsley. Makes 3 or 4 servings.

Spinach-Fish Bake

  1 **11-ounce package frozen breaded**
    fish portions
  1 **10-ounce package frozen**
    chopped spinach

       • • •

  1 **11-ounce can condensed Cheddar**
    cheese soup
  2 **tablespoons milk**
   Dash ground nutmeg
   Lemon wedges

Arrange frozen fish portions in 10x6x1½-inch baking dish. Bake at 425° for 10 minutes. Meanwhile, cook spinach according to package directions; drain thoroughly. Combine with condensed soup, milk, and ground nutmeg. Heat. Spoon over fish in baking dish. Garnish with lemon wedges and return to oven to heat through, about 5 minutes. Serves 4 to 6.

Lemon-Stuffed Fish

½ cup finely chopped celery
¼ cup chopped onion
3 tablespoons butter or margarine
4 cups dry bread cubes
½ teaspoon grated lemon peel
4 teaspoons lemon juice
1 tablespoon snipped parsley
½ teaspoon salt
  Dash pepper
2 16-ounce packages frozen fish
  fillets, partially thawed
1 tablespoon butter or margarine,
  melted
  Paprika

Cook celery and onion in 3 tablespoons butter or margarine till crisp-tender. Pour over bread cubes. Add lemon peel and juice, parsley, salt, and dash pepper; toss together.

Slice each block of partially thawed fish in half horizontally through the center, making 4 thin rectangular pieces. Place 2 pieces in greased 13x9x2-inch baking pan. Spoon *half* the stuffing mixture on each. Top with 1 tablespoon melted butter and sprinkle with salt. Cover pan with foil. Bake at 350° till fish flakes easily with a fork, 20 to 25 minutes. Sprinkle with paprika. Makes 6 servings.

Stuffed Fillet Roll-Ups

Cook 2 tablespoons chopped onion in 2 tablespoons butter till tender. Stir in 2 cups soft bread crumbs, ¼ teaspoon poultry seasoning, ⅛ teaspoon salt, dash pepper, and 2 tablespoons mayonnaise. Partially thaw one 16-ounce package frozen haddock fillets. Cut block of fish in half lengthwise. Then split each piece in half again lengthwise, making 4 strips 8x1½-inches. Completely thaw fish. Spread each piece with bread stuffing; roll up, jelly-roll fashion. Place in 3-cup casserole. Bake, covered, at 375° for 25 minutes. Uncover; bake 10 minutes. Serve with Egg Sauce. Serves 4.

Egg Sauce: Cook 2 tablespoons chopped green onion in 2 tablespoons butter till tender. Blend in 2 tablespoons all-purpose flour, ½ teaspoon salt, and dash pepper. Add 1¼ cups milk, ½ teaspoon prepared mustard, and 1 teaspoon Worcestershire sauce. Cook and stir till bubbly. Add 1 finely chopped hard-cooked egg. Heat.

Herb-Baked Fish

Thaw one 16-ounce package frozen haddock, halibut, *or* cod fillets. Place in 10x6x1½-inch baking dish. Dot the thawed fillets with 1 tablespoon butter or margarine. In saucepan thoroughly blend 1 cup milk and 2 tablespoons all-purpose flour. Cook and stir over medium heat till sauce thickens and bubbles. Cook and stir 1 minute longer. Stir in ¼ teaspoon salt; ¼ teaspoon garlic salt; ⅛ teaspoon pepper; ⅛ teaspoon dried thyme leaves, crushed; dash dried oregano leaves, crushed; and ¼ cup chopped green onion. Mix well.

Pour sauce over fish. Sprinkle lightly with paprika. Bake, uncovered, at 350° till fish tests done, 20 to 25 minutes. Makes 4 servings.

Tuna Italian

½ cup chopped onion
1 tablespoon butter or margarine
1 10½-ounce can condensed cream
  of mushroom soup
1 6-ounce can evaporated milk
⅓ cup grated Parmesan cheese
1 6½- or 7-ounce can tuna, drained
1 3-ounce can sliced mushrooms,
  drained (½ cup)
¼ cup chopped ripe olives
2 tablespoons snipped parsley
2 teaspoons lemon juice
4 ounces noodles, cooked and
  drained (about 2 cups)
  Parmesan cheese
  Paprika

Cook onion in butter till tender but not brown. Add soup, evaporated milk, and cheese; heat and stir. Break tuna in chunks; add with next 5 ingredients. Pour into 2-quart casserole. Sprinkle with additional Parmesan cheese and paprika. Bake at 350° for 25 to 30 minutes. Top with additional snipped parsley and ripe olive slices, if desired. Makes 6 servings.

Tuna and noodle variation

Olives, Parmesan cheese, and lemon juice →
are added to make Tuna Italian a specialized version of the family favorite.

Salmon or Tuna Pie

Sure to be a hit with the family—

        2 beaten eggs
        ½ cup milk
        ¼ cup chopped onion
        2 tablespoons snipped parsley
        1 tablespoon butter, melted
        ¾ teaspoon dried basil leaves,
            crushed
        ¼ teaspoon salt
                •   •   •
        1 16-ounce can salmon, *or* 2 6½- or
            7-ounce cans tuna, drained
        1 stick piecrust mix
          Creamed peas

Combine eggs, milk, onion, parsley, butter, basil, and salt. Break salmon or tuna into chunks, removing bones and skin from salmon. Add to egg mixture. Pour into well-greased 8-inch pie plate. Prepare piecrust mix according to package directions. Roll ⅛ inch thick; cut circle using bottom of 8-inch pie plate as a guide. Cut the circle into 6 wedges; arrange atop salmon or tuna mixture. Bake at 425° till done, about 25 minutes. Serve at once with creamed peas. Makes 6 servings.

Tuna 'n Rice Soufflé

        1 10½-ounce can condensed cream
            of mushroom soup
        1 6½- or 7-ounce can tuna,
            drained and flaked
        1 cup cooked rice
        ¼ cup chopped canned pimiento
        2 tablespoons snipped parsley
                •   •   •
        4 eggs
          Lemon wedges

In saucepan heat and stir soup. Add tuna, rice, pimiento, and parsley; heat through. Remove from heat. Separate eggs. Beat whites till stiff peaks form. Beat yolks till thick and lemon-colored; gradually stir in tuna mixture. Pour slowly onto beaten egg whites, folding together thoroughly. Turn into *ungreased* 2-quart casserole. Bake at 350° till mixture is set in center, 30 to 35 minutes. Serve immediately. Pass lemon wedges. Makes 6 servings.

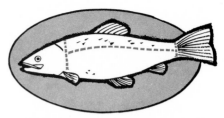

Remove head and tail. Using table knife, make a gentle lengthwise cut 1 inch from upper edge, cutting in just to backbone.

Slide knife along top of backbone gently folding top section away from backbone. Repeat, folding back bottom section.

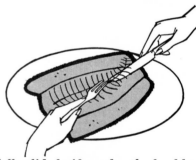

Carefully slide knife under the backbone, lifting it away from body of fish. Use fork to assist. Discard the backbone.

Gently replace the two sections to their original position atop the fish. Head and tail may be replaced, if desired.

Fish in Cheese Sauce

Try this with haddock or halibut—

> 1 pound fresh or frozen fish steaks or fillets, cut in serving-sized pieces
> 1 tablespoon butter or margarine
> ¼ teaspoon salt
>   Dash pepper
> . . .
> 1 10-ounce package frozen cut asparagus
> 1 11-ounce can condensed Cheddar cheese soup
> ¼ cup milk
> 1 cup soft bread crumbs
> 2 tablespoons butter, melted

Thaw frozen fish and place in greased 10x6x1½-inch baking dish; dot with 1 tablespoon butter; sprinkle with salt and pepper. Bake at 350° about 30 minutes. Meanwhile, cook asparagus according to package directions; drain. Place asparagus atop fish. Combine soup and milk; pour over all. Combine crumbs and melted butter; sprinkle atop. Return to oven till lightly browned, 10 minutes. Makes 4 servings.

Seafood Turnovers

Dill sauce adds a finishing touch—

> 1 7¾-ounce can salmon *or*
>   1 7-ounce can tuna
> 1 10½-ounce can condensed cream of mushroom soup
> ¼ cup chopped celery
> . . .
> 2 sticks piecrust mix
> 2 tablespoons milk
>   Dash dried dillweed

Drain and flake salmon or tuna, removing bones and skin from salmon. Combine ½ *cup* of the soup, fish, and celery. Prepare piecrust mix according to package directions; roll into four 6-inch circles. Place ¼ of the filling on ½ of each circle; fold to form turnovers. Seal edges with fork; prick top. Bake on *ungreased* cookie sheet at 450° for 15 to 20 minutes. Combine remaining soup, milk, and dillweed; heat. Serve with turnovers. Makes 4 servings.

Planked Stuffed Walleye

> 1 3-pound dressed walleye *or* pike
>   Salt
> ⅓ cup chopped celery
> 2 tablespoons chopped onion
> 1½ teaspoons snipped parsley
> 2 tablespoons butter
> 2 cups dry bread cubes
> ½ teaspoon salt
> ½ teaspoon ground sage *or* dried marjoram leaves, crushed
>   Dash pepper
>   Melted butter
> 4 slices bacon
> 3 ripe tomatoes, cut in half
>   Garlic salad dressing
>   Duchess Potatoes
> 2 10-ounce packages frozen peas, cooked and drained

Wash fish; remove head, fins, and backbone, but leave tail on. Rinse again and wipe dry. Rub inside and outside of fish with salt. Let stand 10 minutes.

Cook celery, onion, and parsley in 2 tablespoons butter just till tender. Combine with bread cubes, ½ teaspoon salt, sage, and pepper. Toss lightly. Stuff fish loosely. Skewer; lace.

Place the fish on a seasoned plank or a well-greased bake-and-serve platter. Brush the fish with melted butter. Bake the fish, uncovered, at 375° for 25 minutes. Remove from oven.

Lay bacon strips over fish. Place tomato halves beside the fish and brush the cut surfaces with garlic salad dressing. Pipe Duchess Potatoes around edge of plank. Return to oven and bake till fish flakes, about 15 minutes.

To serve, remove skewers; add peas to remaining space on plank. Makes 6 servings.

Duchess Potatoes: Beat 1 tablespoon butter, 1 beaten egg, and salt and pepper to taste into 4 cups hot mashed potatoes. Using a pastry bag with large star tip, pipe hot potatoes around edge of plank. Drizzle 2 tablespoons melted butter or margarine over potatoes.

Broiling: If fish is frozen, it should be thawed before cooking. Thicker pieces, about one inch, are better for broiling because they will not dry out as fast under the high heat. Place fish on greased broiler pan and baste liberally with melted butter.

Broil about three to four inches from heat till fish flakes easily when tested with fork. Fillets or steaks do not need to be turned over, but whole fish should be turned once, halfway during cooking.

Broiled Lake Trout

> **6 1-inch thick lake trout steaks**
> **(or use northern, young muskie, or salmon)**
> **⅓ cup butter or margarine, melted**
> **Salt and pepper**
> **Pickle Sauce**
> **Lemon wedges**

Place fish in a single layer on greased broiler pan. Brush with melted butter or margarine and season with salt and pepper.

Broil about 3 to 4 inches from heat till fish flakes easily when tested with a fork, about 10 to 15 minutes. Brush fish with melted butter once during cooking. Serve with Pickle Sauce lemon wedges. If desired, trim with olive kabobs and parsley sprigs. Makes 6 servings.

Pickle Sauce: Drain ¼ cup chopped dill pickle and 1 tablespoon finely chopped capers on paper toweling. Add to 1 cup mayonnaise or salad dressing. Stir in 1½ teaspoons prepared mustard and 1½ teaspoons snipped parsley.

Herb-Crumb Topped Fish

> **2 12-ounce packages frozen halibut steaks, thawed**
> **¼ cup butter or margarine, melted**
> **Salt and pepper**
> **¼ cup dry bread crumbs**
> **⅛ teaspoon dried thyme leaves, crushed**
> **Dash garlic salt**

Place the fish in a single layer on a greased broiler pan. Brush with some of the melted butter or margarine; season with salt and pepper. Broil about 3 to 4 inches from the heat for 8 minutes. Add dry bread crumbs, crushed thyme leaves, and garlic salt to remaining butter or margarine. Sprinkle on fish. Return to the broiler till crumbs are browned and fish flakes easily when tested with a fork, about 3 to 5 minutes longer. Makes 4 to 6 servings.

Fish with Tarragon Butter

Thaw one 16-ounce package frozen fish fillets. Cut fish in 4 serving-sized pieces. Sprinkle fish with salt and pepper. Place on greased broiler pan. Spread with some of the Tarragon Butter. Broil about 3 to 4 inches from the heat till fish flakes easily when tested with a fork, about 10 to 15 minutes. Pass the remaining Tarragon Butter. Makes 4 servings.

Tarragon Butter: Cream ¼ cup softened butter or margarine till fluffy. Then crush ½ teaspoon dried tarragon leaves. Combine tarragon and ½ teaspoon lemon juice with creamed butter. Keep the butter at room temperature for 1 hour to mellow. Refrigerate any leftover butter.

Charcoal broiling: If fish is frozen, it should be thawed before cooking as for oven broiling. Choose thick cuts of fish, since this is a dry heat method of cooking. The pan-dressed fish should be cooked over moderately hot coals about 16 to 20 minutes, while fillets and steaks should be cooked 10 to 16 minutes, turning the fish once during cooking. Use a greased, wire broiler basket so that the fish will be easier to turn.

For a crispy coating on freshly caught trout, dip cleaned fish in a seasoned cornmeal mixture before frying in a skillet.

Charcoaled Salmon Steaks

Brush six 1-inch thick salmon steaks (or use northern, young muskie, or trout) with ⅓ cup melted butter. Place in a greased, wire broiler basket. Broil over *moderately hot* coals for 5 to 8 minutes. Turn, brush with melted butter, and broil till done, 5 to 8 minutes longer. Season with salt and pepper. Combine 1 cup mayonnaise and 1 tablespoon undrained capers. Pass with fish. Makes 6 servings.

Frying: This is a good and popular method of cooking fish. This method adds crispness and it also adds fat to the lean types of fish. The fish may be dipped in an egg or milk mixture, seasoned, then coated with crumbs, cornmeal, or flour before cooking. It can then be panfried, ovenfried, or deep-fat fried. Drain fish after frying to remove any excess fat.

Trout Amandine

Wash 4 pan-dressed brook trout. (*Or* substitute crappies, bluegills, or yellow perch.) Leave tail on but remove head and backbone. Dry. Dip in seasoned all-purpose flour. Melt ¼ cup butter in skillet. Add fish and fry till browned and fish flakes, 12 to 15 minutes, turning once. Remove from pan and keep warm.

Melt an additional ¼ cup butter in skillet, mixing with crusty bits. Add 2 tablespoons slivered almonds. Brown, stirring occasionally. Stir in ¼ cup lemon juice and 2 tablespoons snipped parsley. Season with salt and pepper. Pour over the fish. Makes 4 servings.

Fried Fish

Wash pan-dressed fish; dry thoroughly. Dip in 1 beaten egg mixed with 1 tablespoon water, then in bread crumbs, seasoned flour, or cornmeal. Brown fish in ¼ inch hot shortening on one side. Turn; brown other side.

Oven-Fried Fish

> 1 pound fresh or frozen fish
>   fillets
> ½ cup milk
> ½ cup fine dry bread crumbs
> 2 tablespoons butter, melted

Thaw frozen fillets; cut in serving-sized pieces. Dip in milk; roll in crumbs. Place in greased baking pan. Sprinkle with salt and pepper. Drizzle butter over fish; bake at 500° till fish flakes easily with fork, 10 to 12 minutes. Makes 3 or 4 servings.

Zippy Fish Fillets

> 2 tablespoons Worcestershire sauce
> 1 tablespoon lemon juice
> 1 pound fresh or frozen fish
>   fillets
> ½ cup dry bread crumbs

Combine Worcestershire and lemon juice. Thaw frozen fillets; Cut in serving-sized pieces. Brush with lemon mixture. Season with salt and pepper. Dip in crumbs. Bake in greased baking pan at 500° about 15 minutes. If desired, serve with tartar sauce. Serves 4.

Poaching and steaming: Two moist-heat methods of cooking fish are steaming and poaching. To steam, cook the fish over the steam rising from boiling water. Sometimes the water is seasoned. For steaming fish special equipment is usually required, either a steam cooker or a deep pan with a rack on which the fish is placed.

To poach, cook the fish in a simmering liquid. Again the cooking liquid can be seasoned water, seasoned milk, or a mixture of water and wine, or water and lemon juice. (See also *Shellfish*.)

Serve Fish Chowder in a crock and let diners help themselves. Bacon, chives, and pats of butter are flavorful and colorful finishing touches for this hearty, main dish soup.

FISH AND CHIPS—A combination of fried fish fillets and deep-fat fried potatoes. It is a traditional English dish and is often sold, wrapped in newspapers.

Fish and Chips

Cut 1 pound peeled baking potatoes into uniform strips slightly larger than for French fries. Fry potatoes, a small amount at a time, in deep hot fat (375°) till golden, about 7 to 8 minutes. Remove; drain and keep warm.

In a bowl blend together ¼ cup all-purpose flour and ½ teaspoon salt. Make a well in the center of the dry ingredients. Add 2 tablespoons water, 1 tablespoon salad oil, and 1 egg yolk. Stir to make a smooth batter. Beat 1 egg white till stiff peaks form. Fold into batter. Cut 1 pound fish fillets into serving-sized pieces. Dip fish pieces in ¼ cup all-purpose flour, then into the egg batter.

Fry in same hot shortening (375°) till golden brown, about 1½ minutes on each side. Season fish and chips with salt. To serve, sprinkle fish with vinegar. Makes 4 servings.

FISH CHOWDER—A hearty, thick soup made with fish, onions, potatoes, and seasonings. It is sometimes made with milk and other vegetables. The name chowder originated from the name for the French kettle, *chaudière*. (See also *Chowder*.)

Fish Chowder

>   1 pound fresh or frozen fish
>   fillets
>   2 slices bacon
>   2 cups diced, peeled potato
>   1 cup water
>   ½ cup chopped onion
>   1½ teaspoons salt
>   ⅛ teaspoon white pepper
>   • • •
>   1 tablespoon all-purpose flour
>   2 cups milk
>   2 tablespoons snipped chives
>   2 tablespoons butter or margarine

Thaw frozen fish. In large saucepan cook bacon till crisp. Remove bacon, drain on paper toweling; crumble and set aside. Pour off excess fat from saucepan. In same saucepan combine potato, fish, water, onion, salt, and pepper. Bring to boiling; cover, reduce heat, and cook till potato is tender, about 15 to 20 minutes. Lift fish from saucepan. Cut into bite-sized pieces. Return to saucepan.

Blend flour and a small amount of the milk till smooth. Blend in remaining milk. Add to fish mixture. Cook and stir over low heat till mixture bubbles. Sprinkle crumbled bacon and chives atop just before serving. Top with pats of butter. Makes 6 servings.

Tuna Chowder

A quick and hearty soup for lunch—

In saucepan combine one 4-ounce envelope dry green pea soup mix, ⅓ cup uncooked packaged precooked rice, and 2 teaspoons instant minced onion. Stir in 3 cups cold water. Cook, stirring frequently, till mixture is boiling. Cover and simmer 3 minutes. Stir in one 6½-or 7-ounce can tuna, drained and flaked. Add salt and pepper to taste. Cook till mixture is heated through. Makes 4 servings.

FISH HOUSE PUNCH—A rum punch usually containing peach liqueur, brandy, lemon juice, and plain or carbonated water.

Fish House Punch

Mix 1¾ cups sugar, 1 quart lemon juice, and 2 quarts water. Chill several hours, stirring occasionally. Add 2 fifths dark rum, 1 fifth grape brandy, and 1 cup peach brandy. At least 1 hour before serving, pour into punch bowl; add 2 quarts ice cubes. Add more ice just before serving. Makes fifty 5-ounce servings.

FISH ROE—The eggs of female fish that are used as a food delicacy, such as shad roe, or caviar from the sturgeon.

FIVE SPICES—A seasoning used in Chinese cookery. It is also called five-flavored spice powder and is a fragrant, red brown powdery substance that is used with poultry or pork dishes. The mixture may include cinnamon, cloves, star anise, anise, pepper, and fennel. A very small amount of the spice combination is needed.

FIZZ—The name given to a tall, bubbly, effervescent beverage that contains sparkling or charged water. It may be alcoholic or non-alcoholic. (See also *Beverage*.)

Rosy Raspberry Fizz

Combine 2 cups pineapple juice; one 10-ounce package frozen raspberries, partially thawed; 1 pint vanilla ice cream; and 1 pint raspberry sherbet in large bowl. Beat till blended. Carefully pour one 16-ounce bottle cream soda down side of bowl; mix gently. Serve at once in tall glasses. Makes 6 to 8 servings.

FLAGEOLET *(fla zhö le')*—A small, green kidney bean imported from France. They are used in casseroles and soups.

FLAKE—1. To break lightly into small pieces as when separating cooked fish into pieces with a fork. 2. The name of cereals that are rolled very thin.

FLAMBÉ (*fläm bā′*)—The French word for the flaming of food during preparation or when brought to the table for serving. Examples include crepes suzette, cherries jubilee, and English plum pudding.

Chicken Jubilee

> 6 small chicken breasts, boned
>   and skinned
> 1 20-ounce can pineapple slices
> 2 tablespoons butter or margarine
> 1 cup finely chopped cooked ham
> 2 tablespoons chopped onion
> ¼ teaspoon ground ginger
> ¼ cup medium crushed saltines
> ¼ cup butter or margarine
> ¾ cup chicken broth
> 2 tablespoons vinegar
> 1 tablespoon cornstarch
> 1 8¾-ounce can pitted dark
>   sweet cherries, drained
> ¼ cup brandy (cognac)

Place chicken pieces, boned side up, on cutting board. Working from center out, pound chicken lightly to make cutlets about ¼ inch thick. Drain pineapple slices, reserving ½ cup syrup. Dice 4 pineapple slices and cook in 2 tablespoons butter with ham and onion. Add ginger and crushed saltines to the mixture; mix well.

Divide stuffing evenly among chicken breasts. Tuck in sides of each and roll up as for jelly roll. Skewer or tie. In skillet, brown chicken slowly in ¼ cup butter. Add chicken broth, vinegar, and ½ teaspoon salt. Cover and cook 20 minutes. Mix cornstarch with reserved ½ cup pineapple syrup. Stir into sauce in skillet. Cook, uncovered, till chicken is tender, about 15 minutes. Remove to serving dish.

Brown remaining pineapple slices lightly in small amount of butter. Add fruits to chicken. Pour sauce into heatproof dish. Heat brandy; pour over sauce. Ignite at table. Spoon flaming sauce over chicken. Makes 6 servings.

An elegant, flaming dinner

← Spoon flaming brandied pineapple sauce over chicken and fruit pieces for a special Chicken Jubilee family or guest dinner.

To prepare a flambé dish, combine brandy or other alcoholic spirits such as rum or kirsch with a sauce, then ignite the sauce and spoon it over a dessert or main dish. Sometimes a highly alcoholic flavoring extract or a sugar cube soaked in spirits is flamed. The spirits are usually warmed before adding to sauce and igniting. Ignite the sauce with a match, keeping your face clear of the high flames. Then spoon sauce over food. (A sauce high in butter or sugar content will produce a higher flame than will an ordinary sauce.)

A splendid effect is achieved at the end of a dinner by serving a flamed dessert. The alcohol vanishes during burning, leaving the food with a subtle spirit flavor.

FLAN (*flan, flän*)—1. A shallow pastry shell filled with custard or fruit. 2. Custard baked in a caramel-coated baking dish. Flan pastries are made in France, England, and the United States, while flan custards are a popular Spanish dessert.

Flan pastry is made by pressing sweet pastry dough into a straight-sided round or square flan ring which is set on a cookie sheet. The ring is removed after baking and the flan is filled with custards, ice cream mixtures, and pie fillings. A flan custard is made by baking a custard in a dish coated with caramel. (See also *Pastry*.)

Flan

> ⅓ cup sugar
> 4 beaten eggs
> 2 14½-ounce cans evaporated milk
> ½ cup sugar
> 2 teaspoons vanilla

In 8-inch skillet heat and stir ⅓ cup sugar over medium heat till melted and golden brown. Quickly pour into 8-inch round baking dish, tilting to spread over entire bottom of dish. Combine beaten eggs, milk, ½ cup sugar, and vanilla; mix well. Pour into caramel-coated dish; place in larger pan. Add boiling water to pan to 1-inch depth. Bake at 325° till knife inserted half-way between center and edge comes out clean, about 45 minutes. (Center will be soft.) Chill thoroughly. Loosen sides and invert on platter. Makes 8 servings.

FLANK STEAK—A boneless beef cut taken from the triangular muscle located on the underside of the hindquarter in front of the round. The lean, relatively thin steak is distinguished by the bundles of muscle fiber which run lengthwise through it.

Several beef cuts are taken from the flank. Besides flank steak, flank fillets (pinwheels) and flank stew meat are two other cuts. A top-quality flank steak is referred to as London Broil and can be satisfactorily broiled if served in thin, diagonal, cross-the-grain slices.

Because flank steak is a less tender cut of meat, it is best to braise or stuff and bake the meat in a sauce. (See *Beef, London Broil* for additional information.)

Braised Flank Steak

Score one 1- to 1½-pound flank steak; coat with all-purpose flour. Brown meat in hot shortening. Season steak to taste with salt and pepper. Add ½ cup hot water to the browned meat.

Cover meat; cook slowly over low heat or bake at 350° till meat is tender, about 1½ hours. Makes 3 or 4 servings.

Herb-Stuffed Flank Steak

  ⅓ cup chopped onion
  2 tablespoons butter or margarine
  2 hard-cooked eggs, chopped
  2 cups herb-seasoned stuffing
     croutons
  1 cup dairy sour cream
  1 beaten egg
  1 pound beef flank steak
    Meat tenderizer
  2 tablespoons shortening

Cook onion in butter till tender. Stir in chopped eggs, croutons, ¼ cup of the sour cream, beaten egg, and ½ cup hot water. Pound steak to thin rectangle. Use tenderizer following label directions. Spread stuffing over meat; roll up from long side. Skewer securely.

Brown meat in hot shortening. Add ½ cup water to meat. Cover; simmer about 1½ hours. Remove meat; add water to drippings to make ½ cup. Stir in remaining sour cream. Heat just to boiling; pass sauce. Makes 4 servings.

Stuffed Flank Steaks

  ⅓ cup chopped onion
  2 tablespoons butter
  4 cups dry bread cubes
  ½ teaspoon poultry seasoning
  2 1½-pound beef flank steaks,
    scored
  1 16-ounce can tomatoes
  ¼ cup chopped onion
  ¼ cup catsup
  ¼ cup chopped green pepper
  1 3-ounce can sliced mushrooms,
    drained (½ cup)

In skillet cook ⅓ cup onion in butter till tender. Add bread cubes, poultry seasoning, ½ teaspoon salt, and dash pepper; toss till bread is lightly toasted. Sprinkle with ¼ to ½ cup water to moisten. Spread stuffing over steaks and roll up lengthwise as for jelly roll; fasten with wooden picks and lace with string.

Roll in flour; brown all sides in small amount hot shortening. Season with salt and pepper. Add tomatoes, ¼ cup chopped onion, catsup, and ½ teaspoon salt. Cover; simmer till tender, about 1½ to 2 hours. Add remaining ingredients last 15 minutes. Remove steaks to warm platter. Mix 1 tablespoon flour with 2 tablespoons cold water till smooth. Stir into sauce; cook till thick and bubbly. Serves 6 to 8.

Flank Steak Teriyaki

  1 8½-ounce can pineapple slices
  ⅓ cup soy sauce
  2 tablespoons dry sherry
  1 tablespoon salad oil
  1 teaspoon ground ginger
  1 clove garlic, crushed

        • • •

  4 flank steak pinwheels, 1½
    inches thick

Drain pineapple reserving syrup. Combine syrup and next 5 ingredients; pour over meat and marinate 1 hour. Broil 4 to 5 inches from heat for 7 minutes, brushing once with marinade. Turn and broil 5 to 7 minutes longer, again brushing once with marinade. Add pineapple slices to broiler during last 3 or 4 minutes of cooking and brush with marinade. Serve with rice, if desired. Makes about 4 servings.

sight, first suggests a particular flavor. A dessert dish filled with large scoops of rich, brown ice cream immediately suggests some chocolate flavor.

Flavor is best obtained by immediate contact with the mouth, although the aroma of a food often gives the person a clue as to what it will taste like. The aroma of freshly brewed coffee or hot, buttery popcorn indicates a particular flavor.

Taste and touch often go hand in hand to identify the flavor still further. The crisp, crunchy texture of a potato chip from an airtight bag compared to a soggy chip that was exposed to the air illustrates the differing flavor effects one gets by chewing each of these foods.

A true flavor is best achieved with the particular food at neither too-hot nor too-cold a temperature with both taste and smell sensations at work.

FLAVORING — That substance which gives added flavor to food. Flavoring may be in the form of liquid flavoring extracts, spices, herbs, liqueurs, condiments, fruits, seasoned sauces, and many others.

Types and kinds: The terms flavoring and seasoning are often used interchangeably to refer to those substances which, in most cases, improve the flavor of a food-stuff or identify the difference between a bland and delectable dish.

The use of aromatic spices and herbs as flavorings brings most foods out of the ordinary category if used properly. Allspice, basil, cinnamon, curry, ginger, nutmeg, oregano, sage, and thyme are just a few of the common spices and herbs.

Liqueurs and brandies are great flavorings for sauces and gravies which are served with fish or wild game. The alcoholic beverages should add a subtle touch of distinction and not overpower the flavor.

Prepared, flavored sauces make basting and seasoning an easy task. A few commercially prepared sauces which are found on most supermarket shelves are barbecue sauce, Worcestershire sauce, steak sauce, hot pepper sauce, mustard, and catsup.

There are many other bottle flavorings available that enhance the appearance of or give additional flavor to foods. Canned meat broths and flavored vinegars relieve the homemaker of an extra step or two when making these things in many recipes. A commercial product called Kitchen Bouquet is used to add color and flavor to gravy. A meat can be given a hickory-smoked flavor right in the kitchen by brushing it with bottled liquid smoke before broiling. Liquid smoke, in concentrated form, can be mixed in a sauce.

Smoked Salmon Bake

Place 1 pound of salmon steaks *or* other fish steaks in greased 10x6x1½-inch baking dish. Sprinkle with ½ teaspoon salt and dash pepper. Combine one 3-ounce can chopped mushrooms, drained; ¼ cup catsup; 2 tablespoons snipped green onions; 2 tablespoons lemon juice; and 10 drops liquid smoke. Spoon over fish.

Bake at 350° until fish flakes with a fork, about 25 to 30 minutes. Makes 5 servings.

Flavoring extracts are probably the most common and widely used flavorings for baking, dessert, and candy needs. Produced by dissolving the oils in alcohol, the extracts make quite an impressive list. Some of the flavoring extracts and flavorings include: almond, anise, banana, brandy, cherry, cinnamon, cloves, coconut, coffee, lemon, maple, mint, mocha, orange, peach, peppermint, pineapple, pistachio, raspberry, rum, sherry, spearmint, strawberry, vanilla, walnut, and wintergreen.

The preceding list of flavoring extracts and flavorings, as well as others, are either pure or imitation in composition. Pure extracts are taken from the fruit or nut, while imitation flavorings are made of compounds to resemble a particular flavor. Generally, pure extracts are more acceptable, but there are several, such as pineapple and black walnut, which do not resemble their respective flavors, so imitation flavorings are more desirable.

Almond is one of the strongest extracts and should be used cautiously because of its concentrated flavor. Almond extract contributes a rich, fragrant flavor to desserts, candies, icings, sauces, and beverages. Delicious ice creams are made flavored with this nut extract. Fruit cups or fruit pies become mouth-watering good with a few drops of almond extract.

Cherry-Peach Pie

Mouth-watering fruit combo with almond flavor—

    1 20-ounce can pitted tart red
        cherries (water pack)
    1 16-ounce can sliced peaches
    ¾ cup sugar
    3 tablespoons all-purpose flour
    ¼ teaspoon salt
    2 tablespoons butter
    4 drops almond extract
    5 drops red food coloring
        Plain Pastry for 9-inch lattice
        top pie (See *Pastry*)

Drain canned cherries and peaches, reserving ½ cup of cherry juice. Combine sugar, all-purpose flour, and salt; gradually stir in cherry juice. Cook and stir over medium heat till mixture is thick and bubbly; cook 1 minute longer. Add fruits, butter, almond extract, and food coloring. Let stand while preparing pastry.

Line 9-inch pie plate with pastry. Fill with cherry-peach mixture. Adjust lattice top; seal lattice edges; flute edge. Bake at 400° till bubbly in center, about 40 to 45 minutes.

Vanilla is the most common and favorite flavoring addition of American bakers and homemakers alike. Available either in pure or imitation form, vanilla blends with and enhances a number of other flavors extremely well, which probably explains its great popularity and wide usage.

Pure vanilla is made from a tropical climbing orchid, while the synthetic, commercially prepared vanillas, artificially flavored and colored with caramel, contain a small amount of pure vanilla extract.

Bottles of vanilla are marked as pure vanilla or imitation vanilla. An established ingredient to baking and dessert recipes, vanilla also adds a special note to mayonnaise salad dressings, waffle batters, and milk beverages. Vanilla is an excellent flavoring companion for chocolate and mocha-flavored desserts and beverages.

Mocha Chiffon Cake

    4 teaspoons instant coffee powder
    ¾ cup water
    2¼ cups sifted cake flour
    1½ cups sugar
    3 teaspoons baking powder
    ½ cup salad oil
    5 egg yolks
    1 teaspoon vanilla
    3 1-ounce squares semisweet
        chocolate, coarsely grated
    ½ teaspoon cream of tartar
    1 cup egg whites (8 eggs)

Dissolve instant coffee powder in water. Sift together cake flour, sugar, baking powder, and 1 teaspoon salt; make well in center of dry mixture. Add in order: salad oil, egg yolks, coffee, and vanilla. Beat mixture till satin smooth. Stir in grated chocolate.

Add cream of tartar to egg whites; beat till *very stiff peaks* form. Pour batter in thin stream over entire surface of egg whites; fold in gently. Bake in *ungreased* 10-inch tube pan at 325° for 1 hour and 10 minutes. Invert pan and cool thoroughly before removing cake.

Rum flavoring is one of the popular examples of an imitation flavor. Add a festive flavor with imitation rum in mincemeats, fruit cakes, pumpkin pies, hard sauces, and a number of other holiday desserts and foods. Spark up an ice cream sundae with lemon juice, orange marmalade, and a bit of imitation rum flavoring.

Waikiki Sundae

    ¼ cup mashed ripe banana
    2 teaspoons lemon juice
    ½ cup orange marmalade
    ½ cup pineapple-apricot preserves
    ¼ teaspoon rum flavoring
        Vanilla ice cream
    ½ cup flaked coconut, toasted

Combine banana and lemon juice; add marmalade and preserves. Cook and stir 5 minutes over low heat. Remove from heat; stir in flavoring. Spoon warm sauce over ice cream. Sprinkle with coconut. Makes 1⅓ cups.

Some extracts, such as oil of cinnamon, are so concentrated that they should be measured in drops. The number of drops may be specifically indicated, or they may be generally stated as a few drops, which leaves the exact number of drops used up to the individual. Cinnamon and peppermint drops are for cookies and candies.

Cinnamon Apples

        8 **crisp, medium apples**
        8 **wooden skewers**
        4 **cups sugar**
    1⅓ **cups light corn syrup**
    1¼ **teaspoons red food coloring**
       10 **drops oil of cinnamon**

Wash and dry apples; remove stems. Insert skewer into each apple. In buttered saucepan combine sugar, corn syrup, 2 cups water, dash salt, and food coloring. Cook, stirring constantly, till sugar dissolves and mixture comes to boiling. Continue cooking, without stirring, till mixture reaches the hard-crack stage (300°).

Remove from heat; stir in the oil of cinnamon. Tilt pan and turn each apple in syrup to coat. Twirl apple to spread coating evenly—let excess syrup drip back in pan. Set apples on buttered cookie sheet. Chill till firm.

Note: If desired, make lollipops to use the remaining syrup. Arrange wooden skewers 4 inches apart on buttered cookie sheet. Drop hot syrup from tip of tablespoon over the skewers to form 2- or 3-inch suckers. Let cool.

Tiny Red Mints

In buttered saucepan combine 2 cups sugar, ½ cup water, ½ cup light corn syrup, and ⅛ teaspoon cream of tartar. Cook, stirring till sugar is dissolved. Continue cooking, without stirring, to thread stage (232°). Let cool, without stirring, for 10 minutes.

Tint mixture with red food coloring; add a few drops peppermint flavoring oil. Beat with spoon till creamy, about 10 minutes. Drop mixture from teaspoon onto waxed paper forming patties, swirling tops. (Keep pan over very hot water while forming patties; mixture hardens when cooling.) Store cooled patties in tightly covered container. Makes about 4 dozen.

Although the word flavoring may first bring flavoring extracts to mind, other substances can also be classified as flavorings. Most foods have a natural flavoring substance called monosodium glutamate. This substance brings out the natural flavor rather than adding a taste or seasoning of its own. Vegetables, meats, fish, and poultry have this flavoring in a more concentrated form than do other foods.

First used in the Orient, monosodium glutamate, in crystalline form, is now commercially prepared from vegetables and sold under various brand names as a flavor enhancer. When used as a recipe ingredient, it is often listed as MSG.

How to buy: Select good brands of flavoring extracts, herbs, and spices to insure quality and freshness. Buy small bottles of flavoring extracts that are not used very often for they are quite volatile due to their high alcohol content.

How to store: Keep all flavoring extracts, herbs, and spices tightly covered immediately after using to retain full flavor. Check spices and herbs periodically to insure fresh and full-bodied flavor. To test whether a seasoning is still fresh or not, depend on your nose to detect the strength. Periodically replace those spices which do not measure up in flavor and aroma.

Volatile extracts are affected by heat and light, so store them in a cool, dark place. Flavoring extracts are often sold in dark bottles to protect them from light.

How to use: There is no specific set of rules for using flavorings. Imagination and individual preferences create some interesting dishes. Some flavoring extracts are stronger than others and should be measured in drops. The recipe will usually indicate how much to use.

Since flavoring extracts are volatile, they may be used in greater amounts for foods to be frozen. Measure the extracts for boiled foods, such as candies and icings, at the last minute after removing from heat so the extract will not evaporate.

Combine two flavorings, such as vanilla and lemon or lemon and almond, to create exciting flavor ideas. (See also *Spice.*)

FLIP—Any of a number of mixed drinks served either hot or cold containing: 1. liquor, sugar, and a beaten egg. 2. fruits and ice cream with a carbonated beverage or with milk. Flips served during eighteenth century in England and America consisted of various liquors or ales served piping hot by heating with a red-hot poker plunged into the drink. The colonial Americans added the raw egg which is believed to have led to the name because the eggs are beaten or flipped in the drink.

The modern flip is served several different ways and is either hot or iced. Chilled in a cocktail shaker, some flips are made with confectioners' sugar, an egg, and liquor. The same ingredients with spices added can be heated and topped with ground nutmeg. It is also fashionable to serve iced flips with ice cream and fruits along with a carbonated beverage or with milk. (See also *Beverage*.)

Fruit Flip

Drop big scoops ice cream amid fruited drink—

> ½ cup fresh red raspberries
> ½ cup diced ripe banana
> ½ cup diced ripe peaches
> ½ cup unsweetened pineapple juice
> • • •
> ¼ cup sugar
> Vanilla ice cream
> Lemon-lime carbonated beverage

Combine raspberries, diced banana, diced peaches, pineapple juice, and sugar. Divide mixture among four 9-ounce glasses; chill. For each glass: Add scoop ice cream; muddle. Tip glass; slowly pour carbonated beverage down side. Add second scoop of ice cream.

FLITCH—An English word for a whole side of bacon. The leg is cut off and the bone is removed from the side of meat before the pork meat is cured and smoked.

FLOAT—A tall, cool drink most popular in the summertime and made of fruit syrup or other sweet syrup, a carbonated beverage, and scoops of ice cream. The name comes from the ice cream floating in the beverage. Delicious, refreshing combinations can be achieved with unusual beverage and ice cream pair-ups along with fruits, spices, and sugar. Floats are great for snacking or served as a dessert at the end of a simple meal. (See also *Beverage*.)

Viennese Coffee Float

> ¼ cup instant coffee powder
> 2 tablespoons sugar
> 3 inches stick cinnamon
> 3 cups water
> 1 pint vanilla ice cream
> ½ cup whipping cream
> Dash ground cinnamon

Combine coffee, sugar, stick cinnamon, and water. Cover and bring to boiling. Remove from heat and let stand, covered, 5 minutes to steep. Remove stick cinnamon and chill mixture well. Chill 4 tall glasses; pour about ⅓ cup cold coffee mixture into each. Add several spoonfuls of ice cream, stirring to muddle slightly. Add remaining coffee; whip whipping cream and top float with a dollop. Sprinkle with ground cinnamon. Makes 4 servings.

Set a cool, tall Viennese Coffee Float and crisp sugar cookies before family or guests on a hot, summer day for a welcome treat.

FLOATING ISLAND — A soft dessert custard topped with meringue puffs. Fresh fruits and berries are often added for extra flavor. (See also *Custard*.)

Strawberry Floating Island

         3 egg whites
    ⅓ cup sugar
         3 cups cold milk
         2 eggs
         3 egg yolks
    ½ cup sugar
         Dash salt
    1½ teaspoons vanilla
         2 cups hulled strawberries

Beat egg whites till soft peaks form. Gradually add ⅓ cup sugar, beating till stiff peaks form. In 10-inch skillet, heat 3 cups milk to simmering. Divide meringue into 8 equal portions; drop each into milk. Simmer, uncovered, till firm, about 5 minutes. Lift meringue puffs from milk (reserve milk for custard); drain meringue puffs on paper toweling. Chill thoroughly.

In medium saucepan beat eggs and egg yolks slightly; add ½ cup sugar and dash salt. Stir in reserved, slightly cooled milk. Cook and stir over low heat till mixture thickens slightly and evenly coats a metal spoon. Remove custard from heat, cooling immediately; add 1½ teaspoons vanilla. Place hulled strawberries in serving dish; pour custard over berries. Top with meringue puffs. Makes 8 servings.

Launch puffy meringue mounds with strawberry anchors atop a chilled, creamy custard dessert named Strawberry Floating Island. Serve along with crisp cookies for dessert.

FLORENTINE—A recipe term used when spinach is an ingredient. Eggs, fish, sweetbreads, or some type of meat are usually served on a bed of spinach; then, a sauce is spooned over the top of the dish.

Franks Florentine

    1 10-ounce package frozen chopped
        spinach
 1½ cups cooked rice
    1 10¾-ounce can condensed
        Cheddar cheese soup
    2 tablespoons finely chopped onion
    ¼ cup milk
    ½ pound (4 or 5) frankfurters,
        halved crosswise

Cook spinach according to package directions; drain thoroughly. Spread the cooked spinach in bottom of 10x6x1¾-inch baking dish.

Combine cooked rice, soup, onion, and milk; spoon over the cooked spinach. Score half the franks with a criss cross-shaped cut. Arrange on casserole, pressing into rice. Bake at 375° till the mixture is heated throughout, about 20 to 25 minutes. Makes 4 servings.

Make easy Franks Florentine by tucking a bed of spinach and a layer of rice and cheese soup under crisscross cut franks.

Salmon Florentine

    2 10-ounce packages frozen
        chopped spinach
    1 10½-ounce can condensed cream
        of chicken soup
    1 ounce (¼ cup) sharp process
        American cheese, shredded
        (¼ cup)
    ¼ cup dry sherry
    2 tablespoons mayonnaise or salad
        dressing
    1 teaspoon lemon juice
    ½ teaspoon Worcestershire sauce
    1 16-ounce can salmon, drained
    1 cup soft bread crumbs
    2 tablespoons butter, melted

Cook spinach according to package directions *using unsalted water;* drain thoroughly.

In saucepan combine soup, cheese, wine, mayonnaise, lemon juice, and Worcestershire; bring to boiling. Blend ½ *cup* of the sauce with spinach. Divide mixture into 6 baking shells or individual casseroles. Break salmon in chunks, discarding bones and skin; layer over spinach. Spoon remaining sauce over top. Combine bread crumbs and butter; sprinkle over casseroles. Bake at 350° till bubbly, about 25 minutes. Makes 6 servings.

FLOUNDER—The family name for a group of saltwater flatfish found in American waters from New England to the tip of southern Florida, and off the Gulf coast. A few varieties of this flatfish family are fished off the Pacific coast.

Some of the more common fish in this family include: fluke (summer flounder), plaice, blackback (winter flounder), dab, gray sole, lemon sole, yellowtail (rusty dab), sole (English sole, dover, petrale, rex) and many others.

Flounder have a number of characteristics that make them peculiar to the fish world. One of these unique traits is its ability to lay and swim on its side. This is an acquired trait because when the fish is hatched, it swims upright as do other fish. At about five to seven weeks of age one of the eyes of the fish moves across the forehead so that both eyes of the fish are on the topside of the head.

In addition to the above mentioned characteristics, flounder, as they mature, also develop a darkish gray coloring on the topside, which is similar to the color of the ocean floor. This coloration is useful to the flounder not only as a protective device but also as an aid in its scavenger chores of preying on fish, shrimp, and crab. While lying in wait for unsuspecting fish, the flounders merge with the ocean floor, leaving only their eyes uncovered.

Flounder is also an excellent source of protein and contains some minerals, such as potassium and phosphorus, and some of the B vitamins, thiamine and riboflavin. One serving of baked flounder will add about 200 calories to the menu.

Flounder is generally sold either whole or as fillets. Along the coast, the fish is often sold fresh; in other parts of the country, a greater percentage of the fish are sold as frozen fillets.

All members of the flounder family have a lean flesh with white, flaky, tender meat having a sweet and distinctive flavor. They can be broiled, baked, or panfried, then served with a sauce, lemon wedges, or stuffed. (See also *Fish*.)

Flounder Provençale

    6 flounder fillets (1½ pounds)
    4 tablespoons butter or margarine
      Salt and paprika
 ¼ cup chopped onion
    1 clove garlic, minced
    1 16-ounce can tomatoes, cut up
    1 3-ounce can chopped mushrooms,
        drained (½ cup)
 ¼ cup dry white wine
    6 lemon wedges
      Parsley

Dot each flounder fillet with *2 teaspoons* butter. Sprinkle with salt and paprika. Roll up fillets; fasten with wooden picks. Place fillet rolls in skillet. Add onion, garlic, tomatoes, mushrooms, and wine. Cover tightly and simmer till fish flakes, about 15 minutes. Remove fish to warm platter; keep hot. Simmer sauce until slightly thickened. Spoon sauce over fish rolls. Garnish the serving platter with lemon wedges and parsley sprigs. Makes 6 servings.

Stuffed Flounder

 ¼ cup chopped onion
 ¼ cup butter or margarine
    1 3-ounce can broiled chopped
        mushrooms, drained (reserve
        liquid)
    1 7½-ounce can crab meat, drained,
        flaked, and cartilage removed
 ½ cup coarse saltine cracker
        crumbs
    2 tablespoons snipped parsley
 ½ teaspoon salt
      Dash pepper
    8 flounder fillets (2 pounds)
    3 tablespoons butter
    3 tablespoons all-purpose flour
 ¼ teaspoon salt
      Milk
 ⅓ cup dry white wine
    4 ounces process Swiss cheese,
        shredded (1 cup)
 ½ teaspoon paprika

In skillet cook onion in ¼ cup butter till tender. Stir drained mushrooms into skillet with crab, cracker crumbs, snipped parsley, ½ teaspoon salt, and dash pepper. Spread mixture over flounder fillets. Roll fillets; place seam side down in 11¾x7½x1¾-inch baking dish.

In saucepan melt 3 tablespoons butter. Blend in flour and ¼ teaspoon salt. Add enough milk to mushroom liquid to make 1½ cups. Add with wine to saucepan. Cook and stir till mixture thickens and bubbles. Pour over fish.

Bake at 400° for 25 minutes. Sprinkle with cheese and paprika. Return to oven and bake till fish flakes when tested with a fork, about 10 minutes longer. Makes 8 servings.

Flounder in Wine

Place 1 pound flounder fillets in greased 11x7x 1½-inch baking pan. Sprinkle with ½ teaspoon salt and dash pepper. Arrange 2 tomatoes, peeled and sliced, on top. Sprinkle with additional salt. Carefully pour ¼ cup dry white wine over all. Sprinkle with ½ teaspoon dried basil leaves, crushed. Bake at 350° for 20 minutes. Sprinkle with 2 ounces shredded sharp process American cheese (½ cup) and bake till fish flakes with a fork, about 5 to 10 minutes longer. Makes 4 servings.

FLOUR (noun) —The finely ground meal of an edible food, particularly a grain. When just the word flour is used, it is understood to mean wheat flour. The names of other flours are preceded by the name of the food from which they are produced or the process involved, for example, potato flour, banana flour, or whole wheat flour.

The story of the evolution of the flour mill, from a simple hand crusher to a complex mechanical mill, is of great historical interest. Primitive man pulverized the grain by pounding or rubbing it between two stones. In time, the stones wore away, fitting together like "saddle stones." The stone used for pounding became a crude pestle and the other stone, a mortar.

Mechanization enabled flour milling to progress from a household task to a commercial operation. About the first century A.D., grinders (both small and large) called querns were designed, using a crude type of mechanics—a convex stone revolved over a concave stone as men or animals provided the power. By the fourteenth century, the millstone began to replace the quern. The millstone provided a center opening or hopper into which the grain was fed. This mill was propelled first by hand, then, years later, by animals, water, wind, and finally, in the 1800s, by steam.

The Hungarian roller process, similar to today's milling techniques, was introduced into the United States around 1870. The kernels of grain were mechanically pulverized between a series of rollers.

Nutritional value: Whole wheat flour is higher in protein content than is white flour, but other nutritive differences vary.

Whole wheat flour, because all the parts of the kernel are present, retains all the fats, carbohydrates, vitamins, and minerals of the natural wheat.

In the processing of white flour, however, some of these nutrients are lost when the bran and germ are discarded. Today in the United States the essential dietary nutrients lost in milling are replaced according to legally defined levels.

How flour is processed: Flour milling involves separation of the basic wheat kernel parts. The kernel is made up of the endosperm, the bran (husk), and the germ (embryo). The bran and germ flake away readily when the kernel is broken. It is the endosperms' starch-protein complex that possesses the most desirable properties for cooking and baking.

Milling involves four major steps: cleaning, tempering (conditioning), separating, and post-treating. Each step is broken down into many smaller progressions so that separation is most effective.

Cleaning and tempering ready the wheat kernels for separation: cleaning disposes of extraneous material: tempering adds or subtracts moisture to reach the optimum moisture level for separation.

Then the grain begins its journey through the grinding and separating systems. First, the whole kernels are broken open between metal corrugated rollers and hammerlike pegs. The size of the kernels is reduced as the particles pass between rollers that are set closer and closer together. After each grinding, the particles are sifted through sieves of increasing fineness. Bran is then separated in purifiers.

This process of separation continues until the particles are sized and graded into many streams of flour. Alternate milling and separating processes continue until the endosperm is separated as much as possible from the bran and germ.

Post-treatment of milled flour includes blending, maturing, and bleaching to give the flour better baking characteristics. The type of flour desired determines how the flour is blended. For whole wheat flour, all the streams are recombined. To make all-purpose flour, hard and soft wheats are blended in specific proportions. Flour streams are also blended to yield varying flour grades. For example, short patent flour, the highest grade, is made of white flour that contains the least amount of bran, germ, and ash.

Aged or matured flour has better baking qualities than freshly milled flour. Natural aging requires long-time storage. Equally good flour is matured by harmless chemical treatment with reduced time and cost.

Another treatment, bleaching, improves baking qualities and intensifies flour whiteness as well. Some bleaching agents function as maturing agents, too.

Flour may undergo additional treatments, depending on its intended use. Some of these processes include instantizing, enriching, and replacing most of the enzymes lost in the milling process.

Kinds of flour: Each kind of flour is identified by the flour varieties, flour grades, or special treatments used in preparation. White, wheat, or plain flour specify any ground, sifted, and cleaned wheat flour except amber or red durum varieties.

Wheat varieties are classified into two main groups: soft wheats and hard wheats. Soft wheats, grown primarily in the eastern United States, are lower in the structure-building protein called gluten. Soft-wheat flours are ideal for a wide variety of delicately textured baked goods such as cakes and quick breads.

Hard wheats, mainly from the Midwest, are higher in gluten than are soft wheats. Thus, these flours are good for yeast breads and rolls. Crops planted in the autumn and harvested the following summer are called hard winter wheats; those planted in the spring are hard spring wheats.

Some of the better-known flours identified by their blends include whole-wheat, pastry, cake, bread, and all-purpose flours. Whole wheat flour is also called entire wheat or graham flour. It contains the same proportions of germ, endosperm, and bran as does unprocessed wheat.

Both cake and pastry flours are soft wheat blends. Cake flour, a short patent flour, is very fine and uniform in texture. The low level of protein present is ideal for cake baking. Pastry flour has properties in-between cake and all-purpose flour and is best for making pastries and cookies. Bread flour, a blend of hard wheats, is only available commercially.

Probably the most well-known type of flour is all-purpose flour. As the name indicates, several wheat varieties are blended to give this flour versatility. It can be used most satisfactorily for yeast breads as well as cakes and quick breads. The blend proportions that are used vary, depending on where the flour is milled and the local baking habits. In the South, for example, all-purpose flour contains a great deal more soft wheat than it does in northern states.

Flour types are also graded—straight, patent, and clear. Straight flour is the general industrial term for all the milled flour that has been separated from germ and bran. Patent flour, the highest grade of white flour, contains only select flour streams with a low percentage of germ and bran. A short patent flour is the most select patent grade. Any flour remaining after patent flour is removed is called clear flour. Clear flour is less refined and is not available for household use.

Specially processed flours are labeled to identify the process involved, such as enriched, self-rising, and instant-type flours. As mentioned previously, the vitamins and minerals lost in milling are replaced in enriched flour. Its standard of identity is strictly controlled by government requirements imposed on flour manufacturers.

Self-rising flour is available particularly in the South where homemakers bake more quick breads. Baking powder and salt are added to the flour base. When using self-rising flour, omit leavening and salt in the recipe. Do not use self-rising flour to replace yeast in a yeast-leavened product.

Instant-type flours are the most recent innovation. A special technique makes the flour granular in texture so that it pours readily. Sifting is unnecessary. Because it is instantly soluble in cold water or other liquids, many homemakers prefer it for use in making gravies and sauces.

How to use: Flour is the indispensable basis for a host of delicious foods. Successful cooking starts by storing the flour properly, at room temperature in a tightly covered container. During hot weather, the on-hand flour supply should be limited to an amount that can be used within a short period of time to maintain quality.

For accurate measure either sift all-purpose and cake flour before measuring or spoon the unsifted flour into a measuring cup. Stir whole wheat, rye, or buckwheat flour before spooning lightly into the cup. Level with the edge of a spatula. Flour need not be sifted when small quantities are used for thickening.

Flour is used as a thickener for sauces, soups, puddings, and as the basic structure for many baked products. For thickening, flour, even the instant-type, requires gentle treatment. It cannot be added to hot liquids without lumps developing. Therefore, flour is usually combined first with a fat, cold liquid, or sugar to disperse the starch which provides the thickening power. Follow the recipe directions exactly for combining flour or flour mixtures and a liquid to insure a good product.

Onion-Cheese Soup

    1 large onion, chopped (1 cup)
    3 tablespoons butter or
        margarine
    3 tablespoons all-purpose flour
    ½ teaspoon salt
        Dash pepper
    4 cups milk
    8 ounces sharp process American
        cheese, shredded (2 cups)

Cook onion in butter till tender but not brown. Blend in flour, salt, and pepper. Add milk all at once. Heat and stir till boiling. Remove from heat. Add cheese to soup, stirring to melt cheese. Makes about 4 to 6 servings.

In cakes, breads, and pastries, gluten protein is the basis for structure and gives the dough its elasticity. For delicate cakes, less gluten is needed than for yeast breads, so cake recipes often specify cake flour. (In an emergency, substitute 1 cup of all-purpose flour minus 2 tablespoons for each cup of cake flour.) For yeast-baked goods, bread flour with its high gluten content is best, but all-purpose flour is also satisfactory for yeast-baked goods.

Sandies

Cream 1 cup butter or margarine and ⅓ cup sugar. Add 2 teaspoons water and 2 teaspoons vanilla; mix well. Blend in 2 cups sifted all-purpose flour and add 1 cup chopped pecans; chill mixture for at least 4 hours.

Shape dough in balls or crescents. Bake on *ungreased* cookie sheet at 325° about 20 minutes. Remove from pan; cool slightly. Roll in confectioners' sugar. Makes about 3 dozen.

Banana Cake

Chocolate frosting makes a delicious addition—

Place ⅔ cup shortening in mixer bowl. Sift in 2½ cups sifted cake flour, 1⅔ cups sugar, 1¼ teaspoons baking powder, 1 teaspoon baking soda, and 1 teaspoon salt. Add 1¼ cups mashed, fully ripe bananas and ⅓ cup buttermilk. Mix till moistened; beat 2 minutes at medium speed on electric mixer.

Add ⅓ cup buttermilk and 2 eggs; beat 2 minutes longer. If desired, fold in ⅔ cup chopped walnuts. Bake in 2 greased and lightly floured 9x1½-inch pans at 350° about 35 minutes. Cool 10 minutes; remove from pans. Cool the Banana Cake thoroughly.

FLOUR *(verb)*—To coat with flour. Baking pans and pastry cloths are floured to prevent food from sticking. To flour a greased baking pan, sprinkle it lightly with flour. Then shake the pan, spreading the flour evenly over the greased surface.

Foods may also be floured. When cooked, the flour coating adds crispy texture to fried and baked meats, vegetables, or fruits. Fruit may also be floured to prevent it from sinking in a batter. For clean-cut flouring, shake the food with the flour in a plastic or paper bag.

FLOWERS USED IN COOKING—Flowers or parts of flowers eaten as foods or used to flavor foods. The art of cooking with flowers is an ancient one, known in oriental and Persian cuisines thousands of years ago. The orientals' most notable contribution to flower cooking was their use of flowers like jasmine, roses, chrysanthemums, and camellias to give teas fragrance. In addition, they used flower petals in wines for bouquet, in cakes for flavor, and in soups for color contrast. The Persians also added a variety of fresh or dried flowers to candies, soups, and meat dishes.

Down through the centuries, cooks have passed on these ways of using whole blossoms or parts of flowers to garnish, flavor, or add appealing aroma to foods. The Romans believed flowers in foods gave their meals elegance. The Roman emperor, Nero, seasoned his foods with rose petals.

Today's cooks use flowers in everyday cooking although they are not always aware of it. The prized portions of broccoli and cauliflower, for example, are clusters of unopened flower buds. Capers are unopened buds that have been pickled or dried. Some herbs and spices are parts of a flower—saffron is the powder rubbed off the stamens of a particular crocus. Rose- and orange-flower water are also used to flavor cookies. And candied flowers such as violets are luxurious, yet delicious garnishes for cakes and confections.

Cooks needn't be limited to these traditional uses of flowers. In some countries fritters are made with squash blossoms, elderflowers, or acacia flower clusters. Squash blossoms have also been used in poultry dishes, plum blossoms in dumplings, sliced banana flowers in shellfish mixtures, and lily petals in soups.

Cooking with flowers can be a taste adventure. Rose petals make an excellent jam or jelly. Custard sauce sparked with orange-flower or rose water is elegant served over fresh berries. Cooked apples take on a new tang with the addition of rose geraniums or lemon verbena.

FLUKE—A saltwater flatfish belonging to the flounder family. Also known as summer flounders, they weigh from ½ to 15 pounds and usually measure one foot.

Flukes are found mainly along the Atlantic and Gulf coasts. Most of these fish are dressed and sold as four- to eight-ounce fillets. Some of the smaller flukes are marketed whole. (See also *Flounder*.)

FLUMMERY—1. In Wales, a thick oatmeal served with meat or poultry. 2. A Scottish pudding similar to blancmange made with cream, rose water, and sherry. 3. A custardy pudding served over berries. Originally English, flummery was introduced to the Virginia colonies by early settlers.

FLUTE—To make small decorative impressions in food. Piecrusts and some cookies are fluted by pressing the pastry edge in various shapes with the fingers. Fruits and vegetables such as cucumbers and peeled bananas may be fluted by scoring the food lengthwise, using the tines of a fork.

FOAM CAKE—A term sometimes used to describe a cake that is leavened with beaten egg whites, such as an angel food cake, sponge cake, or chiffon cake.

FOAMY SAUCE—A long-popular dessert sauce, light and fluffy, that is delicious served over hot or cold puddings.

Foamy Sauce

> 3 egg yolks
> ¾ cup sifted confectioners' sugar
> ½ teaspoon vanilla
>   Rum flavoring (optional)
>   Dash salt
> 1 cup whipping cream

Beat together egg yolks, sugar, vanilla, rum flavoring to taste, and salt. Whip cream; fold into egg mixture. Chill; stir. Makes 3 cups.

FOIE GRAS (*fwä grä*)—Goose or duck livers that are specially fattened by force feeding the bird. Foie gras from ducks are not as costly, but are less versatile than goose foie gras because they disintegrate when cooked. Foie gras are produced in France, Austria, and Czechoslavakia.

Fois gras can be used in an assortment of dishes. The famous *pâté de foie gras*, which literally means "paste of fat livers," is normally used an an appetizer spread.

Use index finger and knife handle to flute the pastry edge. Fluting adds attractive interest and helps reduce shrinking.

FOIL COOKERY—A method of food preparation in which foods are covered with or wrapped in aluminum foil, then placed in the oven or over hot coals for roasting.

Several properties contribute to foil's usefulness in cooking. First, it is lightweight and flexible so that it molds easily to fit the shape of the food. This flexibility makes it reusable, if desired. Next, unless punctured, heavy-duty foil is moistureproof. Natural juices or liquid ingredients packaged with the food stay inside the sealed foil package during cooking.

Finally, although aluminum is a good conductor of heat, the shiny surface of the foil reflects the heat's greatest intensity away from the food to minimize overcooking. This reflecting property is one of the reasons that foil-wrapped foods can be cooked at very high oven temperatures or placed right on the coals.

How to buy: Foil is available in several different widths and weights, but the cooking job will determine which of the weights or thicknesses will be most satisfactory. Two weights are generally marketed. One, designated as standard weight, is used to make a tight-fitting cover for baking pans or casserole dishes or to refrigerate leftovers. The other, a heavy-duty or freezer foil, is a good choice when preparing large cuts of meat or turkeys which require considerable time in the oven. It is also the one to use when wrapping foods for freezer storage as it is strong and pliable.

Because foods for outdoor cookery may receive rough handling over the coals, buy heavy-duty foil or plan on using a double thickness of the light foil.

How to cook meat, poultry, and fish: Foil cookery is satisfactory for all three when a few basics are kept in mind. Remember that the food generally bakes in a closed package of foil which is somewhat like a skillet or dutch oven with a tight-fitting lid. The steam inside the package as well as the heat from the oven or barbecue coals does the cooking of the food.

Some browning takes place, but it is not the same crusty, brown surface associated with open-pan roasted meats. However, when the oven is used, you can open the foil package 20 minutes or so before the end of the roasting time to allow for additional browning of the food.

In the closed package, steam tenderizes the cartilage and connective tissue in meat and poultry, making foil cookery popular for preparing pot roasts and other less tender cuts of meat. The roast, together with desired seasonings, is wrapped in foil and baked until the meat is fork tender. Because the natural juices are held inside the package, there are usually generous amounts of drippings from which to make gravy. Chickens and turkeys can be roasted in the same manner.

Pork chops or ground meat with vegetable combinations are foil-cooked favorites of both campers and masters of the outdoor grill. Packages containing individual servings bake over slow coals until the meat is done and the vegetables are tender. A special bonus is the fact that the foil packets are disposable.

Beef Dinner in Foil

  1 **pound ground beef**
  ¾ **teaspoon salt**
  1 **medium green pepper, cut in**
      8 rings
  1 **medium onion, sliced and**
      separated into rings
  3 **medium carrots, cut in**
      3-inch strips
  8 **cherry tomatoes, halved**

Shape beef into 4 patties, ¾ inch thick. Sprinkle with salt. Tear off four 1-foot lengths of heavy foil. Center meat patty on each piece of foil. Divide vegetables among packets and layer atop meat. Draw up 4 corners of foil to center; twist corners securely. Bake over *slow* coals till meat is done and vegetables are crisp-tender, about 45 to 50 minutes. Pass catsup, if desired. Makes 4 servings.

Dinner at the campsite

Beef Dinner in Foil is an easy-to-fix meal→ of meat and vegetables cooked at the campsite in handy, disposable packets.

Pork Chop Treat

For each serving: Cut off 50-inch length of lightweight foil or 25 of heavy duty; fold regular foil in half. Place ½ acorn squash, cut side up, just off-center of foil. Dot with 1 tablespoon butter and 1 tablespoon brown sugar. Place one pork chop, cut 1 inch thick, on squash; sprinkle with ¼ teaspoon salt and dash pepper.

Bring foil up over food so edges meet on the three open sides. Take hold of one open side and fold toward food two or more times in ½-inch folds. Press hard. Repeat folding and pressing on remaining sides of package.

Place the package over glowing coals; cook till the pork chop is tender and well done, about 1½ hours. Serve in foil package.

Certain cooking results are obtained by modifying the closed packet method previously mentioned. For example, a foil-wrapped, frozen, boneless rib roast of beef can be cooked without being thawed first. The meat is placed in an open roasting pan, and the foil is loosened on top and sides to allow heat to circulate around the meat. At an oven temperature of 400°, a 4-pound roast will take approximately 3 hours to reach medium doneness, an internal temperature of 140°, as indicated on roast meat thermometer. The foil is opened wide during the last 30 minutes.

Another modification, the *loose* tent of foil, is the secret to open-pan roasting a turkey. The tent is not fastened to the sides of the pan. This allows air to circulate around the turkey so that it will cook evenly in a 325° oven. At the same time, the reflecting property of the foil shields the turkey breast from becoming too brown before the thigh and other thick parts of the bird are done.

Cooking fish in foil presents a slightly different set of circumstances from meat and poultry. Fish has little connective tissue, so the steam is not needed for its tenderizing action. However, fish has so little moisture that keeping the steam and juices inside the closed packet of foil assures a moist, juicy serving of fish when the package is opened. To prevent fish and foil from sticking together, the foil is usually well oiled before wrapping.

Chicken-in-the-Garden

For each serving: Cut 40-inch length of lightweight foil; fold in half. Just off center place 2 or 3 pieces of cut-up broiler-fryer chicken; 1 medium potato, peeled; 1 medium tomato; 1 medium onion, peeled; mushroom caps; and 2 green pepper rings. Sprinkle with 2 tablespoons packaged, precooked rice, 1 teaspoon Worcestershire sauce, ¾ teaspoon salt, and dash *each* pepper and paprika. Dot with butter.

Bring foil over food so edges meet on three open sides. Fold one open side toward food two or more times in ½-inch folds. Press hard. Repeat folding and pressing on remaining sides.

Place package over glowing coals. Cook, turning package every 20 to 30 minutes, until all of the foods are tender, about 1½ hours.

Foil-Baked Halibut

    1 16-ounce package frozen halibut
         fillets, thawed
       Salad oil
    4 teaspoons lemon juice
    2 carrots, cut in julienne strips
    1 small green pepper, cut in
         rings
    1 medium onion, sliced

Cut fish into 4 portions. Tear off four 1-foot lengths of heavy foil. Rub salad oil over top side of foil. Center fish portion on each piece of oiled foil. Sprinkle each portion with ¼ teaspoon salt, dash pepper, dash paprika, and 1 teaspoon lemon juice. Divide vegetables among packets; layer atop fish. Draw up 4 corners of foil to center; twist securely. Bake at 450° till fish flakes easily when tested with fork, about 25 minutes. Makes 4 servings.

Crab Rolls

Drain and remove cartilage from one 7½-ounce can crab meat. Coarsely chop crab meat; combine with 4 ounces shredded Cheddar cheese (1 cup), ⅓ cup sliced pimiento-stuffed green olives; ¼ cup butter or margarine, melted; and 1 small clove garlic, minced. Split 6 French rolls; spread crab mixture over bottom halves and replace tops. Wrap in foil; heat in 350° oven for 15 to 20 minutes. Makes 6 servings.

Foil-baked potatoes are never better than when topped with sour cream, cheese, and onion combined in Chef's Cheese Sauce.

How to cook vegetables and fruit: The wrapping of either white or sweet potatoes, ears of corn, blocks of frozen vegetables, or apples in foil is a popular and handy way to prepare these foods for cooking over the coals at the backyard grill.

Whole potatoes with their jackets on are wrapped loosely in foil for charcoal roasting. Butter, seasonings, or special toppers are passed at serving time.

A slightly different procedure is followed when wrapping packets of sliced potatoes or a block of frozen vegetables. Seasonings plus butter or margarine go in the packet with the food. The foil is closed to keep liquids inside, but enough space is allowed for the steam collected during cooking to expand but not to escape.

Apples baked in foil over the coals make a delicious dessert. For best results choose a tart cooking apple. Wash it well and core, but do not peel. Butter or margarine plus brown and/or white sugar, raisins, or cinnamon candies go into the packet with the apples. For variety in the fillings, substitute miniature marshmallows, honey, chopped nuts, chopped dates, or a sprinkling of semisweet chocolate or butterscotch pieces for the cinnamon candies.

Foiled Potatoes

Scrub medium baking potatoes or sweet potatoes. Brush with salad oil. Wrap in foil. Bake 45 to 60 minutes on grill or on top of coals. Turn occasionally. Pinch to test doneness. When done, cut crisscross in top of package; push on ends to fluff. Top with butter; season to taste.

Potatoes with Chef's Cheese Sauce

Make 5 or 6 Foiled Potatoes. Whip together ¼ cup butter, softened, and 4 ounces shredded sharp process American cheese (1 cup). Stir in ½ cup dairy sour cream and 1 tablespoon sliced green onion. Spoon into potatoes. Serves 5 to 6.

Foiled Vegetables

Place one block frozen vegetables on large square of foil. Season; dot with butter. Wrap, leaving room for steam expansion. Cook over *hot* coals 10 to 15 minutes; turn occasionally.

Spicy Cinnamon Apples in Foil

For each serving: Cut off 24-inch length of foil; fold in half. Place one cored, large, tart apple in center. Fill hole with 1 tablespoon *each* red cinnamon candies and raisins. Dot with butter. Bring foil up loosely over apple; twist ends. Cook over coals till done.

Loosely tucking in ends while wrapping roasting ears in foil allows steam to expand, yet keeps seasonings inside.

FOLD—1. A mixing technique involving a gentle motion to add or blend ingredients into a mixture. 2. A step in making puff or Danish pastry whereby layers of dough and chilled butter are repeatedly lapped over one another before being rolled flat. It is the repeated folding and rolling that make the dough flaky.

Folding is a necessary kitchen skill when working with ingredients too delicate to stand up under vigorous beating. The motion involves cutting down through the mixture with a rubber spatula, going across the bottom of the bowl, then bringing the spatula up and over the mixture close to the surface. The process is repeated and the bowl is turned often to assure an even distribution throughout. A rubber spatula or flat wire whisk are the utensils best suited for the blending job. More often than not, egg whites or whipped cream are the foods involved. However, nuts and pieces of fresh or candied fruit keep their shape better when folded into a batter.

Directions in a recipe using egg whites may specify whipping them until soft peaks form. So, to avoid additional beating which would change the structure of the foam, the egg whites are folded into

Layers of dough interspersed with chilled butter are folded and rolled to give puff pastry its characteristic flakiness.

the batter, sauce, or gelatin mixture. Sometimes, however, the sequence is reversed and dry ingredients or melted chocolate are folded into the meringue.

FOLDOVERS—Biscuits, rolled cookie dough, pastries, or thin slices of meat that are folded in half and may contain a filling.

Apricot Foldovers

  ½ **cup butter or margarine**
  4 **ounces sharp process American cheese, grated (1 cup)**
1⅓ **cups sifted all-purpose flour**
  2 **tablespoons water**

      • • •

  1 **cup dried apricots**
  1 **cup sugar**

Cream butter and grated cheese till light. Blend sifted flour into creamed mixture. Add water and mix thoroughly. Chill 4 to 5 hours.

Meanwhile, in a small saucepan cook apricots according to package directions. Drain well. Stir sugar into hot fruit; cook and stir till mixture boils and becomes smooth. Cool.

Divide chilled dough in half. On a lightly floured board, roll each *half* into a 10-inch square; cut dough in 2½-inch squares.

Place 1 teaspoon apricot filling on each square; fold over and seal. Bake on *ungreased* cookie sheet at 375° till lightly browned, about 8 to 10 minutes. Makes 2½ dozen cookies.

Folding chocolate syrup into fluffy whipped cream makes an easy topping for pound or angel cake. Top with sliced toasted almonds.

Both filling and pastry vary according to planned menu use. Miniature foldovers, or turnovers as they are sometimes called, make tempting appetizers or snacks because they are easy to pick up with the fingers. Plain pastry is a good choice as a base, but refrigerated biscuits are a handy shortcut when flattened slightly before filling and folding in half.

Larger meat or cheese-filled versions become the main course of the meal and may be topped with gravy or a colorful creamed vegetable. In Mexico and South America foldovers known as empanadas are eaten with the fingers like a sandwich. These do not need a sauce or gravy.

Dessert foldovers range in size from tender cookies with a sweet or cheese crust to delectable concoctions of pastry-wrapped pie filling to eat with a fork. The crust may be either plain pastry or a flaky puff pastry. Frostings or glazes are often used as a finishing touch.

FONDANT—A smooth, creamy, crystalline candy which is the basis for mint patties, dipped chocolates, and fillings used to make stuffed dates. After cooking and cooling, the candy is wrapped and stored in a covered container to ripen for 24 hours. After ripening, selected flavorings and food colorings are kneaded into the candy before it is shaped. (See also *Candy*.)

Fondant

2 cups granulated sugar
⅛ teaspoon cream of tartar *or*
2 tablespoons light corn syrup

Butter sides of heavy 1½-quart saucepan. In it combine sugar, 1½ cups boiling water, and cream of tartar. Stir over medium heat till sugar dissolves and mixture comes to boiling. Cook without stirring to soft-ball stage (238° on candy thermometer). Immediately pour onto platter. *Do not* scrap pan. Cool till candy feels only slightly warm to the touch, about 30 minutes. *Do not move* candy while it cools.

When fondant has cooled sufficiently, scrape candy from edge of platter toward center, using a spatula or wooden spoon, then work till creamy and stiff. Knead with fingers till free from lumps. Wrap; place in covered container to ripen 24 hours. Tint, flavor, and mold into desired shapes. *Or*, stuff dates, prunes, or figs and roll in confectioners' sugar.

Vanilla Fondant

Prepare 1 recipe of Fondant. After ripening step, knead in 1 tablespoon soft butter and 1 teaspoon vanilla. Mold candy into desired shapes and dip in chocolate, if desired.

Peppermint Fondant

Prepare 1 recipe of Fondant. After ripening step, knead in about 10 drops peppermint extract and 4 drops of red food coloring. Taste candy as you work to achieve a pleasing flavor and color. Mold into desired shapes.

FONDS DE CUISINE (*fôn duh kwē zēn'*)—A French term which refers to the stocks or broths that are the basis or foundation of many French sauces and special dishes.

Draw fork across rim of pan to remove the excess chocolate when dipping fondant. Drop completed candy on a wire rack placed over waxed paper making a curlicue on top as fork is removed. Allow chocolate to set.

FONDUE — 1. Vegetables cooked until soft, like a purée, then used as a garnish for meat or fish. 2. A baked casserole that is thickened with bread crumbs. 3. A dish cooked or kept warm over a burner at the table and eaten communally.

Although the word fondue is derived from the French word *fondre*, which means to melt, it has been applied to three highly diverse types of dishes.

1. At first glance, the vegetable fondue seems to have nothing to do with "melting." A closer examination, however, indicates that vegetables that have been cooked until soft and mushy have a consistency similar to *melted* cheese.

2. The baked fondue usually consists of cheese, milk, bread crumbs, eggs, and seasonings. As the fondue is baked, the cheese melts and the fondue puffs. Although this fondue is very similar to a soufflé, the bread crumbs give it a stronger structure. For this reason, the fondue will not collapse as easily as will a soufflé.

Cheese-Fondue Bake

An elegant brunch dish—

  3 slightly beaten egg yolks
1½ cups soft bread crumbs
  8 ounces sharp process American
      cheese, shredded (2 cups)
  1 cup scalded milk
½ teaspoon dry mustard
¼ teaspoon salt
      Dash pepper
  3 stiffly beaten egg whites

In mixing bowl combine beaten egg yolks, soft bread crumbs, shredded cheese, scalded milk, dry mustard, salt, and pepper. Fold in stiffly beaten egg whites. Pour into 10x6x1¾-inch baking dish. Bake at 325° till firm, about 35 to 40 minutes. Makes 6 servings.

A Swiss specialty

← A ceramic fondue pot holds this delectable Classic Cheese Fondue. Swirl bread cubes in the warm cheese-wine mixture.

3. The last type, the fondue cooked at the table, currently is very popular in this country. The oldest fondue of this type, a cheese fondue, is a delectable cheese-wine dish that originated in Switzerland as a use for hardened cheese and bread. The Swiss found that melting their cheese in wine in a common pot and then gathering around and dipping pieces of bread into this bubbling mixture made a pleasant change from sitting down to a daily diet of wine, cheese, and dry bread.

Although the Classic Cheese Fondue is made with Swiss and Gruyère cheeses, many variations use other kinds of cheese and additional ingredients. By varying the amount per person, cheese fondue can be served as an appetizer or a main dish.

Fondue is so popular that many other ingredients are now used, notably meats and desserts. These dishes take the name fondue because, like cheese fondue, they involve communal eating.

The classic meat fondue is beef fondue. Although it is also called Fondue Bourguignonne or Fondue Burgundian, its claim to these names is unknown. Beef fondue consists of beef tenderloin cubes cooked at the table in hot oil to the desired doneness (rare-15 seconds to well done-about 1 minute) and then dipped in a complementary sauce. Usually several accompanying sauces are offered with the fondue and each person takes his choice. For other meat fondues, fish, seafood, or other meats are substituted for beef.

Salad oil is usually used for meat fondues, but peanut oil or a mixture of three parts salad oil to one part clarified butter works equally well. Neither salad oil nor peanut oil imparts any flavor to the cooked meat. The butter-oil mixture, however, has a buttery aroma, and it also gives the meat a slight richness.

Chocolate fondue, a warm, rich chocolate sauce in which pieces of cake or fruit are dunked, is the best-known dessert fondue. Other dessert fondues are warm sauces of varied flavors or bite-sized desserts that are deep-fat fried at the table.

The common denominator for the cheese, meat, and dessert fondues is the indispensable fondue pot. This saucepan-like pot has its own stand and burner.

Cubes of beef tenderloin are cooked at the table in hot oil for Beef Fondue. The beef is then dipped into one of the zesty sauces.

Fondue equipment: There are three types of fondue pots—metal cookers, ceramic pots, and dessert pots.

1. The metal cooker is a versatile, all-purpose pot suitable for both hot oil and saucelike fondues. Made of stainless steel, plain or color-coated aluminum, copper, or sterling silver, metal cookers frequently offer non-stick linings.

2. The ceramic fondue pot most closely resembles the Swiss *caquelon,* traditionally used for cheese fondue. Usually quite shallow with a larger surface area than the small-mouth metal cookers, these pots are specially designed to provide plenty of room to swirl bread in the cheese-wine mixture. Since ceramic pots will not withstand the high heat necessary for hot oil fondues, they are suitable only for cheese or saucy dessert fondues.

3. The dessert fondue pot may be either metal or ceramic, but it is characteristically smaller than the other two types. Since dessert fondue sauces are very rich, the small-sized pot will still hold enough fondue for six to eight people.

Fondue burners are classified by heat source—denatured alcohol, canned heat (solidified alcohol), electricity, or candle. Other than the candle which provides only enough heat for dessert pots, any of the heat sources can be used for meat, cheese, or dessert fondues. Follow the manufacturers' directions for operating and caring for your fondue burner.

In addition to the fondue cooking unit, fondue entertaining requires long-handled forks or bamboo skewers. The fondue forks, which often have a colored tip for easy identification, have an insulated handle to prevent them from becoming too hot to hold. Fondue plates, divided into several, separate compartments for meat and sauces, are an optional accessory.

In addition to the friendly atmosphere connected with eating around a fondue pot, a fondue party is easy for the hostess. Since the guests take part in the preparation of their food, a fondue meal requires a minimum of preparation. For a light meal, serve a tossed salad, a light dessert, and a beverage with the main dish fondue. If your guests have heartier appetites, add potatoes or a cooked vegetable to the menu. You don't want to crowd the fondue pot, so have one pot for every four people for hot oil fondues or one pot for every six to eight people for cheese or dessert fondues. Center the fondue pot on a heat-proof tray or mat, then complete the table setting with fondue forks, plates, dinner forks, napkins, and appointments needed for the rest of the meal.

Since the fondue requires some last-minute preparation, you should set the table, prepare the rest of the meal, and assemble the fondue ingredients ahead. If you are serving meat fondue, set out the bite-sized meat cubes one to two hours before serving time so they can reach room temperature. As the guests arrive, heat the oil over the range or prepare the cheese fondue by vigorously, yet gradually, stirring the shredded cheese into the warm wine. If a dessert fondue is the climax of an evening, excuse yourself between courses to do last-minute tasks.

At the table, keep the fondue warm over the fondue burner as the guests leisurely enjoy the good food and conversation.

Fontina is easy to slice for appetizers or desserts.

Beef Fondue

    Salad oil
1½ pounds trimmed beef tenderloin,
    cut in ¾-inch cubes
    Basil Butter
    Green Goddess Sauce
    Wine Sauce
    Olive Sauce

Pour salad oil into fondue cooker to no more than ½ capacity or to depth of 2 inches. Heat over range to 425°. Add 1 teaspoon salt to reduce spattering. Transfer cooker to fondue burner. Have meat at room temperature in serving bowl. Spear meat with fondue fork; fry in hot oil to desired doneness (rare—15 seconds; well-done—about 1 minute). Transfer to dinner fork and dip in sauce. Makes 4 servings.

Basil Butter: Cream ½ cup softened butter till fluffy. Beat in 1 teaspoon lemon juice and ¾ teaspoon dried basil leaves, crushed. Let mellow at room temperature for 1 hour.

Green Goddess Sauce: Blend two 3-ounce packages softened cream cheese and 3 tablespoons milk. Add 2 tablespoons finely snipped chives, 1 tablespoon snipped parsley, 1 teaspoon finely chopped onion, and 2 teaspoons anchovy paste; mix well. Makes about 1 cup.

Wine Sauce: In small saucepan stir ¾ cup dry sauterne into ¼ cup catsup. Bring to boiling. Reduce heat; simmer, uncovered, 5 minutes. Blend together 2 tablespoons cold water and 4 teaspoons cornstarch; stir into wine mixture. Cook and stir till thickened and bubbly. Add 1 tablespoon butter or margarine; cook 1 minute more. Makes ¾ cup.

Olive Sauce: In small mixing bowl blend together ½ cup dairy sour cream and one 3-ounce package softened cream cheese. Fold in 2 tablespoons chopped pimiento-stuffed green olives, 1 tablespoon finely chopped onion, and 1 teaspoon snipped parsley. Makes about 1 cup.

Classic Cheese Fondue

Cut French bread, hard rolls, Italian bread, *or* boiled potatoes into bite-sized pieces.

Combine 12 ounces *natural* Swiss cheese, shredded (3 cups), and 4 ounces *natural or process* Gruyère cheese, shredded (1 cup), with 1½ teaspoons cornstarch. Rub inside of heavy saucepan with 1 clove garlic, halved; discard garlic. Pour in 1 cup dry sauterne and 1 tablespoon lemon juice. Warm till air bubbles rise and cover surface. (Do not cover saucepan or allow wine-lemon juice mixture to boil.)

Remember to stir vigorously and constantly from now on. Add a handful of cheeses, keeping heat medium (but *do not boil*). When melted, toss in another handful. After cheese is blended and bubbling gently and while still stirring, add dash ground nutmeg and dash pepper.

Quickly transfer to fondue pot; keep warm over fondue burner. (If fondue becomes too thick, add a little *warmed* sauterne.) Spear bread cube with fondue fork piercing crust last. Dip bread into fondue and using a figure-8 motion, swirl to coat bread. The swirling is important to keep fondue in motion. Serves 5.

Chocolate Fondue

  6 1-ounce squares unsweetened
    chocolate
1½ cups sugar
  1 cup light cream
  ½ cup butter or margarine
  ⅛ teaspoon salt
  3 tablespoons crème de cacao *or*
    orange-flavored liqueur
    Angel cake, pound cake, apples,
    or bananas, cut in bite-sized
    pieces

In saucepan melt chocolate over low heat. Add sugar, cream, butter, and salt. Cook, stirring constantly, till thickened, about 5 minutes. Stir in liqueur. Pour chocolate sauce into fondue pot; place over fondue burner. Spear cake or fruit piece with fondue fork; dip in chocolate sauce. Makes 6 to 8 servings.

FONTINA *(fän tē′ nuh, fŏn)*—An Italian table cheese. This creamy to light yellow cheese has a mellow flavor and scattered "eyes." Although many versions are sold in the United States under the same name, Fontina, from the Aosta Valley in northern Italy, can be recognized by its light brown, mottled crust. Domestic or imported, this firm cheese is a delicate appetizer or dessert cheese and also has excellent melting properties. (See also *Cheese*.)

FOOD—An edible substance that contains proteins, carbohydrates, fats, and/or other nutrients necessary for the growth, repair, and maintenance of body tissues.

FOOD ADDITIVE—A substance or ingredient added in small amounts to a food by a manufacturer or a processor to improve its nutritive value, flavor, texture, tenderness, keeping quality, or stability.

Over the years, additives have been both blessed and cursed. This dilema stems from the fact that processing and shipping food to feed a nation involves time and distance, both of which are enemies of fresh-picked quality. Food technologists have developed numerous additives to extend product quality.

Food additives encompass so many things that a majority of the packaged foods on the market contain them in some form. Sometimes the additive is a food itself. For example, gelatin stabilizes and thickens frozen desserts and confections.

Additives often improve the nutritive value of foods in which they are used. For example, vitamin D is added to milk and iodine to salt to make these nutrients more readily available to the consumer. Nonfat dry milk is frequently added to foods to give them a protein boost.

Other types of additives include those which improve flavor, appearance, or keeping quality of a product. These include salt, artificial flavorings, as well as ingredients that inhibit mold formation in bread or deter development of rancidity in salad oils and shortening.

Because not all additives are safe to use in foods, the government became intererested in their use, and in 1938 passed the Federal Food, Drug, and Cosmetic Act. While this law prevented the addition of substances known to be harmful, it did not give the Food and Drug Administration power to stop use of questionable additives until they were proven harmful. Twenty years later the law was amended so that now the manufacturer must prove an additive's safety to FDA before the product containing the additive can be marketed.

This safety factor is established through animal-feeding tests. If the additive is cleared, the Food and Drug Administration establishes the maximum quantity that can be used in any food, the foods in which it can be used, and any other necessary restrictions on its use. Additives used before 1958 and recognized as safe because no ill effects were found after their prolonged use, are exempt from this amendment, but may be investigated if their safety is doubted.

FOOD ADULTERATION—The intentional or unintentional addition of any foreign substances to food. Although adulteration can occur at any stage of processing, packaging, or distribution, it is related to improper sanitation, mishandling of the original raw product or container, or the use of harmful components.

Food adulteration has always been a problem. As early as 300 B.C., a Sanskrit law prohibited adding foreign substances to grains, salts, or medicines. In ancient Rome, the adulteration of wine was outlawed. The first English laws against this practice date back to the thirteenth century. Because of the problem of food adulteration (or deliberate poisoning), members of royal houses and lesser nobles used to have a royal taster eat a portion of all foods presented at the royal table. People convicted of adding unsafe substances to foods were often punished by making them eat the food or by subjecting them to public ridicule or abuse.

In the United States, the first law prohibiting the adulteration of foods was enacted in 1890. The 1906 Pure Food and Drug Act was the first large-scale attempt to protect consumers from impure foods. This law was a step forward, but it was still vague and allowed so many exemptions that it was difficult to enforce. Fortunately, the 1938 Federal Food, Drug, and Cosmetic Act and its amendments closed most of the loopholes in the 1906 law.

FOOD COLORING—Edible dyes used to tint foods. To assure that food colorings used by food processors or homemakers are safe, they must receive the certification of the Food and Drug Administration.

Pineapple-Mint Freeze

A cooling salad for summertime meals—

Drain one 20½-ounce can crushed pineapple, reserving syrup. Soften 1 envelope unflavored gelatin (1 tablespoon) in reserved syrup. Add one 10-ounce jar mint jelly and dash salt; heat and stir till gelatin is dissolved and jelly melted. If needed, beat to blend jelly. Stir in pineapple. Chill till thickened and syrupy.

Whip 1 cup whipping cream with 1 teaspoon confectioners' sugar; fold into gelatin mixture. Tint with a few drops green food coloring. Spoon into 8½x4½x2½-inch loaf dish. Freeze till firm. Let stand at room temperature 10 to 15 minutes before unmolding. Unmold; slice and place on lettuce-lined plates. Garnish with fresh mint sprigs, if desired. Serves 8.

FOOD MILL—A utensil that sieves or purées food, which is usually cooked, by forcing it through small perforations.

FOOD POISONING—An illness caused by eating a food that is contaminated by harmful bacteria. Although this could include many types of diseases, the definition is usually limited to illnesses caused by the microorganisms *Salmonella, Clostridium perfringens, Staphylococcus aureus,* and *Clostridium botulinum.*

In the latter part of the nineteenth century, food poisoning was often called "ptomaine poisoning." This term comes from the Greek word for corpse and was used because decaying animal and vegetable matter were thought to cause illness if eaten. Although this term is still used occasionally, it is not correct.

Even though food poisoning and food spoilage often affect the same food, one does not necessarily cause the other. A spoiled food does not always contain food poisoning microorganisms, but more importantly, a food that contains food poisoning microorganisms need not and generally does not look spoiled. If it did, it would be much easier to avoid infected foods.

Common types of food poisoning: There are two types of food poisoning—one caused by the presence of live microorganisms and other by toxins (poisons) produced by the microorganisms. The first type is represented by salmonella and perfringens poisoning. The toxin-producing staphylococcus and botulism microorganisms typify the second type of poisoning.

Salmonella organisms are widespread in the environment and are easily spread as most food is handled in unclean work areas. Unfortunately, their presence is not detectable by the development of any off-odor or -flavor, either in the food or surroundings. Meat, poultry, milk, fish, and eggs are particularly good media for the growth of these organisms.

Symptoms of salmonella poisoning, such as nausea, abdominal pains, and a fever, usually appear 12 to 24 hours after eating the contaminated food. Although salmonella poisoning is seldom fatal and can be treated with antibiotics, the symptoms are very uncomfortable and may persist for as long as several weeks.

The presence of the microorganism *Clostridium perfringens* in food also causes food poisoning outbreaks. Although the symptoms of nausea and diarrhea will make the patient very uncomfortable, perfringens poisoning is very seldom fatal.

Unfortunately, food cannot be made safe from these microorganisms by cooking it because the spores will withstand cooking temperatures. However, bacterial growth is inhibited by cold temperatures. This makes it especially important to promptly refrigerate dishes—meat, meat dishes, gravy—that are particularly susceptible to this type of food poisoning.

Staphylococcus microorganisms are also widely distributed wherever people handle food. They are always present on human skin and in the respiratory tract.

The presence of staphylococcus microorganisms or the toxin is impossible to detect outside the laboratory since neither produce changes in the odor, flavor, or color of the food. Furthermore, staphylococci are able to grow in high concentrations of sugar or salt, which other types of food poisoning bacteria cannot do. Milk, cheese, cream pie fillings, mayonnaise dressings, egg-containing mixtures, and meats are particularly susceptible to the staphylococcus organisms when mishandled. Given a warm room or a sunny campsite, they will multiply rapidly and quickly produce the toxin which causes discomfort.

When several people complain of nausea, abodminal cramps, or diarrhea within one to six hours after eating together, staphylococcus poisoning is often the cause. There is no effective treatment for this type of food poisoning, but symptoms are usually mild and recovery is rapid.

The fourth kind of food poisoning, botulism, is rare but very dangerous because the toxin that causes this kind of food poisoning is lethal when consumed even in very small amounts. The microorganism that causes botulism is commonly found in soil and can infect foods, especially vegetables, grown in contaminated soil. Fortunately, as this microorganism grows in a food, it produces a gas and an off-odor which help make it detectable. Boiling the contaminated food for 20 minutes will destroy the harmful toxin.

In recent years, most cases of botulism have been traced to home-canned foods, particularly corn and green beans, which were not heated enough to destroy the microorganisms. (To avoid this, see *Canning* for the correct home-canning methods.) Eaten fresh, these same foods will not cause illness because the microorganisms cannot grow in the presence of oxygen. However, the absence of air in the sealed jar or can provides an ideal environment for them to grow and produce their deadly toxin. Because of the severity of this type of food poisoning, *commercially* canned foods are tested to make sure no *Clostridium botulinum* microorganisms are present in the food after processing.

The early symptoms of botulism—headache and nausea—usually appear within 24 hours after eating the contaminated food. There is a botulism antitoxin, but its effectiveness is dependent on factors such as the quantity of toxin consumed and how soon the antitoxin is given.

How to prevent: The control of food poisoning depends on careful food handling by both the food processor and the homemaker in an effort to make it as difficult as possible for microorganisms to grow. There are three main weapons used in the fight against food poisoning—cleanliness, prolonged heating, and refrigeration.

The best way to prevent food poisoning is to prevent trouble-causing bacteria from getting into the food. You can accomplish this by being particularly careful to wash your hands before handling food, by using clean utensils for cooked food, and by washing thoroughly all counters. Remember that you may transfer food poisoning microorganisms if you fail to wash the utensils and equipment between handling uncooked and cooked food.

Prolonged heating is the second defense against food poisoning. Whenever you cook a food, the heat kills harmful bacteria present except for the heat resistant spores of *Clostridium botulinum* and *perfringens.* Therefore, a baked, boiled, broiled, braised, or fried food is safe when cooking is completed. However, it is easy to reintroduce harmful bacteria by poking the food with serving utensils, transferring it to a different dish for serving, or allowing it to stand in the open air for extended periods of time. The last condition is doubly dangerous because it provides excellent conditions for spores to produce new bacteria.

The third weapon against food poisoning, refrigeration, is important because it inhibits the growth of harmful bacteria and the outgrowth of the spores even though it does not kill them. Since the optimum temperature for bacterial growth corresponds to room temperature, it is important to chill food quickly and to return it to the refrigerator as soon as possible after serving. A good rule for food is "keep it hot (140° or higher) or keep it cold (50° or lower) or don't keep it."

Foods mishandled on picnics are often responsible for outbreaks of food poisoning. A portable, refrigerated chest is essential for keeping foods chilled.

As can be seen, food poisoning outbreaks are usually the result of carelessness and improper food handling. However, if you learn and use the above sanitary rules and careful techniques for food handling, you will be doing your part to prevent food poisoning. If an outbreak does occur, promptly notify the State Health Department. This department, often with help from the Communicable Disease Department of the Public Health Service, will conduct a thorough investigation into the cause of the incident.

FOOL—A dessert made of sieved fruit and custard or cream (either liquid or whipped). This simple, yet delicious dessert is an old English favorite. Because it is refreshing and quick to prepare, fool is a summertime favorite. Almost any fruit can be used when making a fool, but gooseberries are particularly delicious.

FOO YONG (*foo' yông, yuhng*)—A Chinese dish made of eggs and chopped meat, seafood, or vegetables. The foo yong mixture is usually formed into individual portions and then deep-fat or panfried.

Chicken-Egg Foo Yong

¾ cup finely chopped chicken *or* turkey
⅓ cup finely chopped celery
¼ cup finely chopped green pepper
¼ cup finely chopped mushrooms
¼ cup finely chopped water chestnuts
½ teaspoon salt
Dash pepper
6 well-beaten eggs
Chinese Brown Sauce

Combine chicken *or* turkey, celery, green pepper, mushrooms, water chestnuts, salt, and pepper. Add mixture to eggs; mix well.

Making 6 patties pour mixture onto hot, well-greased griddle. Shape with pancake turner by pushing egg back into patties. When set and brown on one side, turn to brown other side. Serve with Chinese Brown Sauce. Serves 3.

Chinese Brown Sauce: Melt 1 tablespoon butter or margarine. Combine 2 teaspoons cornstarch and 1 teaspoon sugar; blend into butter. Add ½ cup water and 1½ tablespoons soy sauce. Cook, stirring constantly, till mixture is thickened and bubbly. Serve hot.

Shrimp Foo Yong

¾ cup chopped, cooked, and cleaned shrimp
1 cup bean sprouts, drained and rinsed
2 tablespoons finely chopped water chestnuts
1 tablespoon chopped green onion
3 fresh mushrooms, chopped
1 teaspoon monosodium glutamate
4 eggs
2 tablespoons salad oil

• • •

Foo Yong Sauce

Combine shrimp, bean sprouts, water chestnuts, onion, mushrooms, monosodium glutamate, and eggs. Mix well. Grease griddle or skillet with oil. Drop about ⅓ cup mixture onto hot griddle; cook over medium heat till lightly browned, turning once. Stack 3 cakes together for a serving. Serve with Sauce. Serves 3.

Foo Yong Sauce: Blend 1 tablespoon cornstarch, 1 teaspoon monosodium glutamate, and ¼ teaspoon sugar. Gradually stir in 2 tablespoons soy sauce. Add 1 cup chicken broth. Cook and stir till thickened and bubbly.

FORBIDDEN FRUIT—A very sweet, citrus-flavored liqueur that is made of brandy and a grapefruit-like fruit called the shaddock. (See also *Liqueur.*)

FORCEMEAT—A highly seasoned mixture of finely chopped or ground meat, fish, or poultry. Forcemeat can be served by itself or used as a stuffing for foods.

FOREIGN COOKERY—The food and food preparation of a country other than one's own. (See also individual countries.)

FORMOSAN TEA—A partially fermented (oolong) type of tea produced on the island of Formosa. (See also *Tea.*)

FORTIFIED—A food that has had nutrients added above the level normally present in the food. Foods are usually fortified to make them a source of nutrients that are relatively scarce in common foods. The fortification of milk with vitamin D began

in the early 1930s. Today, salt is commonly fortified with iodine and most margarines contain added vitamin A.

FORTIFIED WINE—A wine to which a spirit, usually brandy, has been added to increase the alcoholic content. These wines are usually used during the appetizer or dessert course. (See also *Wines and Spirits*.)

FOWL—A seldom used word for a bird of any kind, especially any type of domesticated poultry. (See also *Poultry*.)

FRANCONIA POTATO—A peeled potato that is roasted in the same pan as a meat roast. These potatoes are sometimes partially cooked before putting them in with the roast. (See also *Potato*.)

FRANGIPANE *(fran' ji pān')*—1. A rich, almond-flavored custard used alone as a dessert or as a filling for cakes and tarts. 2. A cream puff-like pastry usually filled with forcemeat and served as a dessert.

FRANKFURTER—A smoked, fully cooked sausage that is either skinless or enclosed in an edible casing. Whether it's called a frankfurter or frank, wiener, hot dog, or coney, this meat is the most popular type of sausage in the United States. Frankfurters range in size from miniature cocktail franks to foot-long versions, with the big seller being the four- to five-inch one.

Although this sausage obtained the name frankfurter from Frankfurt, Germany, just when or where it originated is not known. However, we do know that some time during the nineteenth century, the frankfurter was introduced to the United States. Later, some enterprising merchant placed this mild, hot sausage in a long, slender bun, making a sandwich. This convenient and delicious combination now sells by the millions each year.

Franks with a Hawaiian touch

← Glazed with a sweet-sour apricot sauce, these Hilo Franks and canned pineapple slices sizzle over the coals on a hibachi.

Similarity between the shape of a frankfurter and a dachshund led to the nickname "dachshund sausages." An early twentieth-century newspaper cartoonist, T. A. Dorgan, drew cartoons of talking frankfurters. Finding dachshund hard to spell, he decided to call his cartoon characters "hot dogs." This name retained its popularity and today the American hot dog is known worldwide as well as among all classes of people.

President Franklin D. Roosevelt did much to spread the fame of the frankfurter when he served a hot dog picnic to the visiting King and Queen of England in 1939. It is likely that this novel social event was the deciding factor that later led Queen Elizabeth II to serve frankfurters at a royal lawn party.

How frankfurters are produced: The frankfurter is made of ground beef or a mixture of beef, pork, and veal. After the meats are ground separately, they are combined with curing agents and seasonings, such as allspice, cinnamon, coriander, garlic, ginger, mustard, red pepper, nutmeg, mace, and sage. Preparations vary slightly according to the sausagemaker's own carefully guarded formula. This mixture is then finely chopped until it resembles a batter. After the air is vacuum-removed from the batter, it is forced under pressure into cylindrical casings.

Although casings made from intestines are edible, cellulose casings are not. Therefore, inedible casings are automatically stripped from the frankfurters after processing and cooling, resulting in a skinless frankfurter. The stuffed casings are twisted off into the desired lengths by an automatic linker machine.

The next processing step requires smoking the frankfurters to develop the characteristic flavor and color. After smoking, the frankfurters are cooked with hot water or steam. Cold water spray or refrigeration quickly cools the frankfurters.

Nutritional value: Like other meats, frankfurters are a source of high-quality protein. One four- to five-inch frankfurter supplies about 150 calories as well as small amounts of sodium and the B vitamins.

Types of frankfurters: Frankfurters are divided into types according to their ingredients. 1. *All-meat* frankfurters are made only with skeletal (muscle) meat and no more than 30 percent fat. They contain no fillers. 2. *All beef* frankfurters are made only with beef and contain no fillers. If labeled *Kosher*, they have been produced under conditions approved by Jewish religious authorities. 3. If the label has no specification other than *frankfurters*, *wieners*, or *hot dogs*, the sausages may contain, besides muscle meat, up to 15 percent poultry, no more than 30 percent fat, and up to 3.5 percent fillers. Fillers, usually cereals, soybean flour, or dry milk powder, are added to help bind the meat together. 4. Sausages labeled as *imitation* frankfurters contain more than 3.5 percent fillers or 10 percent moisture.

How to select and store: When selecting frankfurters, check the label for the ingredients used in making them. Frankfurters in natural casings are not usually prepackaged by the processor and packaged frankfurters are sold in see-through packages. You can judge quality by their appearance; frankfurters that look discolored or dried out should not be purchased.

If unopened, packaged frankfurters can be stored in the refrigerator for up to two weeks. Because the curing agents used in frankfurters hasten the development of undesirable flavor changes at low temperatures, freezing frankfurters is not generally recommended. However, if necessary, they can be frozen for about one month.

How to use: Since frankfurters are fully cooked when purchased, they can be eaten right from the package. Usually, however, they are heated before serving. Franks can be heated quickly in the oven, on the grill, in a frypan, in simmering (not boiling) water, or over a campfire.

Kettle-Cooked Frankfurters

Simmer-cooked to perfection—

In saucepan cover frankfurters with cold water; bring to boiling. Simmer about 5 minutes.

Frank Fries

Score frankfurters, making shallow (¼ inch) diagonal cuts 1 inch apart, if desired. In skillet brown in 1 tablespoon hot butter or margarine for 5 minutes. Do not overbrown.

Other than the always popular hot-dog-in-a-bun, frankfurters can be served in a variety of ways. Since these sausages are processed in serving-sized portions, take advantage of this by leaving them whole and simmering them in a barbecue sauce. Franks stuffed with cheese or a relish mixture and then broiled make another popular, quickly prepared meal.

Because frankfurters are so easy to prepare, they make an excellent food for teen-age parties. Frankfurters not only provide the young people with much needed protein, but they are also well liked. Just heat them in an electric skillet and provide plenty of buns and condiments. The hungry teen-agers will take care of the rest.

Frankfurters are also suitable for quick-cook meals such as Frank-Reuben Sandwiches or Glazed Apples and Franks. If you only have an hour to prepare supper, bring out the frankfurters and serve Hot Dogs Delicious. A package of frankfurters can even become the main dish for company when you serve Frank and Corn Crown or Savory Frank-Noodle Bake.

Hilo Franks

As shown on the cover—

Combine 1 cup apricot preserves, half of 8-ounce can tomato sauce (½ cup), ⅓ cup vinegar, ¼ cup sherry, 2 tablespoons soy sauce, 2 tablespoons honey, 1 tablespoon salad oil, 1 teaspoon salt, and 1 teaspoon grated, fresh gingerroot *or* ¼ teaspoon ground ginger; mix well.

Score 2 pounds frankfurters on the bias and grill slowly over *medium* coals, turning and basting often with the sauce, till hot through and glazed. Last few minutes place one 20-ounce can pineapple slices, drained, on grill; brush with sauce, grill, and turn. Brush again with sauce. Heat remaining sauce to pass with grilled frankfurters. Makes 8 to 10 servings.

Chili-Cheese Franks

    2 15-ounce cans chili with beans
    1 11-ounce can condensed Cheddar
       cheese soup
    2 tablespoons instant minced onion
    1 pound frankfurters (8 to 10)
    8 to 10 frankfurter buns, split
       and toasted
      Corn chips, coarsely crushed

In large saucepan combine chili with beans, Cheddar cheese soup, and instant minced onion. Add frankfurters; heat to boiling. Simmer mixture about 5 minutes to blend flavors.

    To serve, place a frankfurter on each toasted frankfurter bun; top each generously with chili-cheese sauce. Sprinkle with coarsely crushed corn chips. Makes 8 to 10 servings.

Cocktail Wieners

In chafing dish or saucepan over low heat mix one 6-ounce jar prepared mustard (¾ cup) and one 10-ounce jar currant jelly (1 cup). Add 1 pound frankfurters (8 to 10), sliced diagonally into bite-sized pieces; heat through. Serve hot as an appetizer.

Frank and Corn Crown

    ½ cup chopped green pepper
    ¼ cup chopped onion
    ¼ cup butter or margarine
    2 cups soft bread crumbs (about
       3 slices)
    1 17-ounce can cream-style corn
    1 12-ounce can whole kernel corn,
       drained
    2 beaten eggs
    1 teaspoon salt

. . .

    ¼ cup fine dry bread crumbs
    1 tablespoon butter or margarine,
      melted
    1 pound frankfurters (8 to 10),
      cut in half crosswise

Cook green pepper and onion in the ¼ cup butter or margarine till tender but not brown. Add soft bread crumbs, cream-style corn, whole kernel corn, eggs, and salt; mix lightly. Spoon into 8x1½-inch round baking dish.

    Combine dry bread crumbs and melted butter or margarine; sprinkle over corn mixture. Bake, uncovered, at 350° for 30 minutes. Stand franks, cut end down, in crown around edge of mixture. Bake 15 minutes longer. Serves 5 or 6.

This quick fix-up for frankfurters uses canned chili, cheese soup, and instant minced onion. Crushed corn chips top the savory Chili-Cheese Franks served in a toasted bun.

For a hearty meal-in-a-dish, serve Chili Con Wiene over toasted buns. Ripe olives and frank slices garnish this spicy dish.

Savory Frank-Noodle Bake

    4 ounces medium noodles (1 cup)
 ½ cup chopped onion
    1 tablespoon butter or margarine
    4 or 5 frankfurters, thinly sliced
        crosswise (½ pound)
    3 slightly beaten eggs
    1 cup dairy sour cream
 ½ cup cream-style cottage cheese
 ½ cup cornflake crumbs
    1 tablespoon butter or margarine,
        melted

Cook noodles in boiling, salted water till tender, about 7 minutes; drain. In small skillet cook onion in the 1 tablespoon butter or margarine till tender but not brown. Set aside a few frankfurter slices for garnish.

In mixing bowl combine noodles, onion, frankfurters, eggs, dairy sour cream, cream-style cottage cheese, ½ teaspoon salt, and dash pepper. Pour mixture into greased 9-inch pie plate. Mix cornflake crumbs and melted butter or margarine; sprinkle over top of casserole.

Bake at 375° for 20 minutes. Top frank-noodle mixture with reserved frankfurter slices; bake 5 minutes more. Let stand 10 minutes; cut in wedges. Makes 4 to 6 servings.

Chili Con Wiene

    1 pound ground beef
 ½ cup chopped onion
    1 15-ounce can chili with beans
        (2 cups)
    4 or 5 frankfurters, cut diagonally
        in ¼- to ½-inch slices
        (½ pound)
    1 10¾-ounce can condensed tomato
        soup
 ½ cup chili sauce
 ¼ cup chopped green pepper
    8 hamburger buns, split and toasted

In large skillet lightly brown ground beef and chopped onion; pour off excess fat. Add chili, frankfurters (reserve a few slices for garnish), tomato soup, chili sauce, and chopped green pepper. Heat thoroughly. Garnish with reserved frankfurter slices and ripe olives, if desired. Serve over toasted bun halves. Serves 8.

Saucy Franks

    1 pound frankfurters (8 to 10)
    2 tablespoons butter or margarine
    1 10¾-ounce can condensed tomato
        soup
 ¼ cup brown sugar
 ¼ cup water
    3 tablespoons vinegar
    1 tablespoon Worcestershire sauce
 ½ lemon, thinly sliced
 ½ onion, thinly sliced
 ¼ cup chopped green pepper
        Hot cooked noodles or
        frankfurter buns

Score franks in corkscrew fashion. In skillet brown franks lightly in butter or margarine. Add tomato soup, brown sugar, water, vinegar, Worcestershire sauce, lemon, and onion. Simmer, covered, about 10 minutes. Add green pepper; and cook, covered, 5 minutes longer. Serve over hot cooked noodles or buns. Serves 4 or 5.

Nutty Pups

Broil frankfurters over *hot* coals. Serve in hot toasted buns spread with chunk-style peanut butter. Pass pickle relish, if desired.

Frank-Vegetable Medley

4 or 5 frankfurters, cut in
1-inch pieces (½ pound)
½ cup uncooked long-grain rice
1 8-ounce can tomato sauce
1 cup water
1 10-ounce package frozen mixed
vegetables, slightly thawed
and broken up with fork
¼ cup chopped onion
1 teaspoon salt
Dash bottled hot pepper sauce

In 2-quart casserole combine franks, long-grain rice, tomato sauce, water, mixed vegetables, onion, salt, and bottled hot pepper sauce.

Bake, covered, at 375° till heated through, about 1 hour. Stir once or twice during baking. Makes 6 servings.

Frank-Reuben Sandwich

8 frankfurters
1 16-ounce can sauerkraut, drained
and snipped
4 slices process Swiss cheese,
quartered in strips
. . .
8 frankfurter buns
Thousand Island salad dressing

Slit frankfurters in half lengthwise. Spread with sauerkraut. Broil 3 to 4 inches from heat till sauerkraut is hot, about 5 minutes. Top *each* frankfurter with 2 cheese strips. Broil till cheese is melted. Split and toast buns; spread with Thousand Island dressing. Serve frankfurters on buns. Makes 8 sandwiches.

Frankfurter Doubles

Slit frankfurters lengthwise, not quite through. Spread cut surfaces with prepared mustard. Stuff with cheese strips, pineapple chunks, baked beans, drained sauerkraut, pickle relish, *or* mashed potatoes. Wrap each frankfurter with bacon; fasten ends with wooden picks. Broil, stuffed side down, on broiler rack 3 to 4 inches from heat about 5 minutes. Turn frankfurters over and broil 3 to 5 minutes longer. Serve in toasted buns.

Tangy Frank Barbecue

2 tablespoons prepared mustard
2 8-ounce cans tomato sauce
(2 cups)
½ cup dark corn syrup
⅓ cup vinegar
⅓ cup minced onion
2 tablespoons Worcestershire
sauce
½ teaspoon celery seed
¼ to ½ teaspoon bottled hot
pepper sauce
. . .
1 pound frankfurters (8 to 10),
scored diagonally
Hot cooked rice

In skillet blend mustard with small amount of tomato sauce; add remaining tomato sauce, corn sryup, vinegar, onion, Worcestershire sauce, celery seed, and hot pepper sauce.

Cook over medium heat, stirring frequently, till mixture comes to boiling; reduce heat and simmer gently 30 minutes. Add scored frankfurters; cook till frankfurters are hot and plumped, about 7 to 8 minutes. Serve over hot cooked rice. Makes 4 or 5 servings.

Best Hamdogs

1 cup finely chopped cooked
ham *or* luncheon meat
3 tablespoons pickle relish
2 tablespoons finely chopped
onion
2 tablespoons prepared mustard
2 tablespoons mayonnaise *or*
salad dressing
1 pound frankfurters (8 to 10)
8 to 10 slices bacon
Bottled barbecue sauce
8 to 10 frankfurter buns, split
and toasted

Mix ham *or* luncheon meat, pickle relish, onion, mustard, and mayonnaise or salad dressing. Slit frankfurters, cutting almost to ends and only ¾ the way through. Stuff with ham mixture; wrap with bacon and secure with wooden picks. Boil over *hot* coals, brushing with barbecue sauce, till filling is hot and bacon crisp. Serve in toasted buns. Makes 8 to 10 servings.

Glazed Apples and Franks

> 3 tablespoons butter or margarine
> ¾ cup light corn syrup
> 2 tablespoons prepared mustard
> 1 pound frankfurters (8 to 10)
> 6 medium tart apples, cored and
>   quartered

In skillet melt butter or margarine; blend in corn syrup and prepared mustard. Score franks at 1-inch intervals; add to sauce with apples. Cover; simmer slowly 10 to 15 minutes, turning apples and franks once. Arrange franks on serving platter; surround with apples. Pass warm syrup mixture. Makes 4 or 5 servings.

Franks and Cabbage

> 4 cups coarsely shredded cabbage
> 4 or 5 frankfurters, cut into
>   1-inch pieces (½ pound)
> 2 tablespoons butter or margarine
> 2 tablespoons all-purpose flour
> 1 cup milk
> 1 tablespoon prepared mustard

Cook cabbage, covered, in small amount of boiling, salted water till barely tender, about 5 to 6 minutes; drain. Place in shallow 1-quart baking dish. Arrange franks on top. Melt butter; blend in flour and ½ teaspoon salt. Add milk all at once; cook and stir till sauce is thickened and bubbly. Cook 1 minute longer. Stir in mustard. Pour sauce over franks. Heat at 350° for 20 to 25 minutes. Serves 3 or 4.

Wiener Bean Pot

> 2 16-ounce cans pork and beans
>   in tomato sauce
> 1 envelope dry onion soup mix
> ⅓ cup catsup
> ¼ cup water
> 2 tablespoons brown sugar
> 1 tablespoon prepared mustard
> 1 pound frankfurters (8 to
>   10), sliced

In 2-quart casserole or bean pot combine all ingredients. Bake, uncovered, at 350° for about 1 hour. Makes 6 to 8 servings.

Hot Dogs Delicious

It's ready in a jiffy—

> ½ cup chopped onion
> 1 tablespoon shortening
> 1 14-ounce bottle extra-hot
>   catsup (1¼ cups)
> 2 tablespoons pickle relish
> 1 tablespoon sugar
> 1 tablespoon vinegar
> ¼ teaspoon salt
>   Dash pepper
> 1 pound frankfurters (8 to 10)
> 8 to 10 frankfurter buns,
>   split and toasted

Cook chopped onion in hot shortening till tender but not brown. Stir in extra-hot catsup, pickle relish, sugar, vinegar, salt, and pepper. Score frankfurters; add to sauce.

Simmer till frankfurters are heated through, about 10 minutes. Serve in toasted frankfurter buns. Makes 8 to 10 servings.

This easy frankfurter dish is ready in minutes. A spicy mustard sauce covers the meat and apples in Glazed Apples and Franks.

Swiss and Frank Spirals

> 2 5½-ounce packages cocktail
>   wieners (32 wieners)
> 32 2-inch strips process Swiss
>   cheese
> 1 8-ounce package refrigerated
>   biscuits (10 biscuits)
>   • • •
> 2 tablespoons butter or margarine,
>   melted
> 2 tablespoons sesame seed

Cut a lengthwise slit in each wiener; insert strip of cheese in each. Quarter 8 biscuits. (Bake remaining biscuits with appetizers.) Shape quarters in 4-inch strips. Wind, spiral fashion, around each wiener. Place on baking sheet; brush with butter and sprinkle with sesame. Bake at 400° till browned, about 10 minutes. Serve warm. Makes 32 appetizers.

Whether you serve frankfurters alone, with a bun, in a casserole, or in a barbecue sauce, your family will be joining others in making frankfurters the most popular sausage in the United States. In fact, the hot dog is enjoyed so much that the phrase "hot dog" is used worldwide, not only in reference to food but also as an expression of delight. Next time you need a meal in a hurry, remember the quick-to-prepare, versatile frankfurter. Your family is sure to be pleased with the choice.

FRAPPÉ (*fra pā'*)—An iced drink or dessert. The beverage called a frappé is made by pouring a liqueur such as crème de menthe over crushed ice. Dessert frappés are partially frozen and then beaten till mushy. (See also *Beverage.*)

Slim-Jim Frappé

In small mixing bowl combine one 10-ounce can vanilla-flavored liquid diet food and ¼ teaspoon rum flavoring. Pour into 3-cup freezer tray. Freeze till almost firm. Spoon the frozen mixture into blender container; cover and blend till slightly mushy. Pour into two chilled sherbet glasses; sprinkle with ground nutmeg. Serve immediately. Makes 2 servings.

FREEZE-DRIED FOOD—A food dehydrated by a process that combines freezing and drying. Although the use of freeze-drying in processed food is a recent development, this phenomenon occurs frequently in nature. A familiar example is clothes that are hung outside to dry in below freezing weather. Although the clothes will freeze first, they will eventually dry.

Water usually evaporates only from its liquid state, but under certain conditions it can go directly from the solid state (ice) to a vapor. This process is known as sublimation. In freeze-dried foods, the uncooked or cooked food is quick-frozen and then placed in a vacuum chamber. In this chamber small amounts of heat are all that is required to make the ice crystals go directly to a vapor without passing through the liquid state. Up to 99 percent of the moisture in the food can be removed by this method of drying foods.

Freeze-dried foods can be successfully stored without refrigeration for over a year. Before using a freeze-dried food, it must be rehydrated with water or other liquid according to package directions.

For centuries, drying has been used as a method of food preservation because dried foods are lightweight, small in volume, and do not require refrigeration. Freeze-dried foods not only have these characteristics of dried foods, but they also retain their original color, shape, and structure better than dried foods. However, the high cost of freeze-drying, the special packaging required to prevent crumbling of some freeze-dried foods, and the prejudice of American consumers against dried foods, has made use of the freeze-drying process unprofitable for most foods.

For many years, the development of freeze-dried foods was largely the domain of the armed forces. As far back as World War II, the army used large quantities of freeze-dried orange juice. Because of the field need for high-quality foods that do not require refrigeration, the armed forces are still the leading developers and users of freeze-dried foods. In recent years, however, freeze-dried foods have gained popularity as camping supplies and a few products, such as freeze-dried coffee, have been widely accepted by the public.

FREEZING

How to preserve top-quality fruits, meats, vegetables, and cooked foods for year-round enjoyment.

Freezing involves hardening a food into a solid mass by removing the heat from it. This method of food preservation is easy to do and satisfactorily maintains the quality of the fresh food. For these reasons, freezing has become an increasingly popular process in both the home and industry.

Long ago, primitive tribes living in cool climates used freezing to preserve foods, but interest in freezing did not really blossom until the 1800s. An English patent, awarded in 1842, introduced freezing food in an ice-salt brine solution. Shortly thereafter, this freezing process was used in the United States to freeze first fish, then poultry, eggs, and meat.

Freezing concepts did not improve markedly until iceless mechanical refrigeration was developed early in the twentieth century. Clarence Birdseye is credited with advancing freezing processes, especially in the frozen vegetable line. These basic freezing techniques were later adopted for use with prepared foods. As freezing advanced, food quality became better and consumer acceptance widened.

Today, home freezing is accepted as a boon to the modern homemaker because it saves her time, money, and energy. It's an easy way to whip up delicious meals at a moment's notice, to keep the taste of summer-garden foods in mid winter meals, or to cook ahead time-consuming meals.

Nutritional value: By using proper freezing, thawing, and cooking techniques, the natural nutritive value of frozen foods is maintained. Soluble nutrients can, however, be lost during thawing and cooking. To prevent this, thaw the food in its unopened container. Use the preserved food immediately after thawing, then cook it as carefully as you would fresh food.

Equipment

Except for the freezer itself, equipment investment is nominal. Special packaging materials must be selected, but standard kitchen tools are used to prepare the food.

Usable freezing units should maintain a temperature of 0° or less. To assure that the bulk freezer or freezer section of your refrigerator meets this temperature requirement, keep a thermometer in the freezer and check it frequently.

Should power failure occur, do not open the freezer. The food will stay frozen about two days during the summer months. Should the power be off longer than this, use dry ice (2½ pounds per cubic foot) or transfer the food to a commercial locker. Dry ice will keep food frozen two to three days when the freezer is half full and three to four days when full. Place dry ice on cardboard set atop the food. (Do not handle dry ice with bare hands.) Also, keep the room well-ventilated.

All containers for freezing must be both moisture- and vapor-resistant to retain the food's juiciness, flavor, texture, color, and nutritive value. Sealing and labeling materials must also be waterproof. Make the final container selection by considering the type of food being frozen, ease of handling the container, and cost.

The kind of food being frozen largely determines whether you will use rigid or flexible containers. Designed for liquid, semiliquid, or dry foods, rigid containers are made of metal, plastic, heavily waxed cardboard, or glass. Flexible wrappings or bags are better for dry packs. Moisture-vaporproof materials of heavy foil, cellophane, plastic, or laminated paper are suitable, flexible container materials that will mold to the food's shape.

A drugstore wrap molds flexible material to the shape of the food. Cut material 1½ times as long as will go around the food.

With shiny coating on inside, place food in center. Bring wrapping sides together at top. Fold edges down with locked folds.

Press wrapping against the food, then crease both ends into points. Press wrapping to remove any entrapped pockets of air.

Turn wrapping ends under; secure with freezer tape. Label with contents and date. Freeze quickly at 0° or less.

The step-by-step freezing techniques that are given have been scientifically tested. Each homemaker can be assured that the work will be easy and the results not only safe but extremely rewarding as well.

Heavily waxed cardboard cartons, plastic containers and bags, and plastic and foil wraps are but a few of the wide assortment of freezing materials available.

Choose a container that is easy to handle and that meets size and shape needs. The container should hold enough food for one meal only. Straight sides and stackable tops and bottoms save freezer space. Openings should be large enough for packing.

Cost reflects the availability and durability of the material. Most rigid containers other than waxed cardboard can be reused indefinitely. Although the initial cost of rigid containers is higher, their overall cost may be less.

Methods of freezing

All foods are frozen by one of two methods: wet (contains water, syrup, brine, or sugar) or dry. With the wet method the food is packed tightly to remove air, and the liquid is then poured into the container. A piece of crumpled parchment paper placed atop the food holds it below the liquid. Leave enough space between the top of the food and the top of the container (headspace) so that there is room for liquid expansion. Dry-packed food is packed tightly in the container, or a sheet of wrapping is molded tightly about it. With little liquid present, less headspace is required.

The quality of the frozen food can be no better than the fresh product. Freezing does not sterilize food, so during storage changes will occur. To minimize these changes, sweeten fruits and blanch vegetables before freezing. Select the highest quality food and handle it gently. Not only

should the food be ripe and free from decay or spoilage, but it should also be a good freezing variety. The nearest agricultural extension service can tell you which varieties are best. Fruits and vegetables should be frozen as soon after they are harvested as possible because changes rapidly lower the quality. If they cannot be processed immediately, keep the fruits or vegetables refrigerated until ready to use.

Additional precautions will assure top-quality results. First, be certain the container seal is leakproof. Second, freeze the food quickly at 0° or below by arranging single layers of packages in the coldest part of the freezer. Rapid freezing produces smaller ice crystals and a more acceptable product. Third, leave some space between each package in the freezer for air circulation. Packages may be stacked after the food is completely frozen. And fourth, don't overload the freezer. Prepare only as much food as will freeze within 24 hours, about 2 to 3 pounds are suggested for each cubic foot of freezer space.

Freezing fruits

Most fruits, except bananas, can be frozen and thawed successfully. Some, when thawed, are softer than the fresh product, but this is alleviated by serving them just before they are completely thawed.

Fruits are frozen in a syrup, sugar, or unsweetened pack, depending to a large extent on what the final use will be. If the fruit is to be eaten uncooked, a syrup pack is best. Sugar-packed fruits work well when the fruit is to be cooked. A dry pack fits into special diet cookery although the storage time for dry pack is reduced.

How to prepare: When preparing fruits for freezing, do not use galvanized or iron utensils or equipment where the enamel or tin coating is chipped because off-flavors may develop, and because fruit acids dissolve poisonous zinc in galvanized ware. If syrup is to be used, prepare the syrup ahead of time and chill. (See Syrup Preparations, page 954.) Freeze fruits, using the following directions:

1. Select fresh, ripe fruit. Carefully wash fruit in cold water and drain.

Headspaces for freezing

Leave the following headspace between food mixture and top of container:

Liquid or Semiliquid Pack

Wide top opening		Narrow top opening	
Pint	Quart	Pint	Quart
½ inch	1 inch	¾ inch	1½ inches

Dry Pack

| ½ inch | ½ inch | ½ inch | ½ inch |

Fruit	Syrup Pack	Sugar Pack
Apples	Wash, pare, and core. Add ½ teaspoon ascorbic acid color keeper per quart Medium Syrup. Slice apples into ½ cup cold syrup in container. Press down; cover with syrup; leave headspace. Seal; label; freeze.	Wash, pare, core, and slice. Steam 1½ to 2 minutes; cool; drain. Sprinkle ½ cup sugar over each quart of fruit; stir. Pack tightly into containers, leaving headspace. Seal; label; freeze.
Apricots	Wash, halve, and pit. Peel and slice, if desired. If not peeled, cook in boiling water ½ minute; cool; drain. Add ¾ teaspoon ascorbic acid color keeper to each quart Medium Syrup. Pack fruit tightly into containers. Cover with cold syrup; leave headspace. Seal; label; freeze.	Wash, halve, and pit. Peel and slice, if desired. If not peeled, cook in boiling water ½ minute; cool; drain. Dissolve ¼ teaspoon ascorbic acid color keeper in ¼ cup cold water; sprinkle over 1 quart apricots. Mix ½ cup sugar with each quart fruit; stir till dissolved. Pack into containers, pressing down till juice covers fruit. Leave headspace; seal; label; freeze.
Blueberries Elderberries Huckleberries	Wash; drain. Steam 1 minute; cool quickly. Pack into containers; cover with cold Medium Syrup. Leave headspace; seal; freeze.	Wash; drain. Steam 1 minute; cool. To 1 quart berries, add ⅔ cup sugar; mix. Place in containers; leave headspace. Seal; label; freeze.
Cherries, sour	Stem, wash, drain, and pit. Pack into containers; cover with cold Very Heavy or Extra Heavy Syrup, depending on tartness. Leave headspace; seal; label; freeze.	Stem; wash; drain; pit. To each quart fruit add ¾ cup sugar; mix till dissolved. Pack into containers, leaving headspace. Seal; label; freeze.
Cherries, sweet	Stem, wash, drain, and pit if desired. Add ½ teaspoon ascorbic acid color keeper to each quart Medium Syrup. Pack fruit into containers; cover with syrup, leaving headspace. Seal; label; freeze.	
Melons	Halve, remove seeds, and peel. Cut into slices, cubes, or balls; pack into containers. Cover with cold Thin Syrup, leaving headspace. Seal; label; freeze.	
Peaches	Wash, pit, and peel (for smooth look, don't scald). Add ½ teaspoon ascorbic acid color keeper per quart Medium Syrup. Slice peaches into ½ cup syrup in container or leave in halves; press fruit down; add syrup to cover; leave headspace; seal; freeze.	Wash, pit, and peel (for smooth look, don't scald). Halve or slice. Dissolve ¼ teaspoon ascorbic acid color keeper in ¼ cup cold water. Sprinkle over 1 quart fruit; add ⅔ cup sugar; mix well. Pack into containers; leave headspace. Seal; label; freeze.
Pears	Wash, pare, halve or quarter, and remove cores. Cook in boiling Medium Syrup for 1 to 2 minutes; drain; cool. Pack pears into containers. Add ¾ teaspoon ascorbic acid color keeper per quart Medium Syrup; cover fruit with syrup, leaving headspace. Seal; label; freeze.	
Plums	Wash, pit, halve or quarter; pack into containers. Add ½ teaspoon ascorbic acid color keeper to each quart Medium or Heavy Syrup, depending on tartness. Cover fruit with syrup; leave headspace. Seal; label; freeze.	Wash; drain. Pit, halve or quarter. To 1 pound fruit add ⅔ cup sugar; mix. Place in containers; leave headspace. Seal; label; freeze.
Raspberries Blackberries Boysenberries Strawberries	Wash and drain. Remove hulls and slice or leave strawberries whole. Place in containers; cover with cold Medium or Heavy Syrup; leave headspace. Seal; label; freeze.	Wash and drain. Remove hulls and slice or leave strawberries whole. Add ¾ cup sugar to each quart berries; mix carefully. Place in containers; leave headspace. Seal; label; freeze.
Rhubarb	Wash, trim, cut into 1- or 2-inch pieces or in lengths to fit container. Cook in boiling water 1 minute; cool in cold water. Pack into containers; cover with cold Medium Syrup; leave headspace; seal; label; freeze.	

2. Prepare the fruit for syrup or sugar pack as indicated on the chart, page 953. For sugar pack, allow sugar to dissolve and juice to form. Special methods for unsweetened (dry) pack are given below.

3. Pack fruit tightly into moisture-vaporproof containers. For syrup pack, pour in enough cooled syrup to cover fruit. Leave headspace as recommended for wet pack (see page 952).

4. Place piece of crumpled parchment paper atop fruit in container.

5. Seal following manufacturer's directions. Label with contents and date.

6. Freeze at 0° or below in small batches. Store frozen fruit 8 to 12 months.

Unsweetened Fruit Pack

Apples: Use directions for sugar pack, omitting the sugar. Leave ½-inch headspace. Seal, label, and freeze.

Blueberries: Use directions for syrup pack, omitting the syrup. Leave ½-inch headspace. Seal, label, and freeze.

Peaches or Strawberries: Wash, pit, and peel peaches; halve or slice. Wash, drain, and hull berries; leave whole or slice. Fill containers (do not use glass). Cover with water containing 1 teaspoon ascorbic acid color keeper per quart. Leave ½-inch headspace in pints or 1-inch headspace in quarts. Seal, label, and freeze.

Plums: Wash. Pack whole in containers; leave ½-inch headspace. Seal; label; freeze.

Raspberries: Wash, then drain. Pack into containers, leaving ½-inch headspace. Seal, label, and freeze the raspberries.

Rhubarb: Use directions for syrup pack, omitting the sugar. Leave ½-inch headspace. Seal, label, and freeze rhubarb.

How to use: Frozen fruits should be thawed in the sealed container just before they are used. Thaw in the refrigerator, at room temperature, or in cool water. Turn the package several times.

The fruit may then be served raw or cooked. Serve uncooked fruit with a few ice crystals remaining to improve texture. For cooking, thaw the fruit just till the pieces can be broken apart. Use like fresh fruit, allowing for sweetening and juice. If the juice is insufficient, add a little water to prevent scorching. If the juice is in excess, use only part of it or add thickening.

Fruit-syrup proportions

Add sugar to boiling water; stir. Chill. Figure on ½ to ⅔ cup syrup per pint of fruit.

Syrup	Sugar (cups)	Water (cups)	Yield (cups)
Thick	2	4	5
Medium	3	4	5½
Heavy	4¾	4	6½
Very Heavy	7	4	7¾
Extra Heavy	8¾	4	8⅔

Freezing meats

Meats usually are frozen in the uncooked state without the addition of liquid, although cooked meats may be frozen, too. Select top-quality meat.

How to prepare: Meats will freeze faster if they are well chilled. The following step-by-step methods will assure success:

Frozen fruit yield

Generally, the following amount of fruit as purchased yields 1 pint frozen fruit.

Fruit	Pounds
Apples	1¼ to 1½ pounds
Apricots	⅔ to 4/5 pound
Berries*	1⅓ to 1½ pints
Peaches	1 to 1½ pounds
Pears	1 to 1¼ pounds
Plums	1 to 1½ pounds
Raspberries	1 pint
Rhubarb	⅔ to 1 pound
Strawberries	⅔ quart

*Includes blackberries, blueberries, boysenberries, elderberries, and loganberries.

Food	Preparation for freezing	Storage time at 0° How to thaw
Meat	Select young, well-finished animals. Chill and age (see page 116). Have cut in desired meat cuts. Avoid packing more bone than necessary. Wrap tightly in moisture-vapor-proof material. Seal, label, and freeze at 0° or below.	Beef roasts and steaks: 8 to 12 months Lamb, Pork, Veal chops: 3 to 4 months Lamb roasts: 8 to 12 months Pork, Veal roasts: 4 to 8 months Ground meat: 2 to 3 months Thaw in refrigerator in original wrap. See pgs. 198-228 for cooking information.
Poultry	Select high-quality birds. Dress, draw, clean, and wash. Chill 12 hours. Wrap and freeze giblets separately. Disjoint and cut up bird or leave whole. Wrap bird or pieces in mois-ture-vaporproof material. Seal, label, and freeze. Never freeze stuffed poultry.	Chicken: 12 months Turkey, Duck, Goose: 6 months Giblets: 3 months Thaw in refrigerator in original wrap. See pgs. 250-259 for cooking information.
Fish	Dress and wash fish as for cooking. Dip in solution of ⅔ cup salt to 1 gallon water for 30 seconds. Wrap in moisture-vaporproof material. Seal, label, and freeze.	Fish: 6 to 9 months Thaw in refrigerator in original wrap or cook frozen allowing extra cooking time. See pgs. 260-263 for cooking information.
Shellfish	*Oysters, clams, and scallops:* Shuck; freeze immediately. Pack in freezer containers leaving ½ inch headspace. Seal, label, freeze.	Oysters, Clams, and Scallops: 3 months Thaw in refrigerator in original wrap. See pgs. 263-264 for cooking information.
	Crabs and lobsters: Cook as for eating; chill in refrigerator. Remove meat from shell. Wrap in moisture-vaporproof material. Seal, label, and freeze.	Crabs and Lobsters: 1 month Thaw in refrigerator in original wrap. See pgs. 263 and 265 for cooking information.
	Shrimp: Freeze uncooked either in shells or shelled. Remove heads. Wrap in moisture-vaporproof material. Seal, label, freeze.	Shrimp: 3 months Cook shrimp while still frozen. See pgs. 262-263 for cooking information.
Whole eggs	Wash eggs. Break into bowl. Stir with fork just to break yolks; mix well with whites; don't whip in air. To each cup eggs, add 1 table-spoon sugar or corn syrup *or* 1 teaspoon salt. Mix; sieve. Pack in freezer containers in amounts for one cake, scrambled eggs for one meal, etc. Skim air bubbles off surface. Leave ½ inch headspace in pints. Seal. Label with date, measure, and number of eggs, what was added, and intended use. Freeze.	Whole eggs: 6 to 8 months Thaw completely in unopened container; use promptly. Allow for sugar, corn syrup, or salt, which was added during preparation for freezing; otherwise use same as fresh eggs. About 2½ tablespoons equal 1 egg.
Egg yolks	Wash eggs. Separate into bowl. Stir with fork to break yolks. To each cup yolks, add 2 tablespoons sugar or corn syrup, *or* 1 tea-spoon salt. Blend carefully; do not whip in air; sieve. Package as above.	Egg yolks: 6 to 8 months Thaw completely in unopened container; use promptly. Allow for sugar, corn syrup, or salt; otherwise use same as fresh yolks. About 1 tablespoon equals 1 yolk.
Egg whites	Wash eggs. Separate into bowl. Do not stir or add anything to whites. Package same as for whole eggs above.	Egg whites: 6 to 8 months Thaw completely in unopened container; use promptly, same as fresh whites. About 1½ tablespoons equal 1 egg white.
Butter	Select fresh, high-quality butter. Wrap in moisture-vaporproof material; seal, label, and freeze.	Butter or margarine: 3 to 6 months Thaw unopened in package. Use same as fresh.
Ice cream	Seal in freezer container or overwrap carton with moisture-vaporproof material; seal. Homemade becomes grainy when stored.	Commercial ice cream: 3 weeks Remove from freezer shortly before serving.
Whipped cream mounds	Whip whipping cream with sugar and flavoring. Drop from spoon in mounds on waxed paper-lined baking sheet; freeze firm. Place in freezer container. Seal, label, and freeze.	Whipped cream mounds: 3 months Place frozen mounds on servings of dessert. Let stand at room temperature 20 minutes.

1. Prepare meat for freezing (see chart, page 955). For freshly slaughtered meat, chill and age. Fresh fish and poultry are dressed, drawn, washed, and chilled. Remove grocery wrap from store-purchased meat if being kept for more than a few days. Cut meat into family-sized portions. Remove excess bone and fat.

2. Wrap meat tightly in moisture-vapor-proof material. Rewrap fresh grocery-purchased cuts. Separate individual portions such as chops, patties, or fillets with two pieces of waxed paper for easy separation, or wrap separately. Cover sharp bones with double thickness of foil. Mold wrapping material to shape of meat, removing as much air as possible.

3. Seal with freezer tape and label with contents, weight or servings, and date.

4. Freeze quickly at 0° or below in small batches. (Place single layer of meat in coldest part of freezer.) Keep frozen at constant temperature of 0° or less. Storage varies with the type and cut of meat. Smoked or salted meats have a much shorter storage time than do fresh meats.

How to use: Frozen meats may be thawed before cooking. Red meats and fish also can be cooked right from the frozen state. The latter method is just as satisfactory but requires more cooking time.

Thaw meat, poultry, or fish in its original wrap in the refrigerator. Meat and poultry that are to be cooked in liquid may also be thawed in cold water. Place the wrapped meat or poultry in cold water, changing water often as the meat is thawing. When thawed, cook like fresh meat.

Freezing vegetables

Although vegetables can be frozen equally well in a salt brine, improved packaging materials make the dry pack a more convenient method. Some vegetables, such as salad greens, celery, green onions, cucumbers, radishes, and raw tomatoes, should not be frozen. They lose their crispness.

How to prepare: Frozen vegetables maintain the best quality when prepared right after they have been harvested. Directions for dry pack are given here:

1. Select fresh, tender, ripe food.

2. Wash, trim, and sort vegetables according to size following chart, page 957.

3. Blanch vegetables before freezing to slow enzyme action. This helps retain good flavor, texture, and appearance. It also cleanses and softens the vegetables for easier packing. Water blanching is best for most vegetables. Broccoli, sweet potatoes, and winter squash may be blanched using either the water or steam method. Blanching is more effective when the pieces of the vegetables are the same size.

Water blanching: Place one pound prepared vegetables in a wire-mesh basket. Immerse in one gallon boiling water in kettle. Cover: boil for time indicated on chart, page 957. Start counting time immediately. Allow 1 minute longer at 5,000 or more feet above sea level.

Steam blanching: Use kettle with tight lid and rack three inches off bottom. Add one to two inches water; bring to rapid boil. Keep heat high. Place vegetables in single layer in basket; lower onto rack. Cover and steam for time indicated on chart, page 957. Start counting time immediately. Steam 1 minute longer at 5,000 or more feet above sea level.

Frozen vegetable yield

Generally, the following amount of vegetable as purchased yields 1 pint frozen.

Vegetable	Pounds
Asparagus	1 to 1½
Beans, limas in pods	2 to 2½
Beans, snap green	⅔ to 1
Beets, without tops	1¼ to 1½
Broccoli	1
Brussels sprouts	1
Carrots, without tops	1¼ to 1½
Cauliflower	1⅓
Corn, sweet in husks	2 to 2½
Peas	2 to 2½
Spinach	1 to 1½
Squash, summer	1 to 1¼
Squash, winter	1½
Sweet potatoes	⅔

Vegetable	Preparation	Blanching Boiling water	Blanching Steam (on rack over boiling water)
Asparagus	Wash. Trim; cut to package length or in 2-inch pieces. Sort according to stalk thickness.	Small stalks—2 min. Large stalks—4 min.	
Beans, green	Wash; remove ends. Cut in 1- or 2-inch pieces, or French cut.	3 min.	
lima	Shell. Or leave in pods and shell after blanching.	Small—2 min. Large—4 min.	
Beets	Wash and sort according to size; leave ½-inch stems. Cook till tender. Peel; cut up.	Small—25 to 30 min. Medium—45 to 50 min.	
Broccoli	Wash; peel stalks; trim; cut into medium pieces 5-6 inches long, no thicker than 1½ inches.	3 min.	5 min.
Brussels sprouts	Cut from stem; wash carefully. Remove outer leaves. Sort according to size.	Small—3 min. Large—5 min.	
Carrots	Wash; scrape or pare. Cut into ¼-inch slices or leave whole if small and tender.	Sliced—2 min. Whole—5 min.	
Cauliflower	Wash; cut into 1-inch pieces.	3 min.	
Corn, on cob	Husk, remove silk, wash, and sort. Don't use overmature corn.	Small ears—7 min. Medium ears—9 min. Large ears—11 min.	
kernel	Blanch ears; cool, then cut off corn.	4 min.	
Greens Beet or chard Kale Mustard Spinach Collard	Wash thoroughly. Cut and discard thick stems and imperfect leaves.	2 min. 2 min. 2 min. 2 min. 3 min.	
Mixed vegetables	Prepare. Blanch separately for times given; mix together after cooling.		
Peas	Shell peas. Discard starchy peas.	1½ min.	
Potatoes, sweet	Cook till almost tender with jackets on. Cool; pare and slice. Dip in solution of ½ cup lemon juice to 1 quart water. Or mash; mix 2 tablespoons lemon juice with each quart.	Cook 30-40 min.	Cook 45-60 min.
Rutabagas and Turnips	Wash, cut off tops, peel, and cut into ½-inch cubes.	2 min.	
Squash, summer	Wash. Cut in ½-inch slices.	3 min.	
winter	Cut into pieces; remove seeds. Cook till soft; remove pulp; mash. Cook quickly.	Cook 15 min.	Cook about 20 min.

To water blanch vegetables, lower the vegetables into boiling water. Keep the heat high. Cover and start timing immediately.

When blanching time is up, plunge the vegetables into ice water. Chill about as long as you blanched. Remove from water; drain.

Spoon the vegetables into freezing container. Here, a special frame holds the bag open. A funnel directs the vegetables into the bag.

4. Remove promptly when time is up. Cool quickly by putting basket of vegetables into pan of very cold or ice water. Change water frequently. Allow as much time for cooling as for blanching. Drain.

5. Package family-sized units of vegetables tightly in moisture-vaporproof containers. Leave headspace as recommended for dry pack on chart, page 952.

6. Seal, following manufacturers' directions. Label with contents and date.

7. Freeze in small batches at 0° or less. Frozen vegetables may be stored satisfactorily for 8 to 12 months.

How to use: Except for corn frozen on the cob and spinach, all frozen vegetables are cooked right from the freezer to reduce the danger of spoilage. Corn on the cob is thawed so that the entire cob will cook evenly; spinach is thawed to allow for the separation of the leaves.

Cook in a minimum amount of boiling, salted water, about ½ cup water per pint of vegetables. Add the frozen block to the boiling water. Cover; separate pieces with a fork, if necessary. When the water returns to boiling, reduce heat and cook just till the vegetables are tender.

Freezing cooked foods

A variety of prepared foods freeze well, but of most value to the homemaker are the frozen dishes that she can make ahead and freeze. She can then serve the dish with a minimum of preparations.

How to prepare: Except for some types of pies, most mixtures are cooked or partially cooked before freezing. For best results, season the food lightly, (some flavors intensify in freezing, while others decrease), undercook the food slightly, (freezing and reheating soften the structure of food), and use fat sparingly in sauces (it doesn't blend well when reheated). Add toppers to the food at heating time.

1. Prepare food as indicated on the charts, pages 959 to 961.

2. Before packaging the dish that is to be frozen, cool the food quickly to room temperature by placing the pan of cooked food in a sink which contains ice water.

3. Package the food properly in moisture-vaporproof material. Allow headspace for liquid, semiliquid, or dry food as indicated on page 952. Pack tightly to remove as much air as possible. (To save freezer space and to free the dish for reuse, line casserole or pan with heavy foil, leaving long ends. Fill, seal, and place container in freezer. When food is frozen, remove from container. Reheat foil-wrapped food in same casserole or pan.)

4. Seal; label with contents and date.

5. Freeze at 0° or below.

How to store

Frozen foods must be stored at a constant temperature of 0° or lower. If the freezer temperature runs higher than this or if it fluctuates greatly, rapid quality deterioration results. Keep a thermometer in the freezer so that you know the foods are staying frozen at the proper temperature.

Frozen foods should not be stored too long. As a guide, the freezer shelf-life for many foods has been determined. Although keeping them beyond this time does not make them unfit to eat, the quality is sufficiently reduced to make the food less desirable in flavor, appearance, and texture. Label all frozen foods as to the contents and date of packaging, then keep a chart beside the freezer that indicates when foods are put in and taken out. A complete turnover of food within one year is highly recommended and probably necessary to maintain high quality.

Refreezing thawed foods is not generally advised. It can be done safely with meats (not poultry, fish, or shellfish) and fruits if ice crystals are still present in the food, but the quality of a refrozen food will be low. Texture especially becomes undesirable—fruits are mushier; meats, less juicy. Therefore, avoid refreezing any foods that have been previously thawed.

Food	Preparation for freezing	How to serve	Storage time
Breads: Baking powder biscuits	Bake as usual; cool. Seal in freezer container, or wrap in foil and seal.	Thaw in package in 250° to 300° oven about 20 minutes.	2 months
Doughnuts	Fry; cool; wrap and seal.	Reheat in oven.	2 to 4 weeks
Muffins	Bake as usual; cool. Seal in freezer container, or wrap in foil and seal.	Thaw in package at room temperature 1 hour or in 250° to 300° oven.	2 months
Yeast bread	Bake as usual; cool quickly. Wrap and seal.	Thaw, wrapped, at room temperature 3 hours.	2 months
Yeast rolls	Use either plain or sweet dough recipe. Bake as usual; cool quickly. Wrap in foil and seal. Freeze at once.	Thaw baked rolls in package at room temperature or in 250° to 300° oven about 15 minutes. Use at once.	2 months
	Or partially bake at 325° about 30 minutes; do not let brown. Cool, wrap, and freeze at once.	Thaw partially baked rolls 10 to 15 minutes at room temperature. Unwrap; bake in very hot oven (450°) for 5 to 10 minutes. Serve at once.	2 months
Cakes: General	*Baked.* Remove from pan; cool thoroughly. If you frost cake, freeze it before wrapping. Wrap; seal. If desired, place in sturdy container. Freeze at once. (Unfrosted cakes freeze better. Frosted and filled cakes may become soggy.)	Thaw in wrapping at room temperature (2 to 3 hours for large cake, 1 hour for layers). If frosted or filled, thaw loosely covered in the refrigerator.	Unfrosted 6 months Frosted 2 months

Food	Preparation for freezing	How to serve	Storage time
Cupcakes	Bake as usual; cool. If frosted, freeze before wrapping. Seal in freezer container or wrap and seal. Freeze. (Unfrosted cupcakes freeze better.)	Thaw, wrapped, at room temperature 40 minutes. If frosted, thaw loosely covered in refrigerator.	2 months
Sponge and angel food	Bake as usual; cool thoroughly. If frosted, freeze it before wrapping. Then wrap and seal. If desired, place in sturdy container.	Thaw in package 2 to 3 hours at room temperature. If frosted, thaw loosely covered in refrigerator.	1 month
Cake frostings and fillings	*Recommended for freezing:* Frostings with confectioners' sugar and fat, cooked-candy type with honey or corn syrup, fudge, penuche, fruit, nut. Seal in freezer containers; freeze. *Not recommended:* Soft frostings, boiled icings, 7-minute frosting, cream fillings.	Thaw in refrigerator.	2 months
Cookies: Unbaked	Pack dough in freezer containers; seal. *Not recommended:* Meringue-type cookies.	Thaw in package at room temperature till dough is soft. Bake as usual.	6 to 12 months
	Bar cookies. Spread dough in baking pan; wrap and seal. Freeze.	Bake without thawing.	
	Refrigerator cookies. Shape into roll; wrap and seal. Freeze.	Thaw slightly at room temperature. Slice roll; bake.	
Baked	Bake as usual; cool thoroughly. Pack in freezer containers with waxed paper between layers and in air spaces. Seal. Freeze.	Thaw in package at room temperature.	6 to 12 months
Pastry	Pastry and graham-cracker shells freeze satisfactorily. Roll out dough; fit it into pie plates. Bake, if desired. Wrap and seal.	Thaw baked at 325° 8 to 10 minutes. Unbaked frozen pastry baked same as fresh.	2 months
Pies: Fruit, general	*Unbaked:* Treat light-colored fruits with ascorbic acid color keeper to prevent darkening. Prepare pie as usual but don't slit top crust. Use glass or metal pie plate. Cover with inverted paper plate. Wrap and seal. If desired, place in sturdy container. Freeze at once.	Unwrap; cut vent holes in top crust. Without thawing, bake at 450° to 475° for 15 to 20 minutes, then at 375° till done. *Berry, cherry:* Unwrap; cut vent holes in top crust. Without thawing, bake at 400°.	2 months
	Baked: Bake as usual in glass or metal pie plate. Cool. Package as above.	Thaw in package at room temperature or in 300° oven.	2 months
Apple, unbaked	Use firmer varieties of apples. Steam slices 2 minutes, cool, and drain; or treat with ascorbic acid color keeper. Prepare and package as above.	Unwrap; cut vent holes in top crust; bake in hot oven (425°) about 1 hour.	2 months
Peach, unbaked	To keep color bright, treat with ascorbic acid color keeper. Prepare and package as above.	Unwrap; cut vent holes in top crust. Bake, without thawing, at 400° for 1 hour.	2 months
Chiffon	Chocolate and lemon freeze satisfactorily.	Thaw in the refrigerator.	2 weeks
Deep-dish fruit pies	Use deep pie plates.	Bake or thaw same as two-crust pies above.	2 months

Food	Preparation for freezing	How to serve	Storage time
Main dishes Casseroles: Poultry, fish, or meat with vegetable or pasta	Cool mixture quickly. Turn into freezer container or casserole. Cover tightly. Seal, label, and freeze.	If frozen in ovenproof container, uncover. Bake at 400° for 1 hour for pints, 1¾ hours for quarts, or till hot. Or steam over hot water in double boiler top.	2 to 4 months
Creamed Dishes Chicken, turkey, fish, or seafood	Cool quickly. Freeze any except those containing hard-cooked egg white. Don't overcook. Use fat sparingly when making sauce. This helps prevent separation of sauce when reheating. Cover tightly. Seal, label, and freeze.	Heat without thawing in top of double boiler, stirring occasionally. If sauce separates, stir till smooth. About 30 minutes is needed to thaw and heat 1 pint of creamed mixture.	
Meatballs with tomato sauce	Cook till done; cool quickly. Ladle into jars or freezer containers, allowing headspace. Seal, label, and freeze.	Stir frequently over low heat or occasionally in top of double boiler. Or defrost overnight in refrigerator. Heat in saucepan.	3 months
Meat pies and scalloped dishes	Cook meat till tender. Cook vegetables till almost tender. Cool quickly. Put in baking dish. Top with pastry, or freeze pastry separately. Wrap tightly. Seal, label, and freeze.	Bake frozen pies with pastry topper at 400° for 45 minutes for pints and 1 hour for quarts, or till hot and crust is browned.	2 to 3 months
Roast beef, pork, other meats, poultry	Do not freeze fried meats or poultry. Prepare as for serving. Remove excess fat and bone. Cool quickly. Wrap tightly. Best to freeze small pieces or slices; cover with broth, gravy, or sauce. Wrap tightly, seal, label, and freeze.	Thaw large pieces of meat in the refrigerator before heating. Heat meat in sauces in top of double boiler.	2 to 4 months
Spaghetti sauce	Cool sauce quickly; ladle into jars or freezer containers, allowing headspace. Seal, label, and freeze.	Heat over low heat or in top of double boiler stirring frequently.	2 to 3 months
Vegetables Baked beans with tomato sauce	Chill mixture quickly. Package in moisture-vaporproof container. Cover tightly.	Partially thaw in package. Heat in casserole or top of double boiler.	6 months
Spanish rice	Use converted rice. Cook till rice is tender, but not mushy. Cool quickly, package. Seal, label, and freeze.	Heat in top of double boiler about 50 minutes. Add a little water if needed.	3 months
Stews and Soups	Select vegetables that freeze well. Omit potatoes. Onions lose flavor. Green pepper and garlic become more intense in flavor. Omit salt and thickening if stew is to be kept longer than 2 months. Do not completely cook vegetables. Cool quickly, wrap. Seal, label, and freeze.	Heat quickly from frozen state. Do not overcook. Separate with fork as it thaws. Do not stir enough to make the mixture mushy.	2 to 4 months
Sandwiches	*These freeze well:* Cream cheese, hard-cooked egg yolk, sliced or ground meat and poultry, tuna or salmon, peanut butter. Spread slice of bread with softened butter; fill; place second buttered bread slice atop. Wrap tightly. Seal; label with contents and date; freeze. *Not recommended:* Lettuce, celery, tomatoes, cucumber, watercress, whites of hard-cooked eggs, jelly, mayonnaise.	Thaw sandwiches in wrapping at room temperature about 3 hours. Serve immediately.	2 weeks

FRENCH ARTICHOKE—Another name for the globe artichoke. (See also *Artichoke*.)

FRENCH BREAD—A long, cylindrical loaf of thick-crusted white bread. This yeast-raised product usually contains water rather than milk as the liquid. In France, the bread loaves are slender and two-feet long with more crust than soft crumb.

Saucy Beef Boat

Studded with olives—

   1 unsliced loaf French bread
   1 pound ground beef
  ½ cup chopped onion
   1 8-ounce can tomato sauce
   1 1½-ounce envelope spaghetti
       sauce mix
  ¼ cup sliced pitted ripe olives

Cut thin slice from top of loaf; set aside. Scoop out bottom, leaving ½-inch shell. Tear bread in small pieces; reserve. Brown meat with onion; drain. Add tomato sauce, sauce mix, olives, and 1 cup water. Bring to boiling; reduce heat. Simmer, uncovered, for 5 minutes; stir occasionally. Stir in the reserved bread.

Spoon mixture into shell. Place on baking sheet. Bake at 350° for 18 to 20 minutes. Heat top in oven last 5 minutes. To serve, place top on loaf; slice crosswise. Makes 6 servings.

Orange French Toast

  ⅔ cup orange juice
   2 eggs
 10 slices French bread
  ⅔ cup fine dry bread crumbs
   1 cup light corn syrup
   1 teaspoon grated orange peel
  ¼ cup orange juice

Beat together the ⅔ cup orange juice, eggs, and ¼ teaspoon salt. Dip bread slices into egg mixture, then into bread crumbs, coating evenly on both sides. Fry on both sides in small amount of hot shortening till golden.

Meanwhile, combine corn syrup, orange peel, and ¼ cup orange juice in saucepan; simmer for 5 minutes. Serve with toast. Serves 5.

Chili-Burger Rarebit

In saucepan mix one 15-ounce can chili with beans, ½ cup shredded process American cheese, and 2 to 3 tablespoons red Burgundy *or* water. Heat and stir till cheese melts. Shape 1 pound ground beef into 4 patties, ¾ inch thick; cook in skillet over medium-high heat 4 to 6 minutes. Turn; season with salt. Cook 4 to 6 minutes. Serve each patty on 1 bias-cut slice French bread, cut 1 inch thick. Top with chili. Sprinkle each serving with 2 tablespoons shredded process American cheese. Serves 4.

After French bread dough has risen to double, roll to a rectangle. Form loaf by rolling dough tightly, starting at long side.

Add a professional touch to the loaf by cutting diagonal gashes, 2½ inches apart and ¼ inch deep. Brush with egg white mixture.

The family soon heads to the kitchen as the irresistible aroma of freshly baked French Bread wafts through the house. Be sure to make enough for both snack- and mealtime.

French Bread

In large mixer bowl combine 2 packages active dry yeast, 2½ cups sifted all-purpose flour, and 1 tablespoon salt. Add 2½ cups warm water to dry mixture. Beat at low speed with electric mixer for ½ minute, scraping sides of bowl constantly. Beat 3 minutes at high speed.

Stir in 4 cups sifted all-purpose flour or enough to make a moderately stiff dough. Turn out on lightly floured surface. Knead till elastic, about 10 to 15 minutes, working in an additional ½ to 1 cup flour.

Place dough in lightly greased bowl, turning once to grease surface. Cover and let rise in warm place till double (about 1 hour). Punch down; let rise till double (30 to 45 minutes.)

Turn out on lightly floured surface and divide in 2 portions. Cover; let rest 10 minutes. Roll each portion into 15x12-inch rectangle. Beginning at long side, roll up tightly, sealing well as you roll. Taper ends, if desired.

Place each loaf diagonally, seam side down, on greased baking sheet sprinkled with cornmeal. With knife, gash tops diagonally every 2½ inches, ¼ inch deep. Beat 1 egg white till foamy; add 1 tablespoon water. Brush some over tops and sides. Or, for crisp crust brush just with water. Cover with damp cloth, not touching loaves (drape cloth over inverted glasses). Let rise till double (1 to 1¼ hours). Bake at 375° till light brown, about 20 minutes. Brush bread with egg white mixture or water. Bake 15 to 20 minutes. Cool. Makes 2 loaves.

FRENCH COOKERY—A style of cooking that blends simple everyday cooking of provincial France with more elaborate techniques developed by well-trained chefs of the "haute (grand) cuisine." Contrary to most popular opinion, French cookery is not always rich and fancy. It is perhaps better characterized by the artful blending of ingredients, textures, and seasonings to produce aromatic and flavorful foods.

Provincial cooking, more than just peasant cooking, is the background of French cuisine. The specialties of each region were developed long ago to make best use of the foods available locally. In their long history, too, the provinces have been occupied by other nations who ultimately influenced the cooking style.

Haute cuisine, in which master chefs prepare gourmet recipes in elegant restaurants, is usually identified as French cookery. Many of these recipes have evolved from provincial foods.

Historically, what today typifies French cookery developed simultaneously throughout France. Prior to the fourteenth century, frequent turmoil, famine, and military invasion held back cuisine development. During this time, monks were the only individuals who were developing any sort of cooking style. The fame of their stews, sauces, pastries, and soups soon spread, and monasteries became centers for travelers seeking good food and shelter.

The greatest advances in French cookery were made during the Renaissance. Although monks continued to be good cooks, other people began to concentrate on food preparation. Early in this period, Guillaume Tirel (he called himself Taillevant) began refining the French cuisine. As master cook for Charles V, he developed many sauce recipes using bread as a thickening agent and instigated an acceptance of cooked vegetables. He is also the author of the oldest known French cookbook.

Elegant haute cuisine

←Baked Liver Pâté, moist roast turkey with Savory Chestnut Stuffing, and Pain d'Épice carry out a French dinner theme.

Other trends of this period included an increasing use of herbs, spices, and wines in cooking. Most of the seasonings that were used were regionally available, but some were imported from other lands at great expense. Wines were always preferred very sweet and spiced.

To a great extent, the growth of French cookery can be credited to Italian-born Catherine de Medici who married Henry II in 1533. Unable to adjust to the French cookery of that time, she imported Italian chefs. They introduced many foods that were soon accepted by all of France—artichoke hearts, sweetbreads, truffles, Parmesan cheese, veal, and macaroons.

In the seventeenth century, Louis XIV gave French cookery a new grandeur. Large kitchens were built on his palatial estate in Versailles. His best known chef, Francois La Vareene, did away with heavy spicing and complicated menus. He introduced such classics as, Béchamel sauce, marinades, pâtés, and the *roux*.

Exquisite dining had reached the middle class by the following century. Coffee, tea, and chocolate became popular beverages. Exciting new dishes such as filet of sole Pompadour were developed, and cooking moved from a hearth to a separate unit, the stove. The restaurant, as we know it, was developed during this time.

As in other areas of life, new food production and distribution methods changed French cookery in the 1800s. Escoffier, one of the greatest French chefs, adapted French cooking styles. His theory of serving the heaviest foods first and the lightest foods last continues today.

Characteristics of French cookery: To most visitors in France, the food served in restaurants is "typical" French cooking. But the food eaten by the largest number of French people is home-cooked. The French homemaker cooks very much as her mother and grandmother did, using traditional ingredients. Today, however, she may yield to the temptation of using an occasional convenience food.

Making the right sauce for a food to give it appearance and taste appeal is a highly developed French cooking art. To homemaker and chef alike, good meat, fish, poultry, or vegetable stocks are important bases. So are *roux,* a mixture of butter and flour cooked to the right blond or brown shade, and the uncooked *"beurre manie,"* a butter-flour mixture. Both are discretely used as thickening agents and provide the foundation for many of the world-famous French sauces.

Another important technique is that of cooking flavor into rather than out of a food. *Bouquet garni* (a small bundle of herbs), the right hint of onion or garlic, or the use of wine as a part of the cooking liquid, skillfully brings about the desired flavor. By contrast, the delicate character of specially bred Bresse chickens is preserved by seasoning with salt only. Still another French cooking technique that adds flavor is the roasting or sautéing of meat or poultry on a *mirepoix,* a mixture of finely cut vegetables that always includes onions and carrots.

Regional French cookery: It's been said that one can tell quite easily what part of France a person comes from by the way he cooks. Foods prepared with wines exemplify a distinctive regional flavor. Although no longer separate political provinces, those regions noted for the personality of their foods include Ile de France, Normandy, Brittany, Bordeaux, Burgundy, Alsace-Lorraine, Touraine, Franche-Compté, Languedoc, and Provence.

In the province of Ile de France, which includes Paris and the surrounding area, a true regional food personality is lacking although most French cooking as an art was developed in this area. All provinces have influenced this region's cookery which, over the years, has developed into the haute cuisine. To the expertly trained chefs of France goes much of the credit for classic recipes that are now used all over the world.

In northern France, Normandy borders the English Channel, and its neighbor, Brittany, juts out into the Atlantic. Both have an abundant supply of fish and seafood including superb oysters, delicate channel sole, and spiny lobsters.

In Normandy, apples and dairy products are plentiful. Cream is used as poaching liquid for oysters, in a fish sauce with cider and butter, and even in piecrusts. Near here Camembert cheese originated late in the eighteenth century.

Brittany is famous for fish dishes and desserts. Lobster à l'Armoricaine (from Amorique, the ancient name for Brittany) is cooked with tomatoes and herbs, then flamed with brandy. Other Breton fish dishes are often cooked in butter and wine or in a cream sauce. Dessert-favorite crepes were first made in this area.

French-Fried Camembert

6 1⅓-ounce triangles Camembert
    cheese
Beaten egg
Fine dry bread crumbs
Cooking oil

Cut triangles in half lengthwise, then crosswise (24 pieces). Shape crust around soft center to cover as much cheese as possible. Dip in egg, then in bread crumbs. Dip again for second coating. (A thick coat of crumbs prevents the cheese from leaking through.)

Fry in deep, hot fat (375°) till crumbs are golden brown. Drain and serve hot. Offer cocktail picks or forks. Makes 24 appetizers.

The Bordeaux region, in addition to having fine wines and the truffles of Perigord, is where the brandies Cognac and Armagnac are produced and used widely. A baked cream custard is often flavored with Armagnac, while the French homemaker who cooks pâté de fois gras simmers the goose livers in white wine and Cognac. The luscious prunes of this area are bathed in Cognac or wine, or are used in a variety of tarts and puddings.

Burgundy, famous for its red and white wines, combines its plenteous wine with meat as is exemplified by the well-known *French bourguignonne.* Dijon mustard, also Burgundian, is flavored with the juice of unripe grapes. In this region, the homemaker also poaches snails in a wine court bouillon before packing the shells with garlic butter. She makes a *matelote* (fish stew) with red wine and Cognac, bakes a cake like *Pain d'Épice,* cooks chicken with red wine to make *coq au vin*, and makes *lyonnaise* potatoes by frying them and the onions separately, then combining them for serving.

Pain d'Épice

Originated in Dijon, France—

    1 cup honey
    ½ cup hot water
    2 tablespoons sugar
    1½ teaspoons crushed aniseed
    1 teaspoon grated lemon peel
    2½ cups sifted all-purpose flour
    1 teaspoon baking soda

Stir together honey, water, sugar, aniseed, and grated lemon peel. Sift together flour and baking soda; gradually add flour and baking soda to honey mixture, mixing well. Spread in greased and floured 9x9x2-inch baking pan. Bake at 350° for 40 minutes. Cool 10 minutes; remove from pan. Garnish with candied peel and cherries, if desired. Thinly slice to serve.

Alsace-Lorraine cooking reflects history. Alsace, bordering on Germany and having gone through periods of German control, has German cooking influence. Food is hearty—sauerkraut is cooked in many ways, goose fat is preferred as shortening, and roast goose is combined with sauerkraut or chestnuts for holidays. Other Christmas specialties include *kugelhopf* and cookies of many kinds.

Savory Chestnut Stuffing

In saucepan boil 2 pounds fresh chestnuts in shells with water to cover for 15 minutes; drain. Make a cut in each with sharp knife and peel off shell; chop chestnuts. Cook 2 cups chopped celery and ⅓ cup chopped onion in ¾ cup butter till tender but not brown.

In large bowl combine onion mixture, chestnuts, 8 cups dry bread cubes, 2 teaspoons salt, 1 teaspoon poultry seasoning, 1 teaspoon ground sage, and ½ teaspoon pepper. Toss mixture lightly with ½ cup chicken broth. Makes stuffing for one 10- to 12-pound turkey.

In Lorraine, much of which lies farther from the German border, food is cooked more in French fashion. The egg-bacon custard in a pastry shell called *quiche Lorraine* and little tea cakes called *madeleines* originated in Lorraine as did almond macaroons which have been made for centuries. Pork roasted with rosemary and sage is served with plums.

Pork or goose potted meat called *rillettes* or *rillons de tours* is prepared in Touraine. For a stew, eel is browned with onions and flamed with brandy; sauces are based on red wine and herbs. Prunes, fine table grapes, and other fruits are favored in meals, often in an open fruit tart. Small game birds, such as quail, are often wrapped in grape leaves before being broiled over charcoal.

The Franche-Comté region borders Switzerland and Italy. This is dairy country where two fine cheeses, Comté and Reblochon, are produced. Because the area is mountainous, wild herbs grow profusely and are used subtly to flavor many dishes. Freshwater fish abound in this region.

In southern France, the cooking of Languedoc, bordering on the Pyrenees, shows some Spanish influence with traces of the customs left long ago by the Romans. Omelets are prepared with tomatoes and green peppers; *cassoulets* combine white beans with a variety of meats such as pork, mutton, duck, goose, and sausage.

In neighboring Provence, a definite Italian influence is apparent. Every kitchen has strings of garlic and bunches of fresh herbs or jars of dried herbs. Firm in the belief that garlic loses its lingering taste if cooked a long time, especially in liquid, these people use it lavishly. The Provencale sauce of tomatoes, garlic, shallots and oil, and the multifish stew concoction called *bouillabaisse* are both famous. Olive oil is used for all types of cooking, even in the making of pastry.

American versions of French cookery: The recipes given here are French in origin but keyed to foods and cooking equipment found in American markets. With a little time, patience, and skill, you can easily add a French touch to foods prepared in your own kitchen.

Champignons Sautés
(Fresh Mushroom Sauté)

Wash 1 pint fresh mushrooms; trim off stem ends. Slice through cap and stem. Melt 3 tablespoons butter or margarine in skillet; add sliced mushrooms. Sprinkle with 2 teaspoons all-purpose flour; toss together to coat.

Cover and cook over low heat till tender, about 8 to 10 minutes, turning occasionally. Season with salt and pepper. Serves 4.

Caneton à l'Orange
(Duckling with Orange Sauce)

    1 4- to 5-pound ready-to-cook
        duckling
    Orange Sauce

Remove wing joints and tips of duckling, leaving only meaty second joints. Rub inside of duckling cavity with salt and pepper. Skewer opening; lace. Place, breast side up, on rack in shallow roasting pan. Do not add water.

Roast at 425° for 15 minutes; turn oven down to 350° and continue roasting till done, about 1 hour and 40 minutes, spooning off fat occasionally. Duck is done when meaty part of leg feels tender (use paper toweling). Meanwhile, begin preparing the Orange Sauce.

When duck is done, tip slightly so inside juices drain into pan. Remove skewers; place bird on hot platter. Sprinkle lightly with salt; keep warm. Finish Orange Sauce. Spoon part of sauce over duck; pass remainder. Garnish with orange sections, if desired. Serves 4.

Orange Sauce: Grate peel from one orange (2 teaspoons). With vegetable peeler, shave peel from another orange in long thin strips (¼ cup). Squeeze juice from both oranges (⅔ cup). In heavy skillet cook and stir ½ cup sugar and 1 tablespoon red wine vinegar just till sugar caramelizes to a rich brown. Remove from heat at once; add grated orange peel, orange juice, and ¼ cup orange-flavored liqueur. Return to heat and simmer, stirring till caramelized sugar dissolves. After transferring roast duck to platter, skim off fat from juices in roasting pan. Add orange-juice mixture to juices in pan. Cook, stirring constantly and scraping sides of pan till desired sauce consistency, a few minutes. Stir in strips of peel. Add a little lemon juice to the sauce.

Baked Liver Pâté

    1 pound chicken livers
    ¼ cup chopped onion
    1 cup water
    1 cup milk
    1 slightly beaten egg
    2 slices zwieback, crushed
    1 tablespoon cornstarch
    1 teaspoon salt
    ⅛ teaspoon pepper
    Assorted crackers

Cook chicken livers and onion in water for 10 minutes; drain, reserving ⅓ cup liquid. Cool liver mixture; put through fine blade of food grinder. Stir in reserved liquid and milk. Combine egg, zwieback, cornstarch, salt, and pepper. Add to liver mixture; mix well.

Pour into 1-quart casserole; place in shallow pan. Pour hot water into pan to depth of ½ inch. Bake at 325° till knife comes out clean, about 1 hour. Serve chilled with crackers.

Chocolate Truffles

    6 1-ounce squares semisweet
        chocolate
    ¼ cup sifted confectioners' sugar
    3 tablespoons butter or margarine
        • • •
    3 slightly beaten egg yolks
    1 tablespoon rum *or* brandy
    2 1-ounce squares semisweet
        chocolate, grated

In top of double boiler melt the 6 squares chocolate, confectioners' sugar, and butter over *hot not boiling* water. Remove from heat. Stir a small amount of hot mixture into egg yolks; return to hot mixture, stirring well. Blend the rum into the hot mixture.

Chill, without stirring, for 1 to 2 hours. Shape into 1-inch balls. Roll balls in grated chocolate; chill. Makes about 2 dozen.

Satisfies a sweet tooth

French cooks enjoy preparing foods like→ Buche de Noel, Chocolate Truffles, and Raisin Brioche Ring for festive occasions.

Pâté Feuilleté au Fromage
(French Cheese Pastries)

        2 cups sifted all-purpose flour
    ¾ cup shortening
        5 to 7 tablespoons cold water
        3 tablespoons butter or margarine
    ¼ cup all-purpose flour
    ¼ teaspoon salt
        1 cup milk
        1 cup shredded sharp process cheese
    ½ cup shredded Parmesan cheese

Sift together flour and 1 teaspoon salt. Cut in shortening till pieces are the size of small peas. Sprinkle water over mixture, a tablespoon at a time, tossing gently with fork. Repeat till all the mixture is moistened.

Prepare sauce by melting butter in saucepan over low heat. Blend in flour and salt. Add milk all at once. Cook quickly, stirring constantly, till mixture is thickened and bubbly. Add process cheese and stir till it is completely melted; set cheese aside.

Cut pastry in half; roll each half to 11½x7½-inch rectangle, a little less than ¼ inch thick. Line bottom of 11½x7½x1¾-inch baking dish with one piece of pastry. Spread cheese sauce over. Top with remaining pastry. Sprinkle top with shredded Parmesan cheese.

Bake at 450° till pastry is golden, about 20 minutes. Cut the pastry in rectangles and serve hot. Makes 12 servings.

Céleri au Jus
(Braised Celery Hearts)

        3 celery hearts
        1 10½-ounce can condensed chicken
            consommé
        1 teaspoon fresh basil *or*
            ¼ teaspoon dried whole basil
        2 teaspoons cornstarch

Split celery hearts lengthwise in half; trim to 6-inch lengths. Place in skillet; add consommé and basil. Simmer 15 to 20 minutes. Remove to warm serving dish.

Combine cornstarch and 2 tablespoons cold water; gradually stir into consommé in skillet. Cook and stir till thickened and bubbly. Pour small amount of sauce over hot celery. Sprinkle with basil. Pass remaining sauce. Serves 6.

Raisin Brioche Ring

Cover 1½ cups raisins with water; bring to boiling. Drain. In large mixer bowl combine 2 packages active dry yeast and 2 cups sifted all-purpose flour. Heat 1½ cups milk, ⅓ cup sugar, 4 tablespoons butter, and 1 teaspoon salt just till warm, stirring occasionally.

Add to dry mixture; add 3 eggs. Beat at low speed with electric mixer for ½ minute, scraping sides of bowl constantly. Beat 3 minutes at high speed. By hand, stir in raisins and 3½ to 4 cups sifted all-purpose flour, to make a soft dough. Turn dough out onto floured surface; knead 5 minutes. Place in greased bowl, turning to grease surface. Cover; let rise till double, 45 to 60 minutes.

Divide dough in half; cut each half into 8 parts. Pinch off ⅕ of each part. Shape large pieces into balls; place 8 balls against edge of each of two greased 9x1½-inch round baking pans. With kitchen shears, snip dough crisscross fashion in center of each ball. With finger, make hole where cross intersects. Shape smaller dough pieces into teardrops and press pointed ends well into holes in larger balls. Cover; let rise till double, about 45 minutes. Bake at 350° for 30 minutes. Remove from pans. Beat 1 egg yolk with 1 tablespoon water; brush on bread while still hot.

Onion Soup

    1½ large onions, thinly sliced and
            separated into rings (3 cups)
        2 tablespoons butter or margarine
        1 tablespoon all-purpose flour
        4 cups milk
        1 teaspoon salt
        2 beaten egg yolks
            Grated Parmesan cheese
            Sliced French bread

Cook onion in butter or margarine till tender but not brown, about 10 minutes. Sprinkle with flour; cook and stir over low heat till blended. Add milk all at once; cover and simmer for approximately 20 minutes.

Add salt and dash pepper. Stir a small amount of hot mixture into egg yolks. Return to soup mixture, stirring till blended. Season to taste. Sprinkle each serving with grated Parmesan; serve with French bread slices. Serves 8.

Buche de Noel

The French preserve the old Christmas custom of burning a Yule log by serving a log-shaped cake—

    4 egg yolks
    1 cup sugar
    ½ teaspoon vanilla
    4 egg whites
        • • •
    1 cup sifted cake flour
    ½ teaspoon baking powder
    ¼ teaspoon salt
      Confectioners' sugar
    2 tablespoons rum
        • • •
      Chocolate Filling

In small mixing bowl beat egg yolks with electric mixer or rotary beater till thick and lemon-colored. Gradually add ½ cup sugar, beating constantly. Stir in vanilla. In large mixer bowl beat egg whites till soft peaks form; gradually add the remaining sugar, beating till stiff peaks form. Gently fold in egg yolk mixture.

Sift together flour, baking powder, and salt; fold flour mixture into egg mixture. Spread mixture evenly in greased and floured 15½x10½ x1-inch baking pan. Bake at 375° for 10 to 12 minutes. Loosen edges of cake and immediately turn out onto towel sprinkled with confectioners' sugar. Sprinkle cake evenly with rum. Roll up cake and towel jelly-roll fashion, starting with long side; cool thoroughly on rack.

Unroll cake; spread evenly with *half* the filling; roll up cake starting with long side. Cutting on the diagonal, slice a 4-inch piece from end of roll. On serving plate, place 4-inch piece along side of log roll. Frost log with remaining filling; mark with tines of fork to resemble bark. Decorate with pink and green frosting, if desired.

Chocolate Filling: In small saucepan heat ⅔ cup sugar and ⅓ cup water to boiling; cook to soft-ball stage (240°). In small mixer bowl beat 2 egg yolks with electric mixer till thick and lemon-colored. Very gradually add the hot syrup, beating constantly; continue beating till mixture is completely cool. Beat in ½ cup softened butter or margarine, 1 tablespoon at a time. Add one and one-half 1-ounce squares unsweetened chocolate, melted and cooled; 1 tablespoon rum; and 1 teaspoon instant coffee powder. Continue beating till thick.

French Veal Stew

Roll 2 pounds veal shoulder, cut in ¾-inch cubes, in a mixture of ¼ cup all-purpose flour, 1 teaspoon salt, and ¼ teaspoon pepper. In Dutch oven brown meat cubes slowly in a small amount of hot shortening.

Add 2 cups hot water; ½ cup dry sherry; 1 large, whole onion, studded with 2 whole cloves; 2 carrots, cut in 1-inch pieces; 2 cloves garlic, crushed; Bouquet Garni*; ½ teaspoon dried basil leaves, crushed; ½ teaspoon dried thyme leaves, crushed; and ½ teaspoon ground nutmeg. Simmer 1 hour. Discard Bouquet Garni.

Combine 3 beaten egg yolks, 2 tablespoons lemon juice, and 1 tablespoon light cream. Blend some of hot mixture with egg yolk mixture. Add egg yolk mixture to stew. Heat and stir just till mixture is thickened. Serve over hot cooked rice. Makes 6 to 8 servings.

Bouquet Garni: Tie a few sprigs of parsley, fresh celery leaves, and fresh or dried bay leaves in cheesecloth.

French Strawberry Tart

Combine one 8-ounce package softened cream cheese, ¼ cup sugar, and ½ teaspoon vanilla; mix well. Spread cream cheese mixture in bottom of 1 baked 9-inch Rich Tart Shell. Top with 1 quart fresh strawberries, sliced.

Combine 2 tablespoons cornstarch and ¼ cup cold water; add one 10-ounce jar strawberry *or* currant jelly (1 cup). Bring to boiling, stirring constantly; cook tlll thickened and clear. Remove from heat; stir in 2 tablespoons lemon juice and few drops red food coloring. Cool. Spoon over berries; chill. Garnish with whipped cream, if desired. Makes 12 servings.

Rich Tart Shell: Stir ½ cup butter or margarine to soften; blend in ¼ cup sugar and ¼ teaspoon salt. Add 1 egg; mix well. Stir in 1½ cups sifted all-purpose flour. Chill slightly. On floured surface, roll out in 12-inch circle. Using rolling pin to transfer dough, carefully place over *outside* of 9-inch round cake pan or fit into flan pan. (Shape dough to sides of pan *almost* to rim. Be sure there are *no thin places*, especially at corner.) Trim.

Place pan, crust up, on baking sheet. Bake at 450° till lightly browned, about 8 to 10 minutes. Cool a few minutes; while slightly warm, transfer crust to serving plate.

FRENCH CUSTARD—A rich, stirred custard that is made with the addition of egg yolks. Whipped cream is often added to custards that are to be used as a filling for pastries and desserts. (See also *Custard*.)

French Custard Filling

⅓ cup sugar
1 tablespoon all-purpose flour
1 tablespoon cornstarch
1½ cups milk
1 slightly beaten egg yolk
1 teaspoon vanilla
½ cup whipping cream

In saucepan combine sugar, flour, cornstarch, and ¼ teaspoon salt. Gradually stir in milk. Cook and stir till mixture thickens and boils; cook and stir 2 to 3 minutes longer. Stir a little hot mixture into egg yolk; return to hot mixture. Cook and stir till mixture just boils. Add vanilla; cool. Beat smooth; whip whipping cream and fold into cooled mixture.

FRENCH DOUGHNUT—A type of doughnut made in France, usually of cream puff dough. The dough is placed in a pastry tube and then forced out to form rings in the hot fat. A thin frosting or confectioners' icing is usually spread over the cooled doughnut. (See also *Doughnut*.)

FRENCH ENDIVE—Another name, along with Belgian endive and witloff chicory, for the small, tightly packed head of a chicory plant, which is used as a salad green. The crown of bleached foliage, when torn in pieces, pairs up well with other vegetables in tossed salads. (See also *Endive*.)

FRENCH FRY—An American phrase for a method of cooking food in deep, hot fat till brown and crisp. It is usually associated with fried potatoes. Foods suitable for french frying include shrimp, meat croquettes, chicken, potatoes, onions, and some pastries, such as doughnuts. A special pan fitted with a wire basket or an electric deep-fat fryer is of great assistance when french frying, but heavy, deep pans or fondue pots can also be used.

French-Fried Vegetable Bites

1 cup fine dry bread crumbs
¼ cup grated Parmesan cheese
1 teaspoon paprika
1 teaspoon salt
2 slightly beaten eggs
1 tablespoon water
1 cup bite-sized raw cauliflowerets
1 cup crosswise-sliced carrots
1 cup peeled eggplant, cut in
1-inch cubes
Salad oil

Combine bread crumbs, grated cheese, paprika, and ½ *teaspoon* salt. Combine eggs, water, and remaining salt. Dip vegetables in egg, then in crumb mixture; repeat dipping.

Pour salad oil into fondue cooker to no more than ½ capacity or to a depth of 2 inches. Heat over range to 375°. Transfer cooker to fondue burner. Have vegetables at room temperature in serving bowl. Spear vegetables with fondue fork; fry in hot oil for 2 to 3 minutes. Transfer hot, browned vegetable bites to dinner fork before eating. Makes 6 to 8 servings.

French-Fried Potato Puffs

Packaged instant mashed potatoes
(enough for 4 servings)
⅓ cup pancake mix
1 tablespoon dry onion soup mix
1 teaspoon finely snipped parsley

Prepare potatoes according to package directions. Add pancake mix, onion soup mix, and snipped parsley. Drop from tablespoon, a few at a time, into deep, hot fat (365°). Fry till golden brown, about 1 to 1½ minutes, turning occasionally to brown all sides. Drain on absorbent paper toweling. Makes 18 puffs.

French Fries

Peel and cut potatoes lengthwise in strips. Fry small amount of potato strips at a time in deep, hot fat (360°) till crisp and golden, about 6 to 7 minutes. Drain on paper toweling. Sprinkle with salt and serve at once.

Note: Do not french fry new potatoes because they contain a high water content.

French-Fried Onion Rings

Slice 6 medium Bermuda or white onions into ¼-inch thick slices. Combine 2 cups milk and 3 eggs; beat. Follow picture directions below.

Serve crisp, golden, french fried onion rings with hamburgers or steaks. Delicious as a snack or table vegetable, a few onion rings also make a perfect topper for casseroles and salads. (See also *Deep-Fat Fry*.)

Pour beaten egg and milk mixture into shallow pan. Separate onions into rings and swish around till well coated with liquid.

Lift onions out of liquid; shake over pan to drain. Drop a few rings at a time in pan of all-purpose flour, coating each well.

Fill french-frying basket ¼ full to brown onions evenly. Set basket in deep, hot fat (375°). Separate rings with fork.

Remove onion rings from hot fat when golden brown; drain on paper toweling. Sprinkle with salt before serving. Serves 8.

FRENCH KNIFE—A well-balanced, multi-purpose, kitchen knife with a long, tapered blade that widens at the handle and that is used for chopping and slicing food.

To chop food, position tip of knife blade on cutting board and cut food by moving knife up and down quickly without lifting tip of knife from board. Use finger tips of other hand to hold the knife tip against the board while cutting the food.

To slice meat, cut across grain of meat with French knife. (See also *Knife*.)

FRENCH SALAD DRESSING—1. In the United States the name of a salad dressing that is made of oil, vinegar, seasonings, and a tomato ingredient such as tomato juice, catsup, or chili sauce. 2. In France the salad dressing, also called sauce vinaigrette, is made with oil, vinegar, and seasonings but with no tomato product.

Both types usually separate on standing and must be shaken vigorously just before serving. (See also *Salad Dressing*.)

French Dressing

  ½ cup salad oil
  2 tablespoons vinegar
  2 tablespoons lemon juice
  2 teaspoons sugar
  ½ teaspoon dry mustard
  ½ teaspoon paprika
  Dash cayenne

Combine all ingredients and ½ teaspoon salt in screw-top jar; cover and shake. Chill. Shake again just before serving. Makes ¾ cup.

Creamy French Dressing

  1 tablespoon paprika
  2 teaspoons sugar
  Dash cayenne
  ⅓ cup vinegar
  1 egg
  1 cup salad oil

Combine dry ingredients and 1 teaspoon salt. Add vinegar and egg; beat well. Add oil in slow stream, beating constantly with electric or rotary beater till thick. Makes 1⅔ cups.

Fill a big basket with warm French Toast slices sprinkled with confectioners' sugar and serve to your hungry breakfast eaters.

FRENCH TOAST—Slices of bread dipped in an egg and milk mixture, panfried, and served with syrup or a topping. The crunchy crust covers a moist, tender inside.

French toast, most often served for breakfast, can be varied by using orange or raisin bread and a multitude of toppings. Jelly or jam, cinnamon and sugar, or hot applesauce are delicious toppings.

French Toast

In a shallow bowl combine 2 slightly beaten eggs, ½ cup milk, and ¼ teaspoon salt. Dip day-old bread into milk-egg mixture (enough for 4 to 6 slices of bread). Fry in small amount hot shortening in skillet till golden brown. Serve toast hot with maple-flavored syrup, confectioners' sugar, or tart jelly, as desired.

French-Toasted Fondue

> French bread
> 2 well-beaten eggs
> ½ cup milk
> ¼ teaspoon salt
>
> . . .
>
> Salad oil
> Fluffy Maple Sauce

Cut bread into about 50 bite-sized pieces, each with one crust. Combine eggs, milk, and salt.

Pour salad oil into fondue cooker to no more than ½ capacity or to depth of 2 inches. Heat over range to 375°. Add 1 teaspoon salt. Transfer cooker to fondue burner. Spear bread through crust with fondue fork; dip in egg mixture, letting excess drip off. Fry in hot oil till golden brown. Transfer to dinner fork; dip in Fluffy Maple Sauce. Makes 6 to 8 servings.

Fluffy Maple Sauce: Thoroughly cream together 1½ cups sifted confectioners' sugar, ½ cut butter or margarine, ½ cup maple-flavored syrup, and 1 egg yolk. Fold in 1 stiffly beaten egg white. Chill. Makes 2 cups.

FRICADELLE *(frē ka del')* — Small, well-seasoned meatballs or patties that are sautéed or fried till crisp and brown. The meat, which is either ground beef, veal, pork, lamb, or any combination of these meats, is mixed with eggs, milk, grated onion, bread crumbs, and seasonings and formed into balls or patties. Sometimes the meatballs are floured before frying or sautéeing.

FRICASSEE *(frik' uh sē)* — A French word for meat or poultry cooked in a cream sauce which is made with the meat stock. In early times a fricassee was referred to as a stew, probably because it was a good way to use leftover meat and vegetables.

To prepare, the meat is first browned in butter or other fat. A sauce is then made from the meat stock (acquired from the browning process) and simmered along with vegetables, seasonings, and the meat until the latter is tender.

This is a good method of cooking the less tender cuts of meat because the moist heat cooking tenderizes the meat. Chicken and veal are the two most common foods which are served in a fricassee dish.

Simmer drumsticks in a creamy sauce with vegetables. Serve Chicken Fricassee and Dumplings with crisp vegetable relishes.

Chicken Fricassee and Dumplings

> 4 chicken drumsticks
> ¼ cup diced celery
> 1 tablespoon chopped onion
> 1 teaspoon chicken-flavored
>   gravy base
> ½ teaspoon salt
> 3 tablespoons all-purpose flour
> ½ 10-ounce package frozen mixed
>   vegetables (about 1 cup)
> Lemon Dumplings

In 2-quart saucepan simmer drumsticks with 1 cup water, celery, onion, gravy base, salt, and dash pepper till chicken is tender, about 20 minutes. Blend flour and ½ cup cold water; stir into broth. Cook over medium heat, stirring constantly, till gravy is thick and bubbly. Add frozen, mixed vegetables.

For *Lemon Dumplings:* Combine ⅓ cup all-purpose flour, ½ teaspoon baking powder, and ¼ teaspoon salt. Combine ¼ cup milk, ½ teaspoon snipped parsley, ¼ teaspoon grated lemon peel, and ½ teaspoon lemon juice. Add to dry ingredients; stir just till dry ingredients are moistened. Drop batter in mounds atop *bubbling hot* chicken mixture. Cover; simmer mixture for 20 minutes. Makes 2 servings.

FRIED CAKE—A sweet dough shaped into various forms and fried in hot fat. Typical examples of fried cakes include doughnuts, crullers, and fruit fritters.

FRIED CREAM—A French dessert of stirred custard that has been cooled and cut into shapes to be breaded and fried in deep fat. The stirred custard is spread in a thin layer in a pan to cool. This is to allow it to become very firm for cutting into various shapes. The custard pieces are then dipped in batter and deep-fat fried.

FRIED PIE—A dessert made of sweet dough that is wrapped around fruit and then deep-fat fried. To prevent the filling from leaking out during cooking, be sure edges of dough are thoroughly sealed around the fruit. Pies may be frosted with a thin icing or sprinkled with confectioners' sugar. Serve the fried pies warm. (See also *Pie*.)

Pop open a package of refrigerated biscuits and make easy Fried Peach Pies. Sprinkle with confectioners' sugar, then serve warm.

Cover canned peach slices with biscuit dough and tightly seal edges by pressing with tines of fork. Cook fried pie in hot fat.

Fried Peach Pies

1 16-ounce can sliced peaches, well drained (1½ cups)
3 tablespoons honey
2 tablespoons butter or margarine
1 teaspoon shredded lemon peel
1 tablespoon lemon juice
¼ teaspoon ground cinnamon
1 package refrigerated biscuits (10 biscuits)

In large saucepan combine first 6 ingredients. Cook over medium heat, stirring frequently, till thick and glossy, about 15 minutes.

Separate biscuits; roll each biscuit to an oval shape, about 5 inches long. Place a rounded tablespoon of peach filling just off center, lengthwise, of each biscuit. Fold dough over filling and seal edges with tines of fork. Fry in deep, hot fat (375°), turning once, till golden brown, about 1 minute. Drain on paper toweling. Sprinkle with confectioners' sugar, if desired. Makes 10 pies.

FRIJOL (*frē' hol*)—Spanish name for bean, usually referring to a red kidney bean.

FRIJOLES REFRITOS (*frē' hōlz rā frē' tōs, -hō' lēz*)—A Mexican dish in which beans are cooked with tomatoes, onion, chili pepper, and seasonings, then mashed and fried. American refried beans are usually not as spicy. (See also *Mexican Cookery*.)

Frijoles Refritos

Soak ½ pound pink or red beans (1⅓ cups) in 3 cups water overnight for faster cooking or bring to boil in water; simmer 2 minutes. Let stand, covered, for 1 hour. Add ½ teaspoon salt. Cook slowly till tender, about 1 hour and 45 minutes to 2 hours. Drain, reserving liquid. Coarsely mash beans. Stir in ¼ cup shortening, ⅓ cup reserved cooking liquid, and ½ teaspoon salt till shortening melts. Fry beans, stirring to prevent sticking. (These steps may be done ahead of time and beans stored in refrigerator. Serve by heating beans in additional shortening, if needed.) For softer consistency, add more reserved cooking liquid to beans. Serve hot. Makes 4 servings.

FRITTER—Fruit, vegetable, meat, or poultry pieces that have been dipped in batter and cooked in hot fat. The recipe title usually includes the name of the main ingredient used in the fritter. (See also *Bread*.)

Vegetable Fritters

    1½ cups sifted all-purpose flour
    3   teaspoons baking powder
    ¾   teaspoon salt
    1   beaten egg
    1   cup milk
    1   cup cooked corn, cooked peas, or
        diced, cooked carrots

Drop fritter batter from a tablespoon into deep, hot fat. Fry fritters until golden brown on both sides. Drain on paper toweling.

Sift together the all-purpose flour, baking powder, and salt; set aside. Combine beaten egg and milk. Add desired cooked vegetable—corn, peas, or diced carrots—to egg mixture. Add vegetable mixture to dry ingredients. Mix just until moistened.

Drop batter from tablespoon into deep, hot fat (375°). Fry until fritters are golden brown, about 4 to 5 minutes. Drain fritters on paper toweling. Serve fritters with warm cheese sauce or maple syrup. Makes 16 to 18 fritters.

Apple Fritters

Combine 1 beaten egg, 1 cup milk, 1 cup finely chopped apple (unpeeled), ¼ cup sugar, 1 teaspoon grated orange peel, 3 tablespoons orange juice, ½ teaspoon vanilla, and ¼ teaspoon salt. Sift 2 cups sifted all-purpose flour and 3 teaspoons baking powder together; fold into egg mixture, stirring *just* till flour is moistened. Drop by rounded teaspoons into deep, hot fat (350°). When fritters rise to surface, turn and fry till golden, about 3 minutes. Drain. Serve hot. Makes about 42.

FROG LEGS—The long, hind legs of tailless amphibians. The legs, the only part of the frog that is eaten, have tender, white meat that tastes much like chicken.

Frog legs, considered as a gourmet dish, are eaten broiled or fried with lemon, sauce, or mayonnaise. A serving of two large legs, six small legs, or one-third of a pound satisfies the average appetite.

Each large frog leg contains about 70 calories when fried. It also supplies protein, minerals, and some of the B vitamins.

Frog Legs with Sauce

Dip 2 pounds frog legs in ½ cup milk, then ½ cup all-purpose flour. In skillet brown frog legs in ½ cup butter, melted, for 10 to 15 minutes. If legs are large, cook, covered, 15 minutes longer; remove to warm platter. Season with salt and pepper. Add ¼ cup *each* butter and slivered almonds to skillet; brown lightly. Add 2 teaspoons lemon juice. Pour almond mixture over legs; top with ¼ cup snipped parsley. Makes 6 servings.

FROSTING

Ideas for preparing, spreading, storing, and decorating these complementary cake toppings.

Many people think that cake without frosting is as incomplete as bread without butter. While this is not necessarily true, even a simple uncooked frosting often transforms a plain cake into an exotic delight. It can also change pastries and cookies into elegant party delicacies.

By varying the kind of frosting and the way you decorate it, you can dress up a cake for any occasion. For example, a light dusting of sifted confectioners' sugar does wonders for gingerbread or a pound cake, and a simple swirl of frosting on top is enough to decorate a cupcake. On the other hand, a layer cake may have frosting that completely covers the top and sides and is spread between the layers, too.

Frosting is a sweet mixture that is often used as the finishing decorative touch for cakes, cookies, or pastries. Whether creamy or fluffy, cooked or uncooked, plain or highly decorative, a single color or variegated, the frosting should always be soft enough to spread easily, yet stiff enough to hold its shape. The terms frosting and icing are sometimes used interchangeably, but the latter term is usually reserved for fairly thin, uncooked types of frostings that closely resemble sweet glazes.

Some frosting emphasizes the color and flavor of a cake. For example, a delicately colored citrus frosting dresses up an orange cake. Others may contrast, such as fudge frosting on a yellow cake.

How to prepare

Frosting is either cooked or uncooked depending on the preparation techniques that are used. Although this division is sometimes hazy, cooked frostings are those that require heat for something other than just melting ingredients.

Cooked: Cooked frostings range from creamy chocolate ones to fluffy white ones. Probably the best known cooked frostings are Fudge Frosting, Seven-Minute Frosting, and Boiled Frosting.

Since Fudge Frosting is really a soft chocolate fudge, the techniques that are used when making fudge also apply to fudge frosting. The critical points are cooking the sugar-milk mixture to the soft-ball stage (check this with a candy thermometer) and beating the frosting just till it reaches spreading consistency. Overbeating the frosting will cause it to harden like fudge. If this happens the result is a delicious candy, but you won't have any frosting to spread on the cake!

Seven-Minute Frosting is so named because it takes approximately seven minutes of beating and cooking to get the frosting to form stiff peaks. A double boiler is often used to equalize the heat when making Seven-Minute Frosting. For a soft, fluffy frosting, be sure to stop cooking the frosting as soon as stiff peaks form.

When you make Boiled Frosting, be sure you cook the sugar syrup just to the soft-ball stage (240°). A candy thermometer is the best way of checking the temperature, but the cold water test can be used instead of, or in conjunction with, the thermometer. If the syrup isn't cooked enough, the frosting will be runny. On the other hand, if the syrup is overcooked, the frosting will be too heavy to spread easily.

A superb cake

Perky chocolate curls crown this lofty →
Double Mocha Cake. The subtly coffee-flavored frosting tops a chocolate-coffee cake.

Fudge Frosting

Butter sides of heavy 3-quart saucepan. In it combine two 1-ounce squares unsweetened chocolate, 3 cups sugar, 1 cup milk, 3 tablespoons light corn syrup, and ¼ teaspoon salt. Cook and stir over low heat till sugar dissolves and chocolate melts. Cook to soft-ball stage (234°) without stirring.

Remove from heat; add ¼ cup butter and cool till warm (110°), without stirring. Add 1 teaspoon vanilla; beat till of spreading consistency. Frosts two 9-inch layers.

Seven–Minute Frosting

   2 unbeaten egg whites
1½ cups sugar
   2 teaspoons light corn syrup *or*
      ¼ teaspoon cream of tartar
   1 teaspoon vanilla

Place egg whites, sugar, light corn syrup *or* cream of tartar, ⅓ cup cold water, and dash salt in top of double boiler (don't place over boiling water); to blend, beat ½ minute at low speed on electric mixer.

Place over, but not touching, boiling water. Cook, beating constantly, till frosting forms stiff peaks, *about* 7 minutes (*don't overcook*). Remove from the boiling water. If desired, pour into the mixing bowl. Add vanilla; beat till of spreading consistency, about 2 minutes. Frosts two 8- or 9-inch layers.

Boiled Frosting

In heavy saucepan combine 2 cups sugar, ¾ cup water, 1 tablespoon light corn syrup *or* ¼ teaspoon cream of tartar, and dash salt. Cook over low heat, stirring till sugar dissolves. Cover saucepan for 2 to 3 minutes to dissolve sugar crystals on sides of pan.

Uncover; add hot syrup to 2 stiffly beaten egg whites, beating constantly with electric mixer. Add 1 teaspoon vanilla; beat till of spreading consistency, about 6 minutes. If too thin, let stand 3 minutes to set up; stir once or twice. Frosts two 8- or 9-inch layers.

Pink Frosting

   2 cups sugar
   1 cup water
   3 tablespoons strawberry-flavored
      gelatin
   ½ teaspoon cream of tartar
      Dash salt
         • • •
   2 unbeaten egg whites
   1 teaspoon vanilla

In saucepan combine sugar, water, strawberry-flavored gelatin, cream of tartar, and salt. Bring to boiling, stirring till the sugar dissolves. Then slowly add to unbeaten egg whites, beating constantly with electric mixer at high speed till stiff peaks form. Add the vanilla to frosting mixture. Frosts two 8- or 9-inch layers.

For a simple cake top design, sift confectioners' sugar onto a paper doily. Press the sugar through, then carefully remove doily.

Using a small, flexible spatula, spread the frosting over the cake. When top is frosted, swirl the remaining frosting on sides.

Coconut Frosting

In a saucepan combine one 6-ounce can evaporated milk, ⅔ cup sugar, ¼ cup butter or margarine, 1 slightly beaten egg, and a dash of salt. Cook over a medium heat, stirring constantly, till the mixture thickens and bubbles, about 12 minutes. Cool slightly; add 1⅓ cups flaked coconut, ½ cup chopped pecans, and 1 teaspoon vanilla. Cool. Frosts two 8-inch layers.

Double Mocha Cake

        2 cups sifted cake flour
        2 cups sugar
        1 teaspoon baking soda
        2 teaspoons instant coffee powder
        ¾ teaspoon salt
        ½ cup butter or margarine,
            softened
                •   •   •
        ¾ cup buttermilk
        ½ cup water
        4 1-ounce squares unsweetened
            chocolate, melted and cooled
        3 eggs
        1½ teaspoons vanilla
                •   •   •
        Coffee Frosting

Sift together cake flour, sugar, baking soda, instant coffee powder, and salt. Add to the butter or the margarine in a mixer bowl. Add the buttermilk, water, and chocolate; beat 2 minutes on low speed of electric mixer. Add eggs and vanilla; beat for 2 minutes more.

Pour the batter into two well-greased and lightly floured 9x1½-inch round cake pans. Bake at 350° for 25 to 30 minutes. Cool 10 minutes; remove from the pans. Cool on a rack.

Frost with *Coffee Frosting:* In top of double boiler, *not over hot water,* place 2 unbeaten egg whites, 1½ cups sugar, 2 teaspoons light corn syrup *or* ¼ teaspoon cream of tartar, ⅓ cup cold water, 1½ tablespoons instant coffee powder, and dash salt. Beat 1 minute with a rotary or an electric beater.

Place over, but not touching, boiling water. Cook, beating constantly, till the frosting forms stiff peaks, about 7 minutes. (Don't overcook.) Remove from the boiling water. Then add 1 teaspoon vanilla extract; beat till of spreading consistency, about 2 minutes.

Why cooked frostings fail

As with most foods, inaccurate measurement or failure to follow directions can cause many cooked frostings to fail. However, many of the common problems can also be due to one or more of the following reasons.

Sticky
    Undercooked
    Underbeaten

Tough, hard
    Overcooked
    Overbeaten

Thin
    Undercooked
    Underbeaten

Coarse, sugary fudge frosting
    Stirring while cooking
    Beating before cool

Granular fluffy frosting
    Underbeaten
    Too little cream of tartar
        or corn syrup

Fluffy frosting with low volume
    Underbeaten

Peanut Butter Quick Cake Frosting

The broiler finishes the cooking. This frosting is especially delicious on a yellow cake—

        ⅓ cup peanut butter
        ⅓ cup light cream *or* evaporated
            milk
        1½ cups brown sugar
                •   •   •
        1 cup flaked coconut

In a saucepan combine peanut butter, light cream *or* evaporated milk, and brown sugar. Cook, stirring constantly, till the mixture is boiling. Spread over 13x9x2-inch cake; broil about 4 inches from heat till frosting is bubbly, about 2 to 3 minutes. Top with flaked coconut; broil just till coconut is toasted.

Uncooked: You can make a variety of kinds of uncooked frostings, such as confectioners' sugar frosting, butter frosting, frostings based on cream cheese or a cooked pudding, whipped cream frostings, and blender-made frostings. The frostings used for making decorative flowers and designs on cakes and cookies are special types of uncooked frostings, made to hold their shape when pushed through a decorating tube. (See also *Cake Decorating.*)

Many cooks use nothing but uncooked frostings for their cakes because these are generally more failure-proof. Unlike cooked frostings, if an uncooked frosting becomes too thick to spread, the proper consistency is usually attained by adding a little more liquid. If the frosting is too thin and won't stay on the cake, simply add more sifted confectioners' sugar.

For frostings in a jiffy or frostings that are similar to cooked frostings, but without the fuss, use packaged frosting mixes according to directions or ready-to-spread frosting in a can. Use frostings in squeeze tubes or pressure cans for quick decorative designs or cake-top writing.

Uncooked Frosting

  1 unbeaten egg white
  ½ cup corn syrup
  ½ teaspoon vanilla
     Dash salt

In mixer bowl combine egg white, corn syrup, vanilla, and salt. Beat with electric mixer till of fluffy spreading consistency. Frosts one 8- or 9-inch square cake or a loaf cake. Serve within a few hours or refrigerate.

Chocolate-Nut Fluff

  1 cup semisweet chocolate pieces
  2 cups whipping cream
  ½ cup toasted slivered almonds

In saucepan melt chocolate pieces over low heat. Cool. Whip whipping cream till it just barely mounds. Fold chocolate and almonds into cream, allowing chocolate to harden in flecks. Frosts one 10-inch tube cake.

Choco-Satin Frosting

  3 1-ounce squares unsweetened
     chocolate, melted and cooled
  ¼ cup hot water
  3 cups sifted confectioners'
     sugar
  1 egg
  ½ cup butter, softened
  1½ teaspoons vanilla

Combine chocolate, water, and sugar; blend with electric mixer. Beat in egg, then butter and vanilla. (Frosting will be thin at this point.) Place mixing bowl in ice water; beat frosting till of spreading consistency. Frosts two 8- or 9-inch layers. Refrigerate frosted cake.

Rocky-Road Frosting

In a small saucepan combine two 1-ounce squares unsweetened chocolate, 1 cup miniature marshmallows, ¼ cup water, and ¼ cup butter or margarine. Cook, stirring constantly, over a low heat till the chocolate and the marshmallows are melted. Then cool slightly.

Add 2 cups sifted confectioners' sugar and 1 teaspoon vanilla; beat till smooth and of spreading consistency, about 2 minutes. Stir in 1 cup miniature marshmallows and ½ cup broken walnuts. Frosts top of 13x9x2-inch cake.

Butter Frosting

  6 tablespoons butter
  1 16-ounce package confectioners'
     sugar, sifted (about 4¾
     cups)
     About ¼ cup light cream
  1½ teaspoons vanilla

In a mixing bowl cream butter; then gradually add about *half* the sifted confectioners' sugar, blending well. Beat in 2 *tablespoons* light cream and vanilla. Gradually blend in remaining confectioners' sugar. Then blend in enough light cream to make of spreading consistency. Frosts two 8- or 9-inch layers.

Note: For a more creamy frosting, beat in 1 egg instead of first 2 tablespoons light cream. After adding remaining sugar, beat in light cream for spreading consistency.

As Seven-Minute Frosting cooks in the top of a double boiler, it is beaten with an electric mixer till stiff peaks form.

Grasshopper Cake

    4 1-ounce squares unsweetened
        chocolate, melted
    ¼ cup sugar
    2¼ cups sifted cake flour
    1½ cups sugar
    3 teaspoons baking powder
    ½ cup cooking oil
    7 egg yolks
    1 teaspoon vanilla
    7 egg whites
    ½ teaspoon cream of tartar
        Grasshopper Filling

Blend chocolate, ½ cup boiling water, and the ¼ cup sugar; cool. Sift together next three ingredients and 1 teaspoon salt. Make a well in the center of the dry ingredients and add oil, egg yolks, ¾ cup cold water, and vanilla, *in order given*. Beat till very smooth. Stir chocolate mixture into egg yolk mixture.

In large mixer bowl beat egg whites with cream of tartar till very stiff peaks form. Pour chocolate batter in thin stream over entire surface of egg whites, gently folding to blend. Turn batter into *ungreased* 10-inch tube pan. Bake at 325° till cake tests done, about 1 hour and 5 minutes. Invert pan; cool.

Split cooled cake crosswise into 3 layers. Spread Grasshopper Filling between layers and on top of cake. Refrigerate till serving time.

Grasshopper Filling: Soften 1 envelope unflavored gelatin (1 tablespoon) in ¼ cup cold water. In a small saucepan heat together ⅓ cup white crème de cacao and ½ cup green crème de menthe. Add softened gelatin and stir till dissolved. Cool. Then whip 2 cups whipping cream; fold gelatin mixture into whipped cream. Refrigerate 15 minutes, then spread.

Caramel Candy Frosting

Try this on a white cake—

    ¼ pound vanilla caramels (16)
    ¼ cup water
    3 tablespoons butter or margarine
        Dash salt
            • • •
    2 cups sifted confectioners'
        sugar
    2 tablespoons chopped walnuts

In 1½-quart saucepan combine caramels and water. Melt caramels over low heat, stirring occasionally. Cool to room temperature.

Cream butter or margarine; add salt. Add confectioners' sugar alternately with caramel sauce, blending till frosting is smooth and creamy. Add chopped walnuts. Chill till of spreading consistency, about 30 minutes. Frosts one 9-inch cake or 1 dozen cupcakes.

For a pretty, smooth finish to Petits Fours, evenly pour on the icing. Keep icing over hot water. (See *Petits Fours* for recipe.)

A pale green, whipped cream-gelatin mixture is sandwiched between layers of cloud-light chocolate chiffon cake in this elegant Grasshopper Cake. White crème de cacao and green crème de menthe subtly flavor and color the fluffy filling. It's the kind of company dessert you make in advance and refrigerate, then serve with pride.

Basic techniques

Preparing the frosting is only half the job —it must also be put on the cake. Most cooked frostings tend to harden upon setting, so be sure to spread them promptly. Unless the uncooked frosting requires chilling, it also should be spread on the cake soon after it is prepared.

How to frost: Since a warm cake is likely to break at the edges as you spread the frosting, always begin with a completely cooked cake. To avoid crumbs in the frosting, brush away all loose crumbs. Keep the serving plate clean while frosting the cake by covering the plate edges with three or four strips of waxed paper.

Position the first layer top side *down* on the plate. Using a small flexible spatula, spread the top of the first layer with about a fourth of the frosting. If using a soft frosting, spread it *almost*, but not completely, to the cake's edge. The second layer, when placed on top, will cause the frosting to flow to the edges. If using a frosting of firmer consistency, spread it completely to the edge of the cake.

Carefully place the second layer top side *up* on the frosted first layer. Holding the spatula vertically, spread a thin layer of frosting around the sides of the cake. This coating holds the crumbs in place. Next, frost the top spreading frosting completely to the edge. Finish the cake by smoothing the remaining frosting on the sides of the cake. Using the spatula or a spoon, make swirls or a decorative design on the top and on the sides of the cake.

When frosting a cake with three or more layers, position the first two layers as above. Always place the last layer top side *up* for a gracefully rounded top on the frosted cake. Then fill in any gaps between the layers with frosting.

The shape of the cake often determines how you frost it. Although a cake baked in an oblong pan can be removed from the pan before frosting, it is often left in the pan and only the top is frosted. A tube cake should be removed from the pan when completely cool and placed top side *down* on the serving plate. You can then frost the cake's top and sides.

Cupcakes are extremely easy to frost if you use a soft, fluffy frosting. Simply grasp the bottom of the cupcake then invert it and dip the top into the frosting. Twirl the cupcake slightly in the frosting, then quickly turn it right side up.

When you are using a thin icing or glaze, pour it rather than spread it. Petits fours and angel cakes are particularly suitable for this method of frosting.

How to cut: Cutting a frosted cake is often a problem because the knife becomes covered with frosting. To prevent this, dip the knife in water before cutting and clean it frequently with a damp cloth.

How to store: Store cakes with whipped cream frostings in the refrigerator. Keep other frosted cakes in a cool place such as a cake keeper with a roomy cover.

If you are going to be rushed for time on the party day, bake and frost the cake ahead, then freeze it. Leftover cake can also be frozen. Butter and fudge frostings freeze well. However, soft frostings, boiled frostings, and cream fillings are not recommended for freezing.

You can make a convenient cake holder for freezing by covering a piece of cardboard with foil. Place the unfrosted cake on this holder. Frost then freeze before packaging. When completely frozen, slip it into an airtight plastic bag and close tightly. Place the cake in a box labeled with the date and the kind of cake. Use frozen angel and sponge cakes within one month and other types of frozen frosted cakes within two months. Unwrap the cake, then thaw it in the refrigerator.

Uses of frosting

Plain cookies and pastries are sometimes frosted. Usually a simple confectioners' sugar frosting adds just the right amount of sweetness. A few drops of food coloring can be used to tint the frosting.

The coupling of cakes and frostings is largely a matter of personal preference. Cakes that are delicately flavored need a delicately flavored frosting that won't overpower the cake's flavor. However, a dark fudge cake can stand a rich frosting.

Many people stick to the traditional combinations of chocolate cake with Fudge or Seven-Minute Frosting, white cake with chocolate frosting, yellow with chocolate frosting, and sponge or angel cake with a glaze or confectioners' sugar frosting.

Although these favorites are delicious, why not try something different? Next time you bake a white cake, frost it with a fluffy lemon frosting or a brown sugar frosting. A cream cheese frosting is particularly good on a yellow cake. A whipped cream frosting with bits of maraschino cherries is scrumptious on an angel cake. A broiled frosting with coconut and nuts makes a quick frosting for spice cake. Chocolate cake with coconut frosting is another delicious combination.

Adding simple designs and decorations to your frosted cake dresses it up even more. For one of the easiest decorations, tint the frosting with food coloring. For a quick topping, sprinkle the frosted cake with plain or lightly tinted coconut. Small, packaged, edible cake and cookie decorations can also be used for a quick fix-up.

Chocolate curls sprinkled on a white frosting make a pretty cake rim. To make perfect curls, use sweet cooking chocolate at room temperature. Using a vegetable peeler, carefully shave off thin slices of chocolate. As you cut, the chocolate will curl. If the chocolate is too cold, the curls will break, while if it's too warm, the curls will become too soft.

Marshmallows, nuts, gumdrops, chocolate kisses, cinnamon candies, and other small candies can be arranged in designs on the cake top. Animal crackers, peppermint sticks, and a construction paper tent top easily convert a frosted cake into a merry-go-round. Flexible licorice shoestrings can be twisted into cowboy brands, names, and other designs. Marshmallows snipped into petals and centered with pieces of gumdrop make pretty flowers.

Tiny umbrellas, baby booties, or other small decorations appropriate for special occasions can be purchased and artfully arranged on the cake to carry out a particular party theme. Whether you prefer simple or elaborately decorated cakes, remember that experimenting is the key to unusual and delicious frosted cakes.

FROZEN CUSTARD—A frozen dessert of eggs or egg yolks added to regular ice cream ingredients. Like ice cream, frozen custard is subject to federal regulations concerning percentage of egg yolk solids, milk fat, and milk solids. Frozen custard is also called French custard or French custard ice cream. (See also *Ice Cream*.)

FROZEN DESSERT—A delicious and eye-appealing homemade or commercial food served at the end of a meal. Traditionally, this group includes water ices, sherbets, ice creams, and custards, as well as other desserts that are made with these foods.

Frozen desserts were popular with the early Chinese, who used snow and ice in their beverages and foods. Sherbet was a favorite of the Persians who used it in a cold, fruit beverage. The combination of ice and sherbet led to the use of ice cream in sixteenth-century Italy. For example, at the wedding of Catherine de Medici to Frances' future King, Henry II, in 1533, a different flavor of the frozen delight was served each day of the wedding festivities.

Today, commercially prepared frozen desserts are produced in great volume to meet the ever-increasing appetites of Americans for these chilly delights. Ice cream, which is the most popular summer-time treat in this country, is made from milk products, sweetenings, and a variety of flavoring ingredients. Sherbets, similar to ices, are made of milk, egg whites, gelatin, and fruit flavoring. Ices, on the other hand, contain no milk products but are composed of water, sugar, and juices.

Many frozen desserts are prepared by combining commercial desserts with smoothing and flavoring ingredients. The addition of these ingredients to frozen desserts and the amount of stirring during preparation influence the rate of crystal formation. For like the sugar crystals in candy, small ice crystals are also desired for a smooth frozen dessert.

Examples of these frozen desserts easily made at home include bombes, mousses, parfaits, frappés, sodas, milk shakes, and malted milks. Ice cream, sherbet, and water ices can be given a special homemade flavor by adding a multitude of other ingredients. (See also *Dessert*.)

Phony Spumoni

Prepare one 2-ounce package dessert topping mix according to package directions. Into dessert topping mix, fold ⅓ cup quartered red and green maraschino cherries, 1 tablespoon chopped candied orange peel, and 1 tablespoon chopped, toasted almonds; set mixture aside.

With large wooden spoon scoop 1 quart rich vanilla ice cream into large bowl; stir ice cream to soften slightly. Press softened ice cream on bottom and sides of 6-cup mold or foil-lined 8½x4½x2½-inch loaf dish, forming uniform shell. Working quickly, spoon dessert topping mixture into center of mold. (If ice cream becomes too soft while forming shell in mold, place mold in freezer long enough to set ice cream before adding dessert topping center.) Freeze 6 to 8 hours or overnight.

To unmold, press hot damp towel closely around mold till ice cream softens slightly and loosens. Garnish with whipped cream piping and gumdrop roses, if desired. Serves 6 to 8.

Lotus Ice Cream

      2⅔ cups light cream
        1 cup sugar
      ⅓ cup lemon juice
      ⅓ cup chopped, toasted almonds
      1½ teaspoons grated lemon peel
      ½ teaspoon vanilla
      ⅛ teaspoon almond extract

Combine all ingredients in a mixing bowl, stirring till sugar is completely dissolved. Freeze the mixture in a hand-turned or electric ice cream freezer. Makes 1 quart ice cream.

Note: To ripen ice cream, remove ice to below lid of can; take off lid. Remove dasher. Plug opening in lid; cover inside of lid with several thicknesses of waxed paper; replace lid. Pack more ice and salt around can. Cover freezer with heavy cloth or newspapers. Let ice cream ripen about 4 hours.

Easy gourmet dessert

Crunchy almonds, candied orange peel, and →
bright red and green cherries are added to the topping mix in Phony Spumoni.

Fresh Garden Mint Ice Cream

1½ cups sugar
1½ cups water
2 cups finely crushed, fresh mint leaves
1 cup light corn syrup
1 cup finely crushed, fresh pineapple
1 cup canned pineapple juice
2 cups milk
2 cups whipping cream
¼ cup crème de menthe

Combine sugar and water; cook and stir till mixture boils. Cook to soft-ball stage (236°). Add mint leaves; cook about 10 minutes longer. Remove from heat; strain the mixture. Add corn syrup; let cool. Add remaining ingredients; freeze in hand-turned or electric ice cream freezer. Let ice cream ripen. Makes 2 quarts.

Cookie-Fruit Freeze

1½ dozen chocolate wafers
1 cup whipping cream
1 tablespoon sugar
1 teaspoon vanilla

• • •

1 30-ounce can fruit cocktail, drained (3½ cups)
1 ripe banana, sliced (1 cup)
½ cup miniature marshmallows
¼ cup chopped walnuts

Line bottom and sides of 8x8x2-inch pan with chocolate wafers. Whip whipping cream and combine with sugar and vanilla. Fold in drained fruit cocktail, sliced banana, marshmallows, and chopped walnuts. Pile the mixture into cookie-lined pan. Freeze till firm. Remove from freezer 30 to 35 minutes before serving. Cut in squares to serve. Makes 9 servings.

Frozen Apricot Torte

1 30-ounce can apricots, drained and chopped
½ cup sugar
1 tablespoon lemon juice
1 cup whipping cream
1 cup soft macaroon crumbs

Combine apricots, sugar, and lemon juice; mix well. Whip whipping cream and fold in. Sprinkle ½ *cup* macaroon crumbs in bottom of 1-quart refrigerator tray; spoon in cream mixture. Top with remaining macaroon crumbs. Freeze till firm, about 5 hours. Makes 6 to 8 servings.

Choco-Mint Freeze

1¼ cups finely crushed vanilla wafers (28 wafers)
¼ cup butter or margarine, melted
1 quart peppermint stick ice cream, softened
½ cup butter
2 1-ounce squares unsweetened chocolate
3 well-beaten egg yolks
1½ cups sifted confectioners' sugar
½ cup chopped pecans
1 teaspoon vanilla
3 egg whites

Toss together crumbs and the butter or margarine. Reserve ¼ cup crumb mixture; press remaining crumb mixture into 9x9x2-inch baking pan. Spread with ice cream; freeze.

Melt ½ cup butter and the chocolate squares over low heat; gradually stir into egg yolks with the confectioners' sugar, nuts, and vanilla. Cool thoroughly. Beat egg whites till stiff peaks form. Beat chocolate mixture; fold in egg whites. Spread chocolate mixture over ice cream; top with the reserved crumb mixture. Freeze till firm. Makes 8 servings.

Frosty Strawberry Cubes

Combine one 8¾-ounce can crushed pineapple, drained (1 cup); 1 cup fresh strawberries, hulled and crushed; and ⅓ cup sugar; mix well.

Soften and blend one 3-ounce package cream cheese with ⅓ cup mayonnaise or salad dressing. Stir into fruit mixture; fold in ½ pint softened vanilla ice cream. Turn into 3-cup refrigerator tray and freeze till firm.

Cut frozen mixture into small cubes and serve in a dish with a fruit, such as strawberries, raspberries, blueberries, pear wedges, peach halves, watermelon wedges, or banana chunks rolled in chopped nuts. Makes 6 servings.

Chocolate-Nut Sundae Cups

    1 3¾-ounce package chocolate
        fudge-flavored whipped dessert
        mix
    ¼ cup chopped pecans
    1 jar butterscotch topping
    ⅓ cup broken pecans
        Vanilla ice cream

Prepare dessert mix with milk and water as directed on package. Chill till almost set, 45 minutes to 1 hour. Stir; fold in nuts. Drop onto waxed paper-lined baking sheet in about ½ cup portions. Make a depression in center of each to make cups to hold a scoop of ice cream. Freeze till firm, about 2 to 3 hours.

Before serving, heat butterscotch topping slightly. Stir in broken pecans. Place a scoop of vanilla ice cream in each chocolate cup. Top with warm butterscotch topping. If desired, garnish with pecan halves. Serves 4.

Frozen Limeade Pudding

Beat 3 egg yolks till thick and lemon colored; add ½ cup thawed frozen limeade concentrate and ¼ cup sugar. Cook and stir over low heat till mixture thickens and is boiling; cool.

Beat 3 egg whites till stiff peaks form; fold into limeade mixture. Whip 1 cup whipping cream and fold into limeade mixture along with 3 to 4 drops green food coloring.

In small bowl combine ⅓ cup chocolate wafer crumbs (6 to 7 wafers) and 1 tablespoon melted butter or margarine; reserve about 2 tablespoons mixture. Spread remainder in 1-quart refrigerator tray; spoon in limeade mixture. Top with reserved crumbs. Freeze till firm, about 4 to 5 hours. Makes 6 servings.

FRUCTOSE—The technical name for sugar found in fruits and honey. It is sometimes called fruit sugar. (See also *Sugar*.)

Jiffy dessert idea

Drizzle warm butterscotch sauce over vanilla ice cream nestled in Chocolate Nut Sundae Cups. Serve with hot coffee.

FRUIT

*Plan colorful, flavorful, and nutritious menus
by using these tantalizing foods.*

In the strictest botanical sense, a fruit is the mature seed-bearing structure of a flowering plant. Nuts, cereal grains, olives, corn, tomatoes, and some spices are literally fruits just as much as bananas and peaches. However, in the cooking sense, only those foods that are succulent, pulpy, sometimes juicy, and either naturally sweet or artificially sweetened before they are eaten are considered fruits.

Fruits in the latter category originate from either of two basic types of plants—deciduous or evergreen.

Deciduous plants are common to colder climates. Portions of the plants die at the end of a growing season, their leaves and fruits drop off, and the plants enter a dormant stage. This type includes apples, peaches, pears, grapes, and strawberries.

The second type, evergreen plants, are better known as tropical fruits because they require high, moist heat for best growth. These climatic conditions abound in the tropics. About 50 varieties of tropical fruits have become important foods throughout the world. Of these, bananas, plantains, coconuts, mangoes, and pineapples are of greatest importance.

Fruit-producing plants develop into one of two forms, trees or shrubs. Well-known tree fruits include apples, cherries, avocados, persimmons, dates, and figs. The chief shrub fruit is the grape, but cranberries, strawberries, pineapples, and bananas are other outstanding varieties.

A bounteous dish

← Fruit Cup Tower, an assortment of succulent melon and berry combinations, illustrates the marvelous, limitless world of fruits.

The development of fruit species extends over thousands and possibly even millions of years. The first fruit plants grew wild. Later, civilized man learned to cultivate, mutate, and preserve these fruits.

Wild forms of most all of today's fruits were available to early man in the regions where the climate was suitable for fruit growth. Historians know the likely centers of origin for some fruits: (1) central Asia—apples, cherries, mulberries, pears, plums, pomegranates, and quinces; (2) Mediterranean area—dates, melons, and figs; (3) Southeast Asia—bananas, peaches, persimmons, and oranges; (4) Central America—avocados, cranberries, and pineapples.

Fruit cultivation began about 3000 B.C. in the Mesopotamia River area of the Middle East. The Babylonians developed good cultivation and land utilization techniques by interplanting date trees with grapes, figs, pomegranates, and apples.

But traders and migratory peoples widened the scope of fruit cultivation by carrying fruits from their places of origin to other parts of the world. Peaches were first grown in China after which ancient caravans brought some of them to Persia. Later, Alexander the Great introduced peaches to Europe. By the Middle Ages, European commercial cultivation and trade were blossoming. Bananas from Malasia and oranges from China were introduced to the Americas in 1500.

The earliest fruit cultivation in what was to become the United States began with the Indians. Fruit orchards were common to their villages where propagation by seed was well known. During colonization, Europeans brought their own fruit cuttings, as in 1566 when the Spaniards planted the first sizable orchards in Georgia. Olives, dates, figs, oranges, lemons, and peaches were some of the varieties cultivated. Orchards in Jamestown, Virginia, were established by 1629.

Fruit continued to come into this country via commercial trading. For example, the trader Metcalf Bowler introduced the Rhode Island Greening apple tree he had received from an oriental prince.

Modification of the original fruits developed both accidentally and intentionally. Grapefruits as we know them are believed to have originated from Nature's crossing of the pear-shaped citrus fruit called shaddock and the sweet orange. Mutations of European apples and Asian varieties are the ancestors of those apples enjoyed today. Most of today's fruits developed from mutated seedlings that were later propagated under controlled conditions.

By scientifically selecting the best seedlings, hybridists have improved fruits in appearance, taste, keeping quality, and disease resistance. For example, the controlled crossings of the Virginian meadow strawberry and the Chilean strawberry produced a more versatile berry. Propagation of the best fruit tree varieties was and still is carried on primarily by budding and grafting. The well-known American plant breeder, Luther Burbank, developed over 113 varieties of plums and prunes in addition to important species of apples, blackberries, cherries, peaches, and quinces.

In order that fruits could be eaten and enjoyed year-round, man also developed preservation techniques. Simple methods were used centuries ago. For example, frigid arctic temperatures enabled Eskimos to freeze brambleberries. Many fruits were sun-dried even before the Christian Era. In fact, natural sun dehydration is the oldest known form of food preservation.

Only within the last two centuries, however, have more modern methods of preservation been introduced. Artificial drying and canning were initiated in the 1800s, while quick freezing was perfected in 1929 by the famous inventor, Clarence Birdseye.

Role in diet: Fruits along with vegetables make up one of the four basic food groups that must be eaten daily to maintain a balanced diet. Fruits themselves provide substantial amounts of many vitamins and minerals but are particularly good contributors of vitamins A and C. They also provide food energy, primarily in the form of carbohydrates, and a bulk or laxative agent in the form of cellulose.

How to select and store

Carefully read package labels and grocery counter signs when selecting fresh, canned, or frozen fruits. These sources contain vital information, such as the name of the product, its weight, the name and address of the packer or distributor, the kind of pack or special treatment the fruit has undergone, and the grade. Counter signs usually give more limited information, but they do include the price.

Grading is one of the most outstanding guidelines to follow when selecting quality fresh or processed fruits. The United States Department of Agriculture has established ratings for most fruits that are shipped between states. Many states have similar supplementary regulations.

Fruit sources of vitamins A and C

At least one serving every day of a good source of vitamin C or 2 servings of a fair source, and 1 serving every other day of a good source of vitamin A are necessary for a well-balanced diet. One serving is equivalent to about ½ cup fruit; 1 medium apple, peach, or orange; or ½ grapefruit or cantaloupe.

Fruit	Vitamin A	Vitamin C
Apricot	Good	
Cantaloupe	Good	Good
Grapefruit		Good
Guava		Good
Lemon		Good
Lime		Fair
Mango	Good	Good
Orange		Good
Papaya	Fair	
Peach	Fair	
Persimmon	Good	
Strawberry		Good
Watermelon	Fair	Good

Guide To Buying Fresh Fruit

Fruit	Peak availability	Characteristics to look for
Apples	September-May	Good color for variety; firm to touch. Avoid those which are soft and mealy.
Apricots	June-July	Golden yellow; plump; fairly firm. Avoid pale yellow or green, extremely hard or soft, or shriveled and wilted ones.
Avocados	All year	Yield to gentle pressure; vary in size, shape, and color from green to black. Brown markings on skin do not lower quality.
Bananas	All year	Firm; bruise-free; yellow touched with green. If riper fruit preferred, ripen at room temperature.
Berries Blueberries Cranberries Strawberries Others	June-August September-December March-July June-August	Firm; plump; full-colored; bright, clean, fresh appearance. Only strawberries should have hull (stem cap) attached when mature.
Cherries	May-June	Fresh appearance; firm; well-matured; good color for variety. Bruise easily.
Coconuts	September-March	Good weight for the size; milk inside still fluid. If no milk, coconuts are spoiled. Reject ones with moldy or wet-looking eyes.
Figs	July-September	Fairly soft to touch. Use immediately; very perishable. Sour odor indicates overripe fruit.
Grapefruit	October-June	Firm; well-rounded; heavy for the size; smooth-textured. Skin color not always good flavor indicator. Even though ripe, grapefruit skin may have green tinge. Russeted fruit often just as good as bright-colored. Avoid coarse, puffy, rough-skinned fruit.
Grapes	June-December	Fairly soft; tender; plump. Well-formed clusters with green, pliable stems. Darker varieties—free of green tinge; green grapes—slight amber blush.
Kiwi	June-August	Soft to touch, like avocado. Sometimes called Chinese gooseberries.
Lemons	All year	Moderately firm; smooth- and glossy-skinned; heavy for the size.
Limes	May-October	Heavy for the size. Green varieties more acidic than yellow.

Fruit	Peak availability	Characteristics to look for
Mangoes	April-August	Solid and not too soft to the touch. Can vary in size, from a plum to an apple, and in color, from yellow to red. Smooth skin often speckled with black. Green mangoes sometimes used in cooking.
Melons Cantaloupes	 May-September	Color and aroma best guides. Delicate aroma; thick netting that stands out; yellow-tinged skin under netting. No evidence of stem at blossom end.
Casabas Crenshaws Honeydews Persians	July-October July-October February-October July-October	Buttery yellow, wrinkled rinds; lengthwise furrows. Yellow gold rind; pleasant aroma. Creamy yellow rinds; pleasant aroma. Thick webbing; gray green to brown skin under webbing.
Watermelons	May-August	Dull surfaces with cream-colored undersides; symmetrical shape.
Nectarines	June-September	Choose as for peaches.
Oranges	November-June	Heavy for the size; firm; skins not too rough. Naval oranges are seedless, slightly thick-skinned, and are easy to peel and segment. Temple oranges are very juicy, easy to peel, and have rich flavor.
Papayas	All year	Greenish yellow to full yellow in color; flesh gives slightly when fruit pressed in palm of hand.
Peaches	June-September	Plump; fairly firm depending on variety. Skin color white or yellow with a red blush.
Pears	August-May	Yield to gentle pressure at stem end. Color ranges from creamy yellow to russet.
Persimmons	October-January	Firm; shapely; plump; highly colored (orange red); attached stem cap. Handle gently. Resemble large ripe tomatoes in shape and firmness.
Pineapples	February-August	"Piney" aroma; golden yellow; slightly soft. Green fruit may not ripen properly. Overmature fruit may show soft, watery decay spots on the bases or sides.
Plums	June-September	Plump; full-colored; soft enough to yield to slight pressure. Softening at tip is usually a sign that fruit is mature. Avoid shriveled and hard plums.
Pomegranates	September-November	Thin-skinned; bright purple red; fresh appearance.
Tangerines and Tangelos	November-January October-January	Deep orange or yellow; glossy skin. Natural tendency is for skin to be loose. Puffy, dry skin indicates overripe fruit.

Fresh fruits: The grade of fresh fruits should be considered even though appearance is the final quality determinant. For most fruits U.S. Fancy is the top grade available. Fruits in this category are free of blemishes and have excellent color and shape. However, for a few fruits U.S. No. 1 or U.S. Extra No. 1 is the top grade; for others it may be only a second or third grade rating. A lower grade fruit is permitted to have more defects.

Buy fresh fruits in season when the price and quality are likely to be best. Consider the amount you can use and store efficiently. In selecting check the grade, then use your eyes in preference to your hands to determine the fruit's overall quality. (For selecting specific fruits, see guide on pages 993 and 994.)

Prior to storing, sort fresh fruits, discarding any that are decayed. Those that need ripening can be left at room temperature in indirect sunlight. Wash and dry firm-skinned fruits such as apples, pears, and oranges. However, do not wash berries, cherries, or grapes until they are eaten, as washing damages their protective skins. Leave on the caps and stems of these latter fruits while they are being stored.

In storage, proper temperature and humidity help maintain quality. Most fruits are best stored in the refrigerator crisper. If the fruits are in a plastic bag, make sure the bag contains holes to allow for air circulation. Storage time for purchased fruits is often relatively short; homegrown fruits hold up longer. (For specific storage information, see page 997.)

Processed fruits: Since most processed fruits cannot be judged visually, the government has established a separate rating scale for them. Fruits with uniform size and shape, good color and ripeness, and without defects are rated U.S. Grade A or U.S. Fancy. Fruits marked U.S. Grade B or U.S. Choice are very good quality but contain a few imperfections. The fruits labeled U.S. Grade C or U.S. Standard are still wholesome, but the pieces may not be uniform and, in some instances, may be broken. Fruits in this last grade are especially suitable for recipes in which the fruits are chopped or puréed.

Canned fruits: To select the most suitable canned fruits, depend on the grade, the appearance, and the type of packing liquid. Avoid leaking or bulging cans. As long as the metal has not been punctured, dented cans are acceptable. Canned fruits may be purchased and packed in assorted liquids—extra heavy, heavy, light, juice, water, or artificially sweetened.

Advantages of canned fruits include their year-round availability and their extended storage life at room temperature. It is desirable to use canned fruits within one year of purchase since quality changes do occur when the fruits are stored for longer periods or when stored in too warm a place (above 75°). Nevertheless, canned fruits are safe to eat as long as the container is intact and no bulges are apparent.

Frozen fruits: Because satisfactory freezing requires the use of quality fruits, most frozen fruits are a good grade. Select solidly frozen packages that are free of juice stains. At home, store the frozen fruits at 0° or less. They can be stored this way for 8 to 12 months.

Dried fruits: When choosing dried fruits, select well-sealed, clean packages. The fruits should be bright-colored and firm, yet pliable. In storage, dark dried fruits such as prunes and raisins retain their color better than do lighter fruits such as apples and apricots. Dried fruits may be stored in a cool place for six months or more. If the weather is excessively hot and humid, refrigeration is best.

Color-bright fruit

When cut, the surfaces of certain fruit varieties will darken on exposure to air unless specially treated. To keep the bright, fresh fruit color, immerse the cut fruit in a sugar syrup, brush with citrus (lemon, orange) or pineapple juice mixed with a little water, or apply ascorbic acid color keeper according to label directions. The following fruits should be prepared in this manner: apples, avocados, bananas, peaches, and pears.

Use in menu

Fruits have great eye appeal when you contrast their rainbow of colors, textures, sizes, and shapes. Fresh fruits should be fully ripe; frozen fruits, partially thawed.

Many outstanding fruit recipes are made by simply simmering, broiling, baking, or frying the fruit. Unless a saucy mixture is desired, fruits used for cooking retain better appearance and shape when they are slightly underripe. Let the delicate fruit flavor predominate, using only enough sugar to sweeten the product a bit. Cook the fruits slowly just till tender.

Versatility describes menu uses for today's fruits. Eaten as is for a snack, breakfast, or dessert, fruits are always delicious. Suitable for almost any cooking use, fruits can be tempting appetizers, flavorful accompaniments, and elegant main dishes and desserts. For garnishes, they're not only pretty, but also good to eat. Molded in gelatin, cooked in piecrusts, cakes, cookies, breads, and puddings, or used in sauces and toppers, the uses for fruits are seemingly endless and inexhaustible.

As an appetizer: Fruits, particularly citrus fruits, are a common first course for breakfast but can be used in a variety of ways—beverages, fruit cups, in spreads and dips, or in bite-sized pieces—to start off other meals of the day, too.

As an appetizer beverage, fruit punch gaily decorated with a fruit ice ring can spark a summer anniversary party. During winter, skiers and ice skaters find warmth and refreshment from a hot, spiced drink.

❖MENU❖

SPRING WEDDING RECEPTION
Wedding Cake
Tea Sandwiches
Mixed Salted Nuts   *Pastel Mints*
Pineapple-Citrus Punch
Coffee

Pineapple Citrus Punch

Mounds of ice cream add richness—

Mix one 12-ounce can unsweetened pineapple juice (1½ cups), 1 cup orange juice, ¼ cup lemon juice, 2 tablespoons honey, and 1 tablespoon maraschino cherry juice; chill well.

Pour juice mixture over ice in punch bowl. Add 1 pint vanilla ice cream in small spoonfuls. Resting bottles on rim of bowl, carefully pour two 7-ounce bottles ginger ale, chilled, down side. Serve immediately. Makes 7 cups.

Fruit cups are welcome additions to breakfast, lunch, or dinner menus, too. Used singly or in combination with one another, fresh, frozen, and canned fruits can be cut in bite-sized pieces and served with a slightly tangy syrup or sauce.

Fruit Cup Combinations

• Section 3 oranges; combine with 2 bananas, sliced, and 2 slices canned or fresh pineapple, diced. Sprinkle with lemon juice and sweeten to taste. Chill. If desired, serve the fruit in hollowed-out halves of orange shells.

• Combine diced fresh pineapple and halved ripe strawberries. Sift confectioners' sugar over fruit mixture. Chill thoroughly. Trim each serving with a sprig of fresh mint.

• Combine canned fruit cocktail with thin red apple slices, orange sections, and avocado balls. Chill well. *Or*, top fruit cocktail with a scoop of orange or lemon sherbet.

• Freeze ginger ale to a mush in freezer tray. Serve in chilled sherbets; top ginger ale slush with chilled, drained canned fruit cocktail.

• Cut balls from melon using a melon-ball cutter or a half-teaspoon measure. Serve very cold, alone or with other fresh fruits.

• Peel ½-inch-thick rings of chilled cantaloupe or honeydew melon. Fill centers with watermelon balls or fresh berries. Sprinkle melon rings with a little lemon juice.

• Toss melon balls with mixture of sweetened, fresh lime juice, finely chopped candied ginger, and a dash of aromatic bitters.

• For variety, sweeten fruits with grape juice, grenadine syrup, apricot cordial, orange-flavored liqueur, or maraschino cherry juice.

Guide To Storing Fresh Fruit		
Fruit	How to store	Holding time
Apples	Refrigerate	1 to 2 weeks
Apricots	Refrigerate, uncovered	3 to 5 days
Avocados	Ripen at room temperature, then refrigerate	3 to 5 days
Bananas	Ripen at room temperature, then refrigerate	1 to 2 days

Berries
  blueberries, strawberries, and others
  cranberries
	Refrigerate, unwashed and uncovered
	
	Refrigerate
		1 to 2 days
		1 to 2 days
		1 week

Cherries	Refrigerate, unwashed and uncovered	1 to 2 days
Citrus Fruits	Refrigerate, uncovered	1 to 2 weeks
Coconuts	Refrigerate	1 to 2 months
Figs	Use immediately; refrigerate briefly	1 day
Grapes	Refrigerate, unwashed and uncovered	3 to 5 days
Kiwi	Refrigerate when ripened	3 weeks
Mangoes	Ripen at room temperature; refrigerate briefly	1 day
Melons	Ripen at room temperature, then refrigerate	1 week
Papayas	Ripen at room temperature, then refrigerate	1 to 2 days
Peaches	Refrigerate, uncovered	3 to 5 days
Pears	Ripen at room temperature, then refrigerate	1 to 2 weeks
Persimmons	Ripen at room temperature, then refrigerate	1 to 2 days
Pineapples	Refrigerate	1 to 2 days
Plums	Refrigerate	3 to 5 days
Pomegratnaes	Room temperature or refrigerate	2 to 3 days

Fruit Cup Tower

• *Melon Cocktail:* Combine cantaloupe balls and watermelon scoops (use a shovel-shaped ice cream scooper). Dash melon balls with orange- or cherry-flavored liqueur to taste. Chill thoroughly. Serve in sherbet dishes.

• *Strawberry Starter:* Rinse, hull, and halve fresh strawberries (or use frozen, unsweetened strawberries, partially thawed). Spoon into sherbet dishes. Combine one 8-ounce carton strawberry-flavored yogurt, ¼ cup sugar, and few drops red food coloring. Drizzle over berries. Garnish with fresh mint sprigs.

• *Blueberry-Honeydew Cup:* Combine honeydew balls, fresh blueberries, and finely snipped candied ginger; chill well. Spoon into sherbet dishes. Resting bottle on rim of dish, slowly pour in chilled ginger ale to cover bottom of dish. Serve with fresh lime wedges.

• *Raspberry-Nectarine Cocktail:* Combine raspberries, nectarine slices, and small chunks of fresh pineapple. Spoon fruit into sherbet dishes. Garnish with sprinkling of confectioners' sugar. Tuck in a sprig of fresh mint.

• *Banana-Berry Cup:* Peel and slice bananas; sprinkle with lemon juice. Combine with fresh blackberries and spoon into sherbet dishes. Drizzle with *Orange-Sour Cream Topper* prepared by combining 1 cup dairy sour cream, ½ teaspoon grated orange peel, ¼ cup orange juice, and 2 tablespoons sugar; mix well.

• *Cantaloupe Supreme:* Halve and seed 2 cantaloupes. Scoop out melon balls, leaving ¼-inch shell on 3 melon halves. Drain two 10-ounce packages frozen raspberries, thawed, reserving syrup. Combine reserved syrup, 3 to 4 tablespoons cream sherry, and the melon balls. Spoon into the 3 melon shells; chill. At serving time, top the melons with scoops of pineapple sherbet and drained raspberries. To serve, spoon the pineapple sherbet into sauce dishes, then spoon melon balls and juice atop.

• *Cantaloupe Especiale:* Cut icy cold cantaloupe into wedges. Trim each with a cluster of sugar-frosted seedless green grapes.

The chef's specialty

←Fruit-Turkey Kabobs can boast of pear, green pepper, turkey, crab apple, and orange that glisten with an apricot glaze.

In spreads and dips, fruit purées and juices help stimulate appetites. The widely favored guacamole dip is based on mashed avocado. Tint fluffy cream cheese or sour cream fruit dips a delicate pink with maraschino cherry juice or raspberry syrup; another time, use green food coloring in combination with lime juice.

Fruit tidbits are simple, yet colorful appetizer specialties. Miniature, assorted fruit or fruit-meat kabobs are colorful and tasty accents at brunches and cocktail parties. Combined in a sweet-sour sauce for a buffet, fruits with cocktail frankfurters or sausages can stay hot for hours in an attractive chafing dish.

As an accompaniment: Fruits are not only vital to accompaniment salads, relishes, and salad dressings, but also to vegetable dishes, breads, jellies, and syrups as well. And as a garnish, fruits often double as the tasty accompaniment.

Fruit and Orange Fluff

This glamorous serve-yourself salad makes an excellent accompaniment for a buffet dinner—

To prepare dressing, slowly beat one 3⅝- or 3¾-ounce package *instant* vanilla pudding mix and 2 cups cold milk in mixing bowl with rotary beater till mixture is well blended, about 1 to 2 minutes. Gently beat in 1 cup dairy sour cream. Fold in ½ teaspoon grated orange peel and ¼ cup orange juice. Chill thoroughly.

Center small bowl of dressing in large shallow bowl. Arrange sliced unpeeled pears*, quartered nectarines *or* peaches*, whole fresh strawberries, seedless green grape clusters, fresh, dark sweet cherries, and fresh blueberries around. To keep cold, place fruit bowl atop bowl of crushed ice. Makes 3 cups dressing.

*To keep freshly cut fruit bright, use ascorbic acid color keeper as directed or dip in lemon juice mixed with a little water.

Popular vegetable-fruit combinations include beets or green beans with pineapple and applesauce with squash. Sweet-sour oriental dishes frequently blend the closely related fruit and vegetable flavors.

Fruit-filled breads are popular for everyday and special occasion affairs. Quick breads like steamy fruit muffins are ideal for in-a-hurry meals, while yeast breads are good for holiday times.

Cherry Puff Rolls

In a large mixer bowl combine 1½ cups sifted all-purpose flour and 1 package active dry yeast. Heat ⅔ cup milk, ¼ cup water, ¼ cup sugar, 3 tablespoons butter or margarine, and 1 teaspoon salt just till warm, stirring occasionally to melt the butter or margarine.

Add milk mixture to flour mixture in mixer bowl; add 1 egg. Beat at low speed of electric mixer for ½ minute, scraping sides of bowl constantly. Beat 3 minutes at high speed. By hand, stir in sifted all-purpose flour to make a soft dough, about 1¾ to 2¼ cups.

Knead on floured surface till smooth, 8 to 10 minutes. Place in greased bowl; turn once to grease surface. Cover; let rise till double, 1½ to 2 hours. Punch down; let rest 10 minutes. Roll ½ inch thick on floured surface. Spread with 2 tablespoons softened butter or margarine. Fold dough in half; pinch edges together. Roll ½ inch thick again; spread with 2 more tablespoons softened butter or margarine. Fold, seal, and roll dough again.

Cut in 2½-inch circles; place on greased baking sheet. Cover; let rise till double, 20 to 30 minutes. Make depressions in centers; fill with cherry preserves. Bake at 400° 10 to 12 minutes. Frost with *Confectioners' Sugar Icing:* Add light cream to 2 cups sifted confectioners' sugar till spreadable. Add dash salt and 1 teaspoon vanilla. Makes 12 rolls.

❋MENU❋

SUNDAY BRUNCH
Cantaloupe Wedges
French Omelet
Sausage Links
Cherry Puff Rolls *   Butter*
Hot Chocolate

Common fruit garnishes include citrus fruit twists and spiced crab apples. Equally simple but less frequently used garnishes give your menus artistic variety. Try kumquats with a pork roast, pomegranate seeds on a fruit salad, and crystallized or candied fruit on a fluffy dessert.

As a main dish: Fruits and main dishes go hand-in-hand morning, noon, or night. Fruit-filled pancakes and waffles are a welcome breakfast or light supper main dish. A luncheon salad platter is a dieter's delight. Arrange large or whole pieces of fruit around a mound of cottage cheese, sherbet, or salad dressing. On another occasion, use a melon half or quarter for the base and pile fruit pieces in the cavity. For sandwiches, insert a pineapple or avocado slice between meat and bread or combine chopped fruit in a salad-sandwich mixture. Glaze meats with a fruit sauce, stuff poultry with fruit stuffing, or alternate meat and fruit for elegant flaming kabobs at the dinner meal.

Hawaiian Fruit Plate

Have salad ingredients chilled. Peel 1 small pineapple; cut in 6 spears and remove core. Cut rind from 6 watermelon wedges. Halve 1 medium papaya and scoop out seeds; cut in 6 wedges and remove rind. Brush 3 fully ripe bananas, peeled and quartered, with pineapple *or* lime juice. Drain one 16-ounce can sliced peaches. Line large chilled platter or individual plates with romaine. Arrange fruits atop, spoke fashion. Garnish with 2 limes, cut in slices and wedges, and ½ pint fresh whole strawberries. Pass Pineapple-French Dressing. Serves 6.

Pineapple-French Dressing: Combine 1 cup salad oil, ¼ cup pineapple juice, ¼ cup lime juice, 1 tablespoon vinegar, ⅓ cup sugar, 1½ teaspoons paprika, and 1 teaspoon salt; cover and shake. Chill. Shake again before serving.

The islands atmosphere

Fresh lime slices accent the luscious fruit → flavors in Hawaiian Fruit Plate. Drizzle with zesty Pineapple-French Dressing.

❧MENU❧

POST-HOLIDAY SUPPER
Cranberry Juice Cocktail
Fruit-Turkey Kabobs
Fluffy Rice
Wilted Lettuce Salad
Gingerbread   Lemon Sauce
Coffee

Fruit-Turkey Kabobs

    ¾ pound cooked boneless turkey
        roast, cut in 1-inch cubes
    1 orange, cut into wedges
    1 pear, cut into wedges
    1 green pepper, cut into squares
    4 small spiced crab apples
    ½ cup apricot preserves
    ¼ cup light corn syrup
    2 tablespoons butter or margarine
    ¼ teaspoon ground cinnamon
      Dash ground cloves
      Hot cooked rice

Thread pieces of meat and fruit onto four 8-
to 10-inch skewers. Combine remaining ingredients. Bring to boiling, stirring occasionally.
Brush over kabobs. Grill 4 inches from coals,
turning and brushing with sauce till heated and
well glazed. Serve hot kabobs on rice with remaining sauce. Makes 4 servings.

❧MENU❧

HE-MAN DINNER
Fruit-Stuffed Pork
Baked Sweet Potatoes
Peas in Cream Sauce
Tossed Green Salad   Assorted Dressings
Pumpkin Pie   Whipped Cream
Coffee

Fruit-Stuffed Pork Chops

There's cheese in the stuffing, too—

    8 double-rib pork chops with
        pockets cut for stuffing
    2 cups small dry bread cubes
    1 cup finely chopped unpeeled
        apple
    1 cup shredded sharp process
        American cheese
    ¼ cup light raisins
    ¼ cup butter or margarine, melted
    ¼ cup orange juice
    ½ teaspoon salt
    ¼ teaspoon ground cinnamon

Sprinkle salt and pepper over chops. Combine
bread cubes, apple, cheese, raisins, butter,
orange juice, salt, and cinnamon. Stuff fruit
mixture into pockets. Press edges of pockets
together to seal. Bake at 350° till chops are
tender, about 1½ hours. Makes 8 servings.

As a dessert: The most widely accepted
use of fruits is at the dessert course.
There's no denying that strawberry short-
cake and apple pie are America's all-time
dessert favorites. Liqueur-drenched fruit
compotes, baked fruits, ice cream fruit
toppings, and fruit-filled gelatin are but a
few other ways to serve fruits as the final
course. And don't forget the hot fruit cob-
blers, crisps, crumbles, and fruit-filled
cakes, candies, and cookies that you can
add to your recipe repertoire.

Fruit Medley Elegante

Wine complements the fruits—

    ⅓ cup port
    ¼ cup orange juice
    1 tablespoon lemon juice
    2 to 3 tablespoons sugar
    1 cup peeled, sliced peaches
    1 cup halved strawberries
    6 pear halves
    1 large banana, peeled and sliced

Combine wine, fruit juices, and sugar. Pour
over combined fruits. Toss; chill. Serves 6.

Peach-Cot Cherry Bake

1 17-ounce can peach slices,
    undrained
1 cup dried apricots
½ cup brown sugar
½ teaspoon grated lemon peel
2 tablespoons lemon juice
1 teaspoon grated orange peel
⅓ cup orange juice
1 16-ounce can pitted dark
    sweet cherries, drained

In 10x6x1¾-inch baking dish mix first 7 ingredients. Cover; bake at 350° for 45 minutes. Add cherries; bake 15 minutes. Serves 8.

Spiced Fruit Sauce

1 8¾-ounce can pineapple tidbits
1 8¾-ounce can apricot halves
3 inches stick cinnamon
12 whole cloves
2 tablespoons sugar
2 teaspoons cornstarch
½ cup raisins

Drain pineapple and apricots, reserving syrups. Quarter apricots. Combine syrups and spices; cover and simmer 5 minutes. Remove spices. Combine sugar and cornstarch; stir in small amount of hot syrup, mixing well. Return to hot mixture. Cook, stirring constantly, till thickened and bubbly. Add fruits. Cook 5 minutes; stir occasionally. If desired, add aromatic bitters to taste. Serve warm. Makes 1¾ cups.

❊MENU❊

GOOD HOME COOKING
Beef Pot Roast
Pot Roasted Parsnips and Carrots
Popovers   Whipped Butter
Peach-Cot Cherry Bake or
Spiced Fruit Sauce with *Vanilla Ice Cream*
Coffee   Milk

❊MENU❊

IN-A-JIFFY SUPPER
Broiled Ham Steak
Buttered Noodles
Relishes
Pink Fruit Dessert
Coffee

Pink Fruit Dessert

1 12-ounce package frozen
    peach slices
1 13½-ounce can frozen
    pineapple chunks
1 10-ounce package frozen
    raspberries, thawed
Dash aromatic bitters

Thaw peaches and pineapple together. To serve, add raspberries. Dash in bitters. Spoon into sherbets. Makes 4 to 6 servings.

Triple Fruit Dessert: Thaw fruits with 1 to 2 teaspoons finely chopped candied ginger; omit bitters. Substitute ½ cup frozen blueberries, thawed, for raspberries.

FRUIT BUTTER—A fruit spread used like jam or jelly. (See also *Butter—fruit.*)

FRUITCAKE—A rich, compact cake containing a high proportion of nuts and dried or candied fruit, peel, and rind. A small amount of spicy batter holds these chopped pieces together. Although traditional at holidays, particularly Christmas, fruitcake can be enjoyed throughout the year.

Unlike other cake types, fruitcake's flavors and textures improve when the cake is aged three to four weeks. Cool the baked cake to room temperature, wrap in brandy-, wine-, or fruit juice-soaked cheesecloth, then in foil. Store in foil, clear plastic wrap, or an airtight container and keep in a cool place. Continue to moisten once a week. For even slicing, chill before serving. (See also *Cake.*)

Golden Fruitcake

Warmed slices are delicious with a hard sauce—

Cut 1 cup dried apricots into small pieces; pour just enough boiling water over apricots to cover. Let stand for 20 minutes, then drain thoroughly. Combine snipped apricots with 2 cups chopped, candied pineapple; 2 cups golden raisins; 1 cup dark raisins; 1 cup candied cherries, halved; 1 cup chopped citron; 1 cup chopped, candied orange peel; 1/2 cup chopped, candied lemon peel; 2 cups coarsely chopped pecans; and 1 cup slivered, blanched almonds.

Cream 1 1/4 cups shortening, 1 1/2 cups honey, and 2 teaspoons rum extract *or* vanilla together thoroughly; beat in 6 eggs. Sift 2 1/2 cups sifted all-purpose flour with 1 1/4 teaspoons salt, 1 teaspoon baking powder, 1 teaspoon ground cinnamon, 1/2 teaspoon ground nutmeg, and 1/4 teaspoon ground cloves. Add to creamed mixture, mixing till smooth. Add fruit.

Turn fruitcake batter into greased pans lined with aluminum foil—either two 11x4x3-inch fruitcake pans and one 5 1/2x3x2 1/4-inch pan *or* one 10-inch tube springform pan and one 7 1/2x3 3/4x2 1/4-inch loaf pan. Bake at 275° about 1 3/4 hours for small loaves, 2 hours for medium loaves, and 2 3/4 hours for tube pan. (Place shallow pan of hot water on bottom of oven.)

Cool cakes thoroughly, then remove from pan. Wrap tightly in fruit juice- or brandy-soaked cloth and foil. Store in cool place for several weeks. Makes 7 pounds fruitcake.

Pecan halves and berry-laden holly make a decorative trim for Golden Fruitcake at Christmas time. Served with coffee, it's a welcome refreshment to have on hand for unexpected guests.

No-Bake Fruitcake

   1 6¼-ounce package miniature
      marshmallows (2 cups)
  ½ cup evaporated milk
   1 teaspoon grated orange peel
  ½ cup orange juice
   1 13¾-ounce package graham
      cracker crumbs (about 4 cups)
   1 cup raisins
   1 cup chopped dates
  ½ pound mixed candied fruits and
      peels, chopped (1 cup)
  ¾ cup chopped walnuts
  ⅓ cup chopped maraschino cherries
  ¼ teaspoon ground cinnamon
  ¼ teaspoon ground nutmeg
  ¼ teaspoon ground cloves

Mix together marshmallows, evaporated milk, and orange juice. In large bowl combine remaining ingredients. Add milk mixture; blend.

    Line 8½x4½x2½-inch loaf pan with waxed paper, extending paper above sides. Press mixture firmly into pan. Cover tightly with foil. Chill several days before serving.

Light Fruitcake

Combine ¾ pound candied cherries (1½ cups), chopped; 1 cup light raisins; ½ pound candied pineapple, chopped (1 cup); ¼ pound chopped mixed candied fruits and peels (½ cup); ¼ pound candied lemon peel (½ cup), chopped; ¼ pound candied orange peel (½ cup), chopped; and 1 cup chopped walnuts. Stir in 1 cup sifted all-purpose flour.

    Cream 1 cup butter and 1 cup sugar till light. Add 4 eggs, one at a time, beating well after each. Combine ¼ cup *each* light corn syrup, orange juice, and dry white wine; add to creamed mixture alternately with 2 cups sifted all-purpose flour. Fold in fruits and nuts.

    Pour into 2 well-greased 5½-cup ring molds.* Bake at 275° for 1¼ hours. If desired, glaze cooled cakes by brushing lightly with hot corn syrup. Trim with candied cherries or nuts. When set, brush with second coating. Let glaze dry; wrap. Makes two 36-ounce cakes.

    *Or, turn into 8 well-greased 4½x2¾x2¼-inch pans. Bake at 275° for 1 hour. Or, fill paper bake cups in muffin pans with ¼ cup batter. Bake at 275° for 45 minutes. Makes 2½ dozen.

Dark Fruitcake

Molasses makes it dark—

Combine one 6-ounce can frozen orange juice concentrate, thawed; ½ cup molasses; and one 15-ounce package raisins (3 cups) in saucepan. Cook till boiling, stirring occasionally. Reduce heat and simmer 5 minutes. Remove from heat. Stir in 1 pound chopped, mixed candied fruits and peels (2 cups).

    Cream ½ cup butter or margarine and ⅔ cup sugar. Add 3 eggs, one at a time, beating well after each. Sift together 1¼ cups sifted all-purpose flour, ⅛ teaspoon baking soda, 1 teaspoon ground cinnamon, ½ teaspoon ground nutmeg, ¼ teaspoon ground allspice, and ¼ teaspoon ground cloves. Stir into creamed mixture. Stir in fruit mixture and ½ cup chopped walnuts; mix well till all fruit is coated.

    Line one 11x4x3-inch pan and two 5½x3x2¼-inch pans with heavy paper, allowing ½ inch to extend above all sides. Pour batter into pans, filling about ¾ full. Bake at 275° about 2¼ to 2½ hours for large loaf and about 1½ hours for smaller loaves. Cool cakes thoroughly in pans; remove. Wrap fruitcakes in foil or clear plastic wrap and store them in cool place for several weeks. Makes 3½ pounds fruitcake.

For a glossy finish, brush fruitcake with hot corn syrup, garnish, then brush on a second coat. Let glaze dry before wrapping.

FRUIT COCKTAIL—1. A chilled, fresh or canned fruit mixture served as a first course. 2. The name of a canned fruit mixture cut in bite-sized pieces. It's ready to serve when chilled and also has many uses as a recipe ingredient.

Fruit Cocktail Mold

    1 17-ounce can fruit cocktail
    1 3-ounce package lime-flavored
        gelatin
    1 7-ounce bottle ginger ale,
        chilled, (about 1 cup)
    2 tablespoons lemon juice

Drain fruit cocktail, reserving syrup. Add enough water to syrup to make 1 cup; heat to boiling. Add gelatin and stir till dissolved; cool. Gently stir in ginger ale and lemon juice. Chill gelatin mixture till partially set. Fold in drained fruit. Pour into 3½-cup mold. Chill till firm. Makes 4 or 5 servings.

Fruit Cocktail Pie

    **Plain Pastry for 2-crust
        9-inch pie (see *Pastry*)**
    ¾ cup sugar
    2½ tablespoons quick-cooking tapioca
    ¼ teaspoon cinnamon
    ¼ teaspoon nutmeg
    2 cups diced peaches
    2 cups diced pears
    1 cup seedless green grapes
    1 tablespoon chopped maraschino
        cherries
    1 tablespoon lemon juice
    1 tablespoon butter or margarine
    Milk

Line 9-inch pie plate with *half* of pastry. Mix sugar, tapioca, spices, and dash salt. Add fruits and lemon juice; mix lightly. Turn into pie plate. Dot with butter. Adjust top crust, cutting slits for escape of steam; seal. Brush top with milk; sprinkle with sugar. Bake at 400° about 30 minutes. Serve slightly warm.

Bite-sized pieces of peaches, pears, green grapes, and maraschino cherries colorfully blend in Fruit Cocktail Pie. Serve this appetizing treat warm topped with vanilla ice cream.

Fruit-Cocktail Cobbler

    1 31-ounce can fruit cocktail
    ¼ cup brown sugar
    2 tablespoons cornstarch
    ½ teaspoon grated orange peel
    ¾ cup diced orange
    2 tablespoons butter or margarine
    1 cup packaged biscuit mix
    ⅓ cup milk
    1 tablespoon butter or margarine,
        melted

Drain fruit cocktail, reserving syrup. In saucepan mix brown sugar and cornstarch; add reserved syrup. Cook and stir till thickened and bubbly. Add fruit cocktail, orange peel, orange, and the 2 tablespoons butter. Heat to boiling.

Pour into 8x8x2-inch baking dish. Combine biscuit mix, milk, and melted butter; mix just to moisten. Quickly drop batter by spoonfuls onto *hot* fruit. Bake at 400° till biscuits are done, about 20 minutes. Serve warm with cream, if desired. Makes 8 servings.

Fruit Cocktail Gems

    1 16-ounce can fruit cocktail
    ½ cup butter or margarine
    ½ cup brown sugar
    ¼ cup granulated sugar
    ½ teaspoon vanilla
    1 egg
    2 cups sifted all-purpose flour
    ½ teaspoon baking powder
    ½ teaspoon baking soda
    ½ teaspoon salt
    ½ teaspoon ground cinnamon
    ¼ teaspoon ground cloves
    ½ cup chopped walnuts
    ½ cup raisins

Drain fruit cocktail, reserving syrup. Cream butter, brown sugar, granulated sugar, and vanilla till fluffy. Add egg; beat well. Sift together flour, baking powder, baking soda, salt, cinnamon, and cloves; add alternately to creamed mixture with ⅓ *cup* of the reserved fruit cocktail syrup. Stir in chopped nuts, raisins, and the drained fruit cocktail.

Drop dough from teaspoon onto greased cookie sheet. Bake at 375° for 10 to 12 minutes. Cool on rack. Makes 3½ dozen cookies.

FRUIT JUICE — Liquid obtained by squeezing or pressing fruit. Available fresh, frozen, or canned, fruit juice is an ingredient in many beverage concoctions as well as cooking ingredients for recipes.

When used as a beverage, fruit juices add nutritional value to the daily menu and quench thirst, too. Orange juice, grapefruit juice, apple juice, and grape juice are popular for drinking without the addition of sweeteners or other ingredients. These as well as other fruit juices and prepared fruit drinks, like lemonade, are often blended for a delightful snack or refreshment. Carbonated beverages combined with fruit juices can add an effervescent note to punches and coolers.

Hot Apple Toddy

    4 cups apple cider
    ⅔ cup brown sugar
    ½ lemon
    ¼ teaspoon aromatic bitters

In saucepan combine apple cider and brown sugar. Slice lemon; add to cider mixture. Bring to full boil; simmer for 5 minutes. Add aromatic bitters. Serve warm. Makes 6 to 8 servings.

Frosty Golden Punch

    1 6-ounce can frozen lemonade
        concentrate
    1 6-ounce can frozen orange juice
        concentrate
    1 6-ounce can frozen pineapple
        juice concentrate
    1 12-ounce can apricot nectar,
        chilled (1½ cups)
    ½ cup lemon juice
                • • •
    1 quart lemon sherbet
    2 28-ounce bottles ginger ale,
        chilled (7 cups)

Add water to concentrates according to directions on cans. Add apricot nectar and lemon juice. Just before serving, pour in bowl; spoon in sherbet; rest bottle on rim and pour ginger ale down side of bowl. Mix with up-and-down motion. Makes 20 to 25 servings.

Favorite Patio Refresher

1 envelope strawberry-flavored
   drink powder
1 envelope cherry-flavored
   drink powder
1 cup sugar
2 12-ounce cans apricot nectar,
   chilled (3 cups)
1 6-ounce can frozen limeade
   concentrate
1 6-ounce can frozen lemonade
   concentrate
     • • •
1 28-ounce bottle lemon-lime
   carbonated beverage, chilled
   (3½ cups)

Combine drink powder, sugar, 8 cups cold water, apricot nectar, limeade, and lemonade;
chill. Place ice cubes in tall chilled glasses; fill
each ¾ full with fruit juice mixture. Tip each
glass and slowly pour carbonated beverage
down *side* to fill. Stir with up-and-down motion. Makes 12 to 16 servings.

Fruit juices are used in recipes when
fruit flavor, but not texture, is desired, or
to prevent color change of cut fruits such
as fresh apples, bananas, pears, and
peaches. Citrus and pineapple juices are
the principle color preservatives.

Ham Baked in Apple Cider

1 large fully cooked ham
   Whole cloves
     • • •
4 cups apple cider *or* apple juice
2 medium onions, quartered
1 tablespoon brown sugar
1 tablespoon lemon juice
½ cup maple-flavored syrup

Place ham, fat side up, on rack in shallow
roasting pan. Score in diamonds; stud with
whole cloves. Combine apple cider, onions,
sugar, and lemon in saucepan; bring to boiling.
Simmer, covered, for 10 minutes. Strain; pour
over ham. Bake ham following label directions.
Baste often with cider mixture. During last 15
minutes, brush twice with maple syrup.

Three-Fruit Sherbet

1 medium ripe banana
½ 6-ounce can frozen orange
   juice concentrate, slightly
   thawed (⅓ cup)
1 13½-ounce can frozen pineapple
   chunks, cut in pieces
½ cup whipping cream

Combine all ingredients in blender container.
Cover; turn blender on and off till mixture is
well blended. Spoon into freezer tray; freeze.

Lemon-Sour Cream Pie

1 cup sugar
3 tablespoons cornstarch
1 cup milk
3 slightly beaten egg yolks
¼ cup butter or margarine
1 teaspoon shredded lemon peel
¼ cup lemon juice
1 cup dairy sour cream
1 *baked* 9-inch pastry shell
   (see *Pastry*)
   Meringue

Combine sugar, cornstarch, and dash salt. Stir
in milk. Cook and stir till mixture is thickened
and bubbly. Blend small amount of hot mixture into egg yolks; return to hot mixture.
Cook and stir 2 minutes. Add butter, lemon
peel, and lemon juice. Cover; cool. Fold in
sour cream. Spoon into baked pastry shell.

Prepare *Meringue:* Beat 3 egg whites with ½
teaspoon vanilla and ¼ teaspoon cream of tartar to soft peaks. Gradually add 6 tablespoons
sugar, beating to stiff peaks. Spread meringue
over filling, sealing to edge of pastry. Bake at
350° for 12 to 15 minutes.

FRUIT SOUP—A sweet soup made with fresh
or dried fruits that have been cooked and
puréed. The addition of wine or brandy
is often used as a flavor enhancer.

Following the tradition established by
Germans and Swedes, fruit soup is usually
served as a dessert course. It can also
make a tantalizing appetizer. In Hungary,
for example, a sweet cherry soup is used
as a stimulating first course.